I Was Stalin's Prisoner

I Was Stalin's Prisoner

ROBERT A. VOGELER

WITH LEIGH WHITE

HARCOURT, BRACE AND COMPANY

NEW YORK

11489

TO MY SONS

Acknowledgments

I wish to express my heartfelt thanks to my wife, my father, my sister-in-law Pia Eykens, and to the following persons and organizations:

The representatives of the American, Belgian, and British press and radio who did so much to keep my case alive, and particularly William James Boyle, Frans van Erps, Charles Foley, Seymour Freidin, Philip Geysen, G. K. Hodenfield, Roy W. Howard, Joseph Israels III, Allan Keller, Irving R. Levine, Wellington Long, John MacCormac, Ritchie McEwen, Leopold Murray, George Pipal, Ernie Reed, Robert Ruark, Earl Wilson, and Walter Winchell;

The officers and men of the United States Army and particularly Lieutenant General Geoffrey Keyes, Major General Ira P. Swift, Major General Ralph Tate, Brigadier General Jesmond D. Balmer, Brigadier General John A. Elmore, Brigadier General James C. Fry, Brigadier General Willard K. Liebel, Brigadier General James A. Samouce, Colonel Robert Koch, Colonel Michael Mulhall, Captain Leo E. Huff, and Sergeant Hollis Graves;

The officers and men of the United States Navy and particularly the late Admiral Forrest P. Sherman, Captain C. F. M. Spotswood Quinby, Captain S. M. Smith, Captain Adelbert V. Wallis, Lieutenant Charles Rocheleau, and Mr. Jack Alberti;

My friends and colleagues of I.T.&T. and the electrical communications industry, particularly Sosthenes Behn, William H. Harrison, Mark A. Sunstrom, the late William H. Freng, Henry Scudder, Goodwin Cooke, Jacob S. Jammer, and Colonel Grant Williams.

Representatives Jacob K. Javits, T. Vincent Quinn, Robert T. Ross, and those other members of the Congress of the United States who spoke out on my behalf;

Señor Acevedo, the Argentine consul general; M. le Comte d'Apremont Linden, the Belgian minister; José La Cerda; Erle Cocke; Mr. Daw, the British chargé d'affaires; the late John G. Erhardt; Herr Feldscher, the Swiss minister; Chancellor Leopold Figl; Culbert L. Olson; Floretta Pomeroy; Señor Russo, the Argentine minister to Hungary; and many other friends and acquaintances in Vienna;

Nathaniel P. Davis, Laurence C. Frank, Walter J. Donnelly, Walter Dowling, and certain other officers of the American Foreign Service, so often maligned, who struggled in the straitjacket of a weak foreign policy imposed by circumstances beyond their control;

My attorney, Morris L. Ernst, and my collaborator, Leigh White;

The American Legion, the Association of the Bar of the City of New York, the New York Board of Trade, the Veterans of Foreign Wars, the Church of St. Joan of Arc of Jackson Heights, New York; the Reverend Dr. William Ward Ayer; George Sondheim; E. E. Willkie; and all those Americans who did so much, in groups and as individuals, to force the Administration to procure my release from prison.

ROBERT A. VOGELER

New York City
March 14, 1952

Contents

I Was Stalin's Prisoner

One | "A Losing Game"

In Budapest, not far from the American Legation, stood a bronze statue of Harry Hill Bandholtz, the American general who had forced the Rumanians to withdraw from the conquered Hungarian capital following the First World War. Both the statue and the legation were located on what is still ironically referred to in Budapest as "Freedom Square."

One day in October, 1949, on my way to the legation from my office on Nádor Street, I paused to stare at Bandholtz's statue. It was the last symbol of American dignity in the capital of a twice-defeated Hungary. No successor to Bandholtz had risen after the Second World War to force the Russians to withdraw from the prostrate city. On the contrary, our military and diplomatic representatives had submitted to such indignities at the hands of the Russians that it was hard to realize that a man like Bandholtz had ever lived.

Three weeks later, when his statue was removed by the Communist authorities, I felt that my own fate was somehow involved. So did Jule Smith, the commercial attaché of the American Legation.

"You're playing a losing game," he said. "Why don't you go back to Vienna before the AVH gets after you?"

The AVH, the State Defense Authority, was the Hungarian section of the MGB, the foreign division of the Russian political police. If I had known then what I know now, I would certainly have done as Smith suggested, for I was soon to be arrested, tried, and convicted, and held for seventeen months—all but two of which were spent in solitary confinement—until I was ransomed by the United States government in April, 1951. At the time, however, I was still not convinced that our government would be unable to protect me.

The Communist officials with whom I was dealing wore miniature Hungarian flags in their buttonholes. Each red-white-and-green flag had a red star, embossed with a gold hammer and sickle, superimposed upon it. I decided to emulate the Swiss and the Swedes and wear a replica of my own flag in my buttonhole. I bought one from a jeweler on Váczi Street who still had several hidden under his counter.

A few days later I wore the miniature American flag to a cocktail party given by Lieutenant Colonel William Du Puy, one of the legation's assistant army attachés. The wife of one of the legation's secretaries, who was also present, twitted me about my little gesture of defiance. I took advantage of the opportunity to ask her husband what the legation would do if I happened to be arrested.

"We'd make the usual representations," he said, "but I don't think they'd have much effect. The AVH knows that the United States isn't going to war with Russia over a lone American prisoner."

"Then why bother to keep a legation here?"

"Oh, it's of some value," he said. "It's a good listening post, for one thing."

I told him what I thought of the listening-post concept of American diplomacy.

"The trouble with you businessmen," he said, "is that you don't take our advice."

It had been impossible for me to do so. I was the only American businessman left in Budapest, and my job was to do what

I could to save the last American company behind the Iron Curtain. If I had taken the legation's usual advice, this company—Standard Electric of Budapest—would long since have been expropriated without compensation.

The International Standard Electric Corporation (ISEC), of which I was an assistant vice-president, supervised the foreign manufacturing subsidiaries of the International Telephone and Telegraph Corporation, of which I was also an assistant vice-president. I had been sent to Vienna in 1945 to supervise I.T.&T.'s operations in Austria. Since then its operations in Czechoslovakia and Hungary had been added to my responsibilities. I had continued to make my headquarters in Vienna, however, where I could keep abreast of developments in all three countries. There was no censorship in the American sector of Vienna (or in the British and French sectors, for that matter), and I could communicate with our New York office without revealing our hopes and fears to the snoops of the Communist Information Bureau. I could also leave my wife and family in the American sector of the city without worrying too much about their safety. In Budapest it was impossible to converse even in the privacy of my office without running the risk of being overheard by agents of the AVH.

An engineer, as they used to say when I was a student at the Massachusetts Institute of Technology, learns more and more about less and less until he knows everything about nothing. I am an engineer who has become a businessman, and a businessman who is still an engineer—an acoustical engineer, to be precise. I am a jack of all trades in the electrical communications field and a master of none. As a boy I built my own radio sets, and thanks to an inheritance from my paternal grandfather, I also built and drove a couple of racing cars. But acoustical problems have always excited my curiosity. In recent years, in my spare time, I have been experimenting with improved methods of sound transmission, and I still hope, before I die, to be instrumental in marketing a really good loud-speaker at a popular price.

I was born in New York City on September 6, 1911, the first and only surviving child of a naturalized German father and a naturalized French mother. My parents met on board the ship that brought them to the United States. My father, Willy Robert Vogeler, was born in Limbach, near Chemnitz, in Saxony; my mother, Marie-Jeanne Besse, in Billom, near Clermont-Ferrand, in Auvergne. My father was a devout Lutheran, my mother a devout Catholic; they were happily married, but they never managed to compose their religious differences, which is why I became an Episcopalian. I have spoken French and German in addition to English since early childhood, but I have yet to master Flemish, the native language of my naturalized Belgian wife.

Almost a third of my forty years has been spent abroad. My mother and father took me to Europe to meet my French and German grandparents before I was six months old. I caught cold on shipboard, and by the time we disembarked near Rotterdam my parents thought I had pneumonia. My mother insisted, in spite of my father's objections, on having me baptized in the nearest Catholic church. Within a few days I was well enough to accompany my parents to Germany and, later on, to France.

In those days my father was an engineer with the old Maxwell-Briscoe Motor Company. He joined a unit of the General Motors Corporation after the First World War and returned to Europe as a sales representative, traveling out of Germany to Austria, Hungary, Czechoslovakia, Poland, and the Baltic states. For several years I attended suburban public schools in New Jersey and New York. I then attended a German school in Wiesbaden, where my grandfather lived, and later a French school in Mainz.

In 1925 my parents sent me back to the United States to complete my secondary education at the Peekskill Military Academy. Four years later, through the good offices of the late Sol Bloom,

Congressman from the Nineteenth District of New York, I was appointed to the United States Naval Academy at Annapolis. In 1931, however, as a result of the depression and the belief that disarmament would delay rather than hasten the Second World War, Congress voted to reduce the size of the Navy and to commission only a portion of the midshipmen then at the Academy.

The class of 1933, of which I was a member, was hard hit by the retrenchment. My classmates and I discussed the problem and agreed that those of us who did not intend to devote their lives to the Navy should resign in favor of those who did. I was still trying to decide what to do when fate, as it often has before and since, intervened to solve the problem for me. First of all I fell in love. Then I fell ill with a throat infection that kept me in the hospital for fourteen weeks. It seemed doubtful, on my recovery, that I would be able to catch up with my work in time to pass my midyear examinations. I therefore resigned on December 21, 1931.

Two days later I married Debe Hubbard. We went to Europe on our honeymoon, visiting France, Germany, Czechoslovakia, Austria, and, of all places, Hungary. I liked Budapest, but not enough to think that I would revisit that unhappy city as often as I have.

After returning to the United States, Debe and I settled down in Mobile, where I entered the tire and rubber business with a friend of mine named Pat Feore. It was not long before I realized that I had made a series of mistakes. Debe and I were divorced in 1936. In the meantime I had sold out to Feore and enrolled as an undergraduate at the Massachusetts Institute of Technology. I had also enlisted in the Naval Reserve, and was commissioned as an ensign.

In 1937, after obtaining a degree in mechanical engineering and business administration, I joined the Cornell-Dubilier Elec-

tric Corporation of South Plainfield, New Jersey—the largest
American manufacturer of electrical condensers. A year later I
was selected to act as Cornell-Dubilier's consultant with ISEC.
Cornell-Dubilier had just signed a contract with I.T.&T. to provide its foreign subsidiaries—supervised by ISEC—with the information necessary to manufacture condensers according to the
latest mechanical methods.

I.T.&T. is not to be confused with the American Telephone
and Telegraph Corporation, from which it was separated after
the First World War. Today it competes with A.T.&T. in the
manufacture of electrical communications equipment in the
United States. Abroad, through ISEC, it competes with British,
German, Dutch, Swedish, and French companies in the manufacture of all sorts of electrical equipment, though principally in
the field of communications. I.T.&T. also operates a number of
foreign telephone companies, chiefly in Latin America, and
several international communications systems, including Commercial Cables, Mackay Radio, and All America Cables and
Radio. Its manufacturing subsidiaries produce everything from
railroad signals through telephone, telegraph, television, and
radio equipment to radar, loran, and other navigational aids for
ships and aircraft. They also produce a number of cybernetic
devices, including the Totalizator, a machine for computing odds
at race tracks, and the Intelex, a machine that automatically reserves space, determines routes, computes mileages, fares, and
taxes, and then issues tickets to railroad and airline passengers,
all in a single operation.

Before going to Europe for Cornell-Dubilier, I took the precaution of resigning my commission in the Naval Reserve. One
of the professors at MIT, a man named Peters, had disappeared
in the course of a visit to his native Germany. Dr. Peters was
reputed to have been the world's leading authority on the ventilation of ships. Whether he was arrested by the Nazis has never
been determined, for Dr. Peters is still among the missing. The

supposition, though, is that he was constrained to assist the Germans in improving their submarines and that he may now be working for the Russians. Although I was a native-born American, the fact that my father had been born in Germany, and had worked there for many years, placed me in an ambiguous position. I was afraid that when I visited Germany, to inspect the condenser plants in operation in I.T.&T.'s subsidiaries, the Nazis would consider me an *Auslandsdeutscher* and, as such, available for military service. I was also afraid that, if I refused to join them, they would accuse me of being an American spy. I felt that by severing my connection with the Navy I would at least avoid the latter danger, and as far as the Nazis were concerned I did.

My job as a Cornell-Dubilier consultant was to inspect I.T.&T.'s principal European factories with a view to installing modern condenser plants wherever they seemed to be economically justified. Machinery for the manufacture of condensers was eventually installed as the result of my recommendations in the Bell Telephone factory in Antwerp, the Matériel Téléphonique factory in Paris, and the Standard Telephone and Radio factory in Zurich. I visited Budapest in the course of my trip, but in view of the low wages paid in Hungary I was unable to recommend the installation of an expensive condenser plant. It would be cheaper, I thought, for the Standard Electric Company of Budapest to continue manufacturing condensers by hand. My recommendation was accepted, and I left Budapest after spending ten days there in May, 1939.

I had meanwhile fallen in love again—with Lucile Eykens, of Wondelgem, a suburb of Ghent. I met Lucile on my way from Antwerp to Zurich, where I was to address a meeting of Standard employees on sales problems. I was traveling with two refrigeration engineers, Brown and Kirkpatrick, who were to address the same meeting. At Brussels, where we changed trains, I went out to buy a bottle of cognac. On my return I found that we were to continue our journey with two extremely attractive women. The one who caught my eye was a slender blonde in a light blue skiing costume. I suggested to Brown that we offer the girls a drink, expecting them to say that they couldn't speak English, whereupon I would be given an opportunity to show off my knowledge of French and German. The only trouble was that the girl in the light blue skiing costume spoke English almost as well as I did. She was not married, I gathered, and she was on her way to Kandersteg with her companion, a young matron named Denise van Parys.

I was so attracted to Luce, as she was called for short, that I suggested that we go to Kandersteg too. It was Friday night, and we had nothing to do in Zurich until Monday morning. But Brown and Kirkpatrick insisted that we go to Grindelwald as we had planned, and so we said good-by to the girls the next morning in Zurich. Their train continued down one shore of Lake Brienz while our train continued down the other. Fortunately, there was so much fog that by the time we reached Interlaken, where the lines rejoined, I had succeeded in convincing my companions that we might as well go on to Kandersteg. Why visit Grindelwald, I argued, if we couldn't see the Jungfrau?

So we changed trains again and rejoined Lucile and Denise. The former feigned annoyance but the latter was amused. I had never skied before, but when we got to Kandersteg I bought a ski suit and proceeded to make such a fool of myself that I had to be sent to the beginners' slope. Now it was Lucile's turn to be amused. Sunday morning, however, I arose at four to take a lesson with the ski instructor. By Sunday afternoon I felt that the time had come to ask Lucile to marry me.

"Don't be ridiculous," she said. "We don't even know each other."

Monday morning I went back to Zurich to give my talk and

then returned to Kandersteg for two more days of skiing. By the
time I left on Wednesday it was no longer possible for Lucile to
say that we didn't know each other. She accepted my invitation
to attend the ball given on Washington's Birthday by the American consul in Antwerp, and invited me in return to Wondelgem
to meet her father and mother, five sisters, two brothers, and
numerous aunts and uncles. We were married in the Ghent
cathedral in June, 1939, soon after my return from Budapest.

On the outbreak of war, in September, 1939, I was ordered
back to the United States. Lucile was pregnant by then, and
Cornell-Dubilier was unwilling to accept responsibility for what
might happen to us in the event of a German invasion. Jacob
Jammer, a vice-president of ISEC with whom I had formed a
lasting friendship in London, wanted me to join I.T.&T. then
and there. I was more than willing, for I had found the manufacture of communications equipment more interesting than the
manufacture of its components. But I.T.&T., as a result of the
war, soon began to constrict its European operations, and Jammer was unable to find for me the place he had in mind. I therefore returned to the United States to become the Middle Western
representative of Cornell-Dubilier, with headquarters in Indianapolis.

Our first son, Robert Alexander Vogeler, Jr., was born in New
York in the spring of 1940. After living in Indianapolis for a time,
we moved to La Grange, a suburb of Chicago. By the time our
second son, William Eykens Vogeler, was born in the fall of
1941, I had resigned from Cornell-Dubilier to become manager
of the special products division of the Kellogg Switchboard and
Supply Company. In addition to producing equipment for the
Army and Navy, I was also charged with producing, for the
Lend-Lease Administration, 50,000 field telephone sets for the
Russian Army.

The Russian inspectors in the Kellogg factory accused me and my colleagues at every opportunity of supplying them with "inferior" products. They rejected large numbers of leather carrying cases, for example, because they were not all the same shade of brown. The character of their complaints can be gauged by the fact that every carrying case and telephone set rejected by the Russians was immediately accepted by the United States. Actually, we gave the Russians the best equipment that American industry could produce. I knew at the time it was better than anything that Russian industry could produce, but it was not until I reached Vienna that I discovered how much better it really was.

Once, after a particularly unpleasant argument with a Russian inspector, I exploded. "I'm not interested in doing a damn thing for such people," I said. "They're just making fools of us."

It was not long before I discovered that a fellow-traveler on my staff had denounced me to the FBI for making "anti-Russian" statements. It is indicative of the atmosphere prevailing in 1942 that Americans were being officially encouraged to denounce their fellow countrymen for criticizing Russia. Perhaps I was denounced because of my German name and background. In any case, nothing ever came of the incident.

Years later, in Budapest, I would be forced to confess that I had joined the FBI in 1942 and had been placed in charge of "a network of fifty agents and provocateurs" at the Kellogg factory in Chicago. Personally, I doubt very much that the FBI was able to spare even one agent for the Kellogg factory, though it could certainly have used one, if only to observe the strange behavior of the Russian inspectors. Their chief interest, aside from lodging complaints, was inspecting everything that the factory produced, including "secret" equipment for the United States Army and Navy. It was galling to me, I must admit, to have been powerless to prevent the Russians from taking advantage of the fact that they were immune to security restrictions.

I left Kellogg at the end of 1942 to become the assistant to the chief engineer of Libby, McNeill, and Libby. My job at Libby's was to organize the production of immersible food containers for the armed services. As soon as my work was completed, I resigned from Libby's to become, with Jammer's help, the Chicago manager of the Federal Telephone and Radio Corporation, a domestic subsidiary of I.T.&T. I was still holding that position when I was sent to Vienna, at Jammer's suggestion, in the summer of 1945.

Thus, for the entire war, I was employed as a civilian engineer in the United States. My selective service rating was II-A ("deferred because of civilian employment"). I would have preferred to serve in the Navy, for which service I was better suited, by training and inclination, than most fathers in my age group. I tried repeatedly to rejoin the Navy, in fact, but on each occasion I was rejected on the ground that my work as a civilian engineer was more important than anything I could do in uniform.

So much for the charge, to which I would also be made to confess in Budapest, that I was a naval intelligence officer holding the rank of lieutenant commander. The fact is that, since I resigned my ensign's commission in 1937, I have had no connection whatsoever with any branch of the United States government, either military or civilian.

The Standard Electric Company of Budapest was the largest of I.T.&T.'s manufacturing subsidiaries in Eastern Europe. Standard Budapest employed some 3,000 workers in the manufacture of telephone, telegraph, and radio equipment. In turn it controlled a company known as Telefongyár, which employed some 1,400 workers in the manufacture of cables, air brakes, railroad signals, and electrical components, and a small company known as Dial, which rented and maintained private telephone exchanges.

I.T.&T.'s three Austrian subsidiaries—Czeija, Nissl and Company, Mix und Genest, and Berliner—together employed about as many workers as Standard Budapest alone. Czeija, Nissl, the largest of the three, was located in the Russian sector of Vienna. It employed some 2,000 workers in the manufacture of telephone, telegraph, and radio equipment.

In the spring of 1945, two of I.T.&T.'s Czechoslovakian subsidiaries—Kablo and Telegrafia—were expropriated. The third, Standard Doms, was not expropriated until later because the original nationalization law exempted companies employing fewer than 100 workers. I.T.&T. also owned rental and maintenance subsidiaries in Rumania and Yugoslavia. The Yugoslavian subsidiary was expropriated without compensation soon after the Titoists seized power in the fall of 1944. The Rumanian subsidiary, despite the best efforts of Henry Burrell, who was sent to Bucharest in 1946, eventually suffered the same fate.

Czechoslovakia's crypto-Communist Fierlinger government, unlike its counterparts in Yugoslavia and Rumania, however, had promised to pay "equitable" compensation to the owners of all nationalized foreign properties. Richard Brown, of I.T.&T.'s export department, who had entered Czechoslovakia as an Army technical adviser, remained in Prague in the hope of persuading the government to keep its promise.

The fate of I.T.&T.'s Hungarian and Austrian subsidiaries was still to be determined. Like the others, they had been seized and operated by the Germans during the war, and it was obvious that, unless prompt action was taken, they would soon be seized and operated by or for the Russians.

Geoffrey Ogilvie, a vice-president of I.T.&T., was accordingly assigned to Hungary, and I was assigned to Austria, to do what we could to prevent the confiscation of the company's properties. Sosthenes Behn, the chairman of I.T.&T., promoted me to the rank of assistant vice-president and arranged for me to fly to Europe with Ogilvie on August 15, 1945.

Two | Assignment to Vienna

August 15 was V-J Day. New York was so busy celebrating our victory over Japan that it was impossible to find a taxi to take us to La Guardia Airport, and so we had to hire a Cadillac funeral limousine.

Together we flew to Paris. From there Ogilvie flew to Frankfort, and I to Naples, whence, by varying routes and means of transportation, we both finally reached Vienna.

The Army put us up at the Hotel Regina, a field-grade mess on the Maximiliansplatz, which was the only hotel then available in the American sector of the city. And even the Regina wasn't available to two civilians, or "carpetbaggers," as we were called, for very long. General Lewis, the commander of the sector, said that we could stay at the Regina for a few days, but that we would have to move out before we established a precedent for letting "carpetbaggers" clutter up his mess. Ogilvie promised to leave as soon as he could find transportation to Budapest, and I promised to leave as soon as I could find another place in which to live.

Finding another place in which to live, however, was easier said than done. The International sector, which corresponded to the old, or inner, city, was still a maze of ruins. The Russians had taken over the Grand, the Imperial, the Bristol, the Astoria, Sacher's, and all the better hotels that were more or less intact,

25

and the remainder had either been reserved for American, British, and French army personnel, or else were not fit for human habitation.

Ogilvie was finally driven to Budapest, 175 miles down the Danube from Vienna, in an Army weapons carrier. He found that all but one of its better hotels, the Szent Gellért, had been destroyed, and the Szent Gellért had been taken over by the Russians. Ogilvie solved his housing problem temporarily by moving into the convent operated by the Sisters of Social Service. He later succeeded in leasing a house in the Buda hills from a disfranchised professor of philosophy.

The convent in Pest became the headquarters of most of the American and British civilians who visited the twin cities of Buda and Pest in the first year after the war. There was no such convent in Vienna, unfortunately, and in the absence of any unoccupied apartments or civilian hotels, General Lewis, who eventually thawed out and became a good friend of mine, adopted me as a civilian ward of the Army. I was duly classified as a CAF-15 (that is, a civilian in the clerical, administrative, and fiscal category, with the assimilated rank of "colonel"). My status was merely a bureaucratic stratagem designed to permit the Army to furnish me with board and lodging at cost until such time as I could establish an independent household of my own. Hundreds of American civilians, in Vienna and other occupied cities, enjoyed the same status for the same reason during the first year of our military occupation. But though there was nothing irregular about my position, the fact that the civilian rating CAF-15 corresponded to the rank of colonel would be used against me at my trial in Budapest.

At the time, however, it was a company joke. I was a junior executive who had inadvertently placed himself on the same level with many senior executives of a company noted for its employment of former Army and Navy officers. Sosthenes Behn, in fact, is usually referred to as Colonel Behn because of his service as the commander of a field signal battalion in the First World War. Among the other senior executives of I.T.&T. are several former generals, including William H. Harrison, Roger B. Colton, and Pedro A. del Valle; two former admirals, Ellery W. Stone and William F. Halsey; and at least a dozen colonels and lieutenant colonels.

I.T.&T.'s reasons for employing so many former Army and Navy officers are not hard to explain. First, a large corporation specializing in foreign operations must be represented abroad by executives who have traveled widely and who have had experience in dealing with foreign government officials. Second, just as the services have supplied I.T.&T. with executives in time of peace, so I.T.&T. has supplied the services with signal officers in time of war. (Neither Admiral Stone nor General Harrison, for example, were professional officers. Stone left I.T.&T. and Harrison left A.T.&T. to join the services during the war; Harrison joined and Stone rejoined I.T.&T. as soon as their work for the services had been completed.) Third, I.T.&T. is continually faced with the problem of dickering with Europeans, Latin Americans, and Asians who attach great importance to rank.

There was nothing sinister, therefore, about the high proportion of former Army and Navy officers among the company's senior executives. I.T.&T.'s relations with the United States government are no different from those of any other large corporation engaged in foreign operations, or, for that matter, any other large corporation engaged in the manufacture of communications equipment. Certainly, as a junior executive of I.T.&T., I was no closer to our government's military and civilian representatives than many other American civilians in Vienna.

The Russian sector of Vienna was by far the most valuable of the four. It embraced the Danube waterfront, the electric power plant, the main telephone exchange, and most of the city's industrial establishments, including the Czeija, Nissl factory. Its one shortcoming, from the Russians' point of view, was its lack of suitable private residences for field-grade officers and their families. The American, British, and French sectors, on the other hand, though economically less important, embraced a number of pleasant residential suburbs.

The disparity eventually resulted in a deal between the Russians and the three Western Allies. In exchange for certain hotels in the International sector, the Allies agreed to permit the Russians to occupy certain residential areas in their own sectors of Vienna.

The Hotel Bristol, on the Kärntner Ring, was thus turned over to the American Army. It was in such a state of disorder when the Russians moved out that it took a battalion of American soldiers a week to make it habitable. Among the other quaint customs that came to light was the Russians' habit of slaughtering pigs and chickens in the bathrooms. I moved out of the Regina and into the Bristol as soon as the latter was ready for occupancy. The former was subsequently converted into a hotel for women employees of USFA—the United States Forces in Austria.

Except for the loss of most of its windows, which it took me the better part of a year to replace, the Czeija, Nissl factory had escaped serious damage during the siege. Immediately afterward, however, it had been used as a barracks for Russian infantry soldiers who had done a lot of damage. When the infantry were removed, Russian signal corpsmen proceeded to remove all the stocks of raw materials on hand, whereupon they began to dismantle the machinery on the ground that the contents of all factories operated by the Germans during the war constituted legitimate booty.

My first task was to put a stop to the dismantling and reinstall as much as I could of the machinery that the Russians had attempted to remove. My second task was to remove the Russians themselves. My third and most difficult task was to constrain the Russians to recognize the fact that the Czeija, Nissl plant, and everything in or pertaining to it, was American property.

I was assisted in my work by Hans Nissl, the factory's general manager. Nissl's father, Franz Nissl, the Austrian founder of the company, had sold out to I.T.&T. in the late 1920's. Hans Nissl had meanwhile become a citizen of Liechtenstein, a Swiss protectorate, and as such was the bearer of a Swiss passport. The Russians refused to respect his new nationality. They insisted on treating him as an Austrian, which is to say as badly as the Germans would have treated a Russian in the same position.

I put up signs reading "AMERICAN PROPERTY", in Russian and German and then went to see the major who commanded the district of Brigittenau, in which the factory was located. The major, whose name I never learned, informed me that the factory's problems were "technical" matters with which he was not competent to deal. I therefore made an appointment to see Major General Kalugin, the chief of an organization that soon came to be known as USIA—the Administration of Soviet Enterprises in Austria. USIA eventually obtained control of a large part of Austria's industrial capacity.

Kalugin's deputy informed me that the general would receive me in his office at the Hotel Imperial, just down the street from the Bristol, at ten-thirty one Tuesday morning. I was refused admittance, however, by the guards at the entrance, who kept me covered with their tommy guns. When I tried to explain that I had an appointment with General Kalugin, they simply stuck their guns in my ribs and told me to be on my way.

I returned to the Bristol to telephone Kalugin's deputy, who assured me that I was expected at the Imperial and that the guards would be instructed to let me enter. But when I got back to the Imperial, the guards still blocked my way. A Russian Wac appeared on the scene with instructions to escort me to the general's office. But the guards still refused to let me pass. The

Wac shrugged her shoulders and disappeared. Finally a Russian police agent in civilian clothes managed to persuade the guards to let me enter the hotel.

General Kalugin, a large, beefy man with dark cropped hair, received me in a third-floor bedroom. He agreed to call a halt to the dismantling of the factory. He also agreed to remove all but a few Russian "inspectors" on condition that I give first priority to Russian reparations orders. I agreed to do so, provided (1) that Czeija, Nissl be paid for its work at acceptable prices; (2) that the Russians supply it with the necessary raw materials; and (3) that its American ownership be formally recognized. Kalugin accepted the first two conditions and promised to consider the third.

Our first job for the Russians consisted of repairing 150,000 field telephone sets of Russian manufacture. They were extremely primitive in comparison with the field telephone sets that Kellogg had manufactured for the Russians in 1941-42. They were equipped with ordinary dry-cell battery clips, for example, instead of screw-type terminals; and instead of being carried in leather cases, of whatever quality, they were carried in crude wooden boxes. In view of their poor quality and the absence of any spare parts, we had to cannibalize two broken sets for every reconditioned set that we delivered to the Russian Army.

Food was so scarce that, to keep the factory working, I had to serve its employees hot lunches every day. Usually it was necessary to send the one company truck that the Russians had refrained from stealing out into the country to buy food directly from the peasants. Occasionally, though, the Russians would sell us salt pork and vegetables that they had collected from the peasants by force.

Although General Kalugin had promised to "consider" recognizing I.T.&T.'s ownership of Czeija, Nissl, his Russian colleagues

on the Allied Council refused at first to recognize the formal claim that was eventually presented. Indeed, the day after our Austrian lawyers presented the claim, the Russians threatened to reoccupy the factory. I telephoned Kalugin to remind him of our agreement. He told me that he would take the matter up with the major in command of the Brigittenau district, who had since been given full authority. A few hours later the major telephoned to upbraid me for interfering with Russian "military operations."

I had learned by that time that the only way to deal with the Russians successfully was to bluster and threaten as much as they did. I therefore warned the major that if he reoccupied the factory I would refuse to authorize any more work on Russian orders.

One part of me hoped that he would force me to carry out my threat. The factory by then had received so many American, British, French, and Austrian orders that its Russian orders were a nuisance. But another part of me realized that, if I attempted to carry out my threat, the Russians would retaliate by making it impossible for the factory to fill its other orders. Czeija, Nissl, after all, was in the Russian sector of Vienna—an inconvenient fact of which the major immediately reminded me.

"I've been wondering for some time," he said, "what right an American has to be working in the Russian sector without an employment permit."

I explained that I was not an employee but a supervisor of an American enterprise, and that I had a Four-Power permit entitling me to direct its operations in the interests of its stockholders.

"As the commander of a district in the Russian sector, I hereby order you to leave at once."

"As the American supervisor of the Czeija, Nissl factory, I refuse to accept your orders."

"Then I'll have to order my soldiers to expel you by force."

"When do you intend to do that?"

The major hesitated for a moment.

"Why do you want to know?" he asked.

"So that I can assemble some photographers to take pictures of the incident."

The major hung up without another word. I was not expelled from his district, the factory was not reoccupied, and I.T.&T.'s claim to ownership was eventually recognized by the Russian High Command.

The American Army in Vienna occasionally resorted to the same tactic. When the Russians decided one day to occupy the Ministry of Internal Affairs, a group of American correspondents and photographers, who had been tipped off in advance, assembled to record the incident for posterity. The Russians were so reluctant to receive unfavorable publicity, at a time when they were still trying to popularize the Austrian Communist Party, that within an hour they moved out of the Ministry and gave it back to the Austrians.

The Germans had made themselves ridiculous, in Vienna as in other conquered capitals, by renaming familiar landmarks in accordance with Nazi propaganda. The Russians had so outdone the Germans, however, in renaming the same landmarks in accordance with Communist propaganda, that the following story was told of a liberated Viennese prisoner of war who returned one day to his native city.

The soldier, who arrived at the State Railway Station, took a streetcar to Schwarzenberg Platz, only to discover that it was now called Stalinsplatz. The streetcar continued down the ring, crossed the Danube Canal over the Red Army Bridge, formerly known as the Franz Bridge, and proceeded to the Danube waterfront, which was the end of the line.

"It's a beautiful river, isn't it?" the conductor said.

"I know," said the soldier. "Don't tell me. It isn't the Danube, it's the Volga."

In Budapest, where there was said to have been more raping than looting, the Russians' monument to their Unknown Soldier was popularly known as the Unknown Raper. In Vienna, however, where the opposite seemed to have been true, the Russian monument was popularly known as the Unknown Looter.

For weeks after my arrival in Vienna, gangs of soldiers armed with gunny sacks and tommy guns systematically plundered every house and apartment in the Russian sector of the city. The pretext for their looting was to make sure that no Austrian household under their jurisdiction was being used for "illegal" purposes—and everything is illegal under Russian jurisdiction except that which is tolerated, at any given moment, by the Russian Ministry of Internal Affairs, the MVD, or its twin, the Ministry of State Security, the MGB. In their search for "illegal" weapons, "illegal" literature, and "illegal" persons, the Russians found occasion to carry off all the watches, jewelry, fountain pens, liquor, art objects, and pretty women that they could find. Once they had cleaned out a house, they would stencil "PROVERENO" on the door. "*Provereno*" is a Russian word that used to mean "examined." In Austria, however, it now means "plundered."

One of the best-known phrases in the Russian-occupied countries is "*Davai chass*," which means, "Let's have your watch." I have heard a lot of Russian watch stories, but none excelled the true stories of what happened to two of my acquaintances in Vienna.

One of them, an Austrian engineer who worked for Czeija, Nissl, showed up one morning with a new gold watch. He said that a Russian, of all people, had given it to him. On his way to work, he explained, he had been stopped by an armed Russian soldier who pronounced the magic words, "*Davai chass!*" He had no alternative but to hand over the cheap steel watch that he had been wearing for fear of losing his gold watch, which he had hidden. The Russian, in exchange, gave him the new gold watch, which he had apparently stolen from somebody else, explaining that it had stopped running and was therefore *"kaput."* The Austrian engineer said nothing, put the watch on his wrist, and continued down the street. Later, in his office, he examined the watch and found that it was in good working order. The Russian had simply neglected to wind it.

On another occasion, a Russian-speaking American, who was really an intelligence agent, stopped to observe the lively commerce in one of the many open-air black markets in the Russian sector of Vienna. He soon found himself conversing with a friendly Russian captain, who asked him if he was well supplied with watches. The American said he wasn't, whereupon the Russian captain pulled up his sleeves and told him to take his pick of the various watches that he was wearing on either wrist. It was foolish, he said, for a Russian in Vienna not to have a watch. The American accepted one of the watches because he couldn't do anything else without revealing to the Russian that he was an American in disguise.

Marauding bands of Russian soldiers periodically invaded the Czeija, Nissl factory. In November, 1945, four of them broke into the paint shop looking for something to drink. The night watchman pleaded with them not to touch the methyl alcohol, which was used in mixing varnish, but they paid no attention to him and drank it down as if it were vodka. All four of them had to be hospitalized, and two of them died in a matter of hours. The next day my friend the Russian major attempted to arrest me for having "poisoned" two of his soldiers. The charge was so absurd that I was able to talk him out of it by emphasizing the embarrassment that I thought my arrest would probably cause. It was a narrow squeak, I knew, but how narrow it was I failed to realize until after I had been imprisoned four years later.

In June, 1946, when Lucile and I were attending a reception in honor of some visiting American congressmen, I was called to the telephone by the same night watchman. Some drunken Russians, he said, had broken into the warehouse and were loading radios onto a truck.

I immediately drove to the factory and warned the Russians that, unless they returned the radios to the warehouse, I would see that they were given long sentences in the worst concentration camp in Siberia. It was an idle threat, of course, but the Russians were too drunk to realize that I was in no position to make it good. I knew from experience that it was useless to call the Russian police. The MVD was simply not interested in protecting property unless it belonged to high Soviet officials, in which case it was very well protected indeed. Fortunately, in this instance, the Russian drunks took fright and did as they were told.

No army in modern times has ever behaved as badly as the Russian Army behaved, and still behaves, in the occupied countries of Eastern Europe. Its behavior in Austria, if anything, has been somewhat better than its behavior in countries where it is the sole occupying force. It has behaved so badly in Austria, even so, that it has by now destroyed whatever chances the Austrian Communists may have had to win a popular following. The Communists may yet come to power in Austria, if we give them the opportunity, but only if Stalin is willing to convert Austria into a European Korea.

One day, as I was driving to the Czeija, Nissl factory in a borrowed Army jeep, I passed a crew of Austrian linemen hanging new trolley wires above the unused streetcar tracks on Währinger Strasse. The American wire they were using was being unreeled from a truck belonging to the Ministry of Railways. The American Army, it developed, had agreed to supply the Austrians with the copper wire needed to rehabilitate the Vienna streetcar system, hoping against hope that the Russians would

not steal the new wire as they had stolen all the old wire remaining in Vienna at the time of the city's surrender.

The place where I had passed the Austrian linemen was in
the Alsergrund district of the American sector. The linemen, I
discovered, had started at the Brigittenauer Bridge (now called
the "Freedom" Bridge) and were working their way through
the American sector to the boulevards, or *ringstrassen,* around
the inner city. A mile farther on, as I neared the "Freedom"
Bridge, I passed another crew of linemen, this time Russians,
who were busily taking down the same wire and reeling it onto
an American lend-lease truck.

The next day both the Austrian government and the American
High Commission protested to the Russians, who gave their
usual excuse—namely, that the Vienna Street Railways, having
been seized and operated by the Germans for a time, constituted German property within the meaning of the Austrian Ar-
mistice Agreement. All property of the Vienna Street Railways,
therefore, regardless of whence it came, or when, was legitimate
booty—or so the Russians pretended to believe. In this instance,
they pretended to believe that the stolen wire was German,
rather than American. It was several months before the Russians, after assessing the political pros and cons, at last agreed
to let the trolley wires stay up if the American Army furnished
the wire. In the end, of course, it was the Americans who furnished almost everything, including a score of streetcars from
New York's abandoned Third Avenue System—a gift from the
Economic Cooperation Administration.

In the meantime the Russians had begun to dismantle Vienna's
telephone system on the same specious ground: having been
seized and operated by the Germans, it constituted legitimate
booty. By the time they agreed to desist, in return for the Austrian government's promise to supply them with new exchanges,
they had removed 40,000 of Vienna's 70,000 lines of telephone
equipment.

Their primitive methods of removal constituted sheer vandalism. The "technicians" of their signal corps went from exchange to exchange, dismantling 1,000-line frames, placing them on dollies, and pushing them outside, where they were left for days exposed to the weather before they were finally loaded onto trucks and driven to the railroad yards, where they were again exposed for days to the weather before they were loaded onto flatcars and hauled off to Russia. It was criminal sabotage from both the Russian and the Austrian points of view. It deprived the Austrians of indispensable telephone equipment without making more than a small fraction of the same equipment available to the peoples of Russia. I would be very much surprised if more than 10 per cent of the delicate equipment thus removed could ever be used again. I am certain that the greater part of it was damaged beyond any hope of repair.

The Russians also went from house to house, ripping out private hand sets, which they tossed into open trucks as if they were so many pairs of shoes. One day, out of morbid curiosity, I followed a truck laden with hand sets to the railroad yards to see what would happen. The driver backed up to a boxcar and dropped his tail gate. Several German prisoners of war then proceeded to transfer the hand sets from the truck to the boxcar— *with shovels.* The prisoners naturally treated the equipment as roughly as they could, in view of its destination, but their Russian guards made no effort to restrain them. Hand sets are not as delicate as the frames of a telephone exchange, but I doubt that even half the sets removed from Austria were in any condition to be used again on reaching Russia.

The most sickening sight of all was the dismantling of the rolling mill that belonged to Felten und Guillaume, a subsidiary of a Luxemburg steel-manufacturing concern. The Russian "technicians" in charge of the dismantling removed the upper rollers carefully enough, but had to blast the lower rollers off their foundations with dynamite. Russia thus acquired a number of upper rollers in fair condition that could be used only with matching lower rollers that had been ruined in the process of removal. Austria lost a steel mill, and Russia failed to gain one, from which proposition it can readily be seen that both countries lost an economic asset worth many millions of dollars.

If it were not for what my chauffeur told me of his experiences as a prisoner of war in Russia, I would be inclined to believe that the Russians had no intention of utilizing the property that they removed from Austria in the guise of "reparations." Indeed, in attempting to discover some method in their madness, I often wondered if their only purpose was vengeance. If they intended merely to destroy as much of the Austrian economy as they could, they were certainly successful. But after what I learned from my chauffeur, and my subsequent experiences in Hungary, I finally decided that they really intended to make use of the stolen property, and were prevented from doing so only by their lack of respect for property as such, and by their concomitant inability to understand that all property, to be useful to man, must be handled with care and properly maintained.

My chauffeur, Rudolf Hönig, was such a slipshod person himself that I was doubly impressed by his horror of the shiftlessness that he had observed in Russia. He had been drafted into the German Army and sent to the Leningrad front as a truck driver and mechanic. He was captured by the Russians in the winter of 1942-43. Since the Germans had classified him as a mechanic, his Russian captors decided that he was qualified to work as a machinist in a sewing-machine factory in the outskirts of Leningrad. Perhaps he was, but as Hönig told the story it made no difference whether he was qualified or not.

He soon discovered that the parts he was making wouldn't fit the machine for which they were designed. For weeks he lived in fear of being shot as a saboteur, until he discovered that the Russian manager also knew that the parts wouldn't fit and was also afraid of being shot.

Actually, it seems, the manager was doing the best he could. The political commissar, however, insisted on producing 150 sewing machines a day in a factory whose absolute capacity was 120. The manager could do only as he was ordered, even if it meant producing parts that wouldn't fit. The commissar was apparently not interested in whether the sewing machines worked or not. What he was after was the Red Banner of Labor, a medal with which both he and the manager were eventually decorated in recognition of their "socialist" prowess in exceeding the factory's "norm" by 25 per cent.

Sooner or later both the manager and the commissar probably were shot, but by that time Hönig and a fellow Austrian prisoner, who also worked for Czeija, Nissl, had escaped. It took them a year to reach Vienna on foot, by way of Byelorussia, Ukrainia, Rumania, and Hungary. They had both learned enough Russian to pass as Russians until they were outside the territorial limits of the old Soviet Union. They earned their board and lodging by performing feats of magic in the villages through which they passed.

Hönig became my chauffeur after I discovered that Czeija, Nissl owned a Steyr convertible sedan that had been hidden in a haystack near the town of Krems, in the Russian zone of Austria. A Steyr, which is made in Austria, is not a very good automobile, but in the fall of 1945 it seemed to me that it would be better to ride around in an underpowered Steyr than in a streetcar or a jeep. The Steyr in question had been hidden the preceding winter to prevent its being stolen by the Russians. Its spark plugs, distributor, and all five wheels and tires had been stored in the factory. The wheels and tires, however, had since disappeared. I therefore had to scrounge some jeep wheels and tires from the American Army and drill new holes in the wheels to fit the studs of the Steyr. I then drove to the village where

the Steyr was hidden, attached the wheels and tires, and towed
it back to Vienna with the help of an Army sergeant and a borrowed weapons carrier.

The Steyr, which was black, was a conspicuous vehicle not
only because of its jeep wheels and tires. Some Russian soldiers
had located it before I had, and they had damaged the trunk in
trying to force it open with their bayonets. Unable to make off
with the car itself, for lack of wheels and tires, they had con-
tented themselves with removing the black rubber knob from
the old-fashioned gearshift lever and one of the yellow plastic
balls on the inside handle of the left front door. Hönig had ham-
mered out the bayonet holes and repainted the trunk. He had
also machined a stainless-steel ball to replace the rubber gearshift knob and a white plastic ball to replace the yellow doorknob that the Russians had removed. Everything was satisfactory
except the steel ball on the gearshift lever. It was so heavy that
every time the car went over a bump it threw the engine out of
gear.

I often visited the theater in the winter of 1945-46. It wasn't
very amusing, in the absence of heating—especially if you lacked
an overcoat, as I did—but it was better, in spite of the cold, than
sitting around the bar of the Bristol every evening. Lucile and
the boys would not be able to join me until the following spring.
In the meantime all I had to wear was an Army trenchcoat. The
Air Transport Command, on one of whose airplanes I had flown
to Europe in the summertime, had allowed me only the usual
twenty kilograms of baggage, and it was impossible, until the
late spring of 1946, to import any clothing from the United
States.

I grew a mustache that winter, for reasons that I have since
forgotten, and my barber persuaded me to let it luxuriate to the
point where I looked like a character out of a novel by Eric
Ambler. Or so it was said until "Professor" Jerry Colonna came

to town with Bob Hope and other members of a traveling company of USO entertainers. From then until the day Lucile persuaded me to shave off the mustache I was known to my friends as the "poor man's Jerry Colonna."

One night in February, I drove to the Theater an der Wien, which took the place of the ruined Opera House, to see the first postwar performance of Beethoven's *Fidelio*. General McCreery, the commander of the British forces in Austria, was also attending the theater, and I parked the Steyr immediately behind his official Daimler. Nobody, I thought, would dare to steal the general's car or any car in its immediate vicinity.

It turned out that I had underestimated the Russians. It was such a cold night that General McCreery's Austrian driver took refuge inside the theater, and once inside he succumbed to temptation and decided to view the opera. He must have enjoyed the performance, because the Russians had left before he emerged to discover that the general's car had disappeared.

It was grand larceny in the grand manner. According to the theater's elderly doorman, who had been too frightened to raise an alarm, several Russian soldiers drove up in a large American van decorated with the insigne of the Red Cross. While two of the soldiers stood guard with tommy guns, the others opened the rear of the van, tied a steel cable to General McCreery's Daimler, and hauled it aboard with the help of some skids and a hand winch that they had installed inside the van. There was room for one more car, and since the Steyr was the closest it, too, was hauled aboard. The job was completed in less than fifteen minutes.

In August, 1946, I visited Budapest for the first time since the war. Standard Budapest had been having production difficulties, and Ogilvie thought that I, as an engineer, would be able to make some useful recommendations.

The difficulties arose from the factory's chronic shortage of raw materials. Standard Budapest, like Czeija, Nissl, had been given a succession of Russian orders to fill as part of what was known as "reparations." It was the Hungarian government's responsibility to supply the factory with all the materials necessary to complete the orders on schedule. In practice, though, certain materials were always late in being delivered. The factory, to keep its employees busy, was thus forced to start work on another order before a previous order had been completed. The staggering of orders made it necessary either to move the uncompleted orders off the production line, and store them, or else move the production line itself.

I recommended ways and means of solving the problem with a minimum loss of efficiency, but the only thanks I ever received was to be blamed at my trial for creating the very problem that I had tried to solve. Actually, the problem was inherent in the controlled economy that the Russians had imposed in Hungary with the help of their Communist stooges. No factory can operate efficiently if it is forced to depend on inefficient government agencies for its supplies of raw materials.

I intended to return to Vienna as soon as I had made my recommendations—which were rejected by the Communist shop stewards—but it turned out to be impossible for me to do so. The alcoholic Russian colonel who was the sole official authorized to issue exit permits was indulging himself in a lengthy spree. Along with a lot of other people, therefore, I had to wait for several days until the colonel had sobered up sufficiently to issue the permits without which it was impossible for anyone, even Allied officers, to leave Hungary.

It was not the first time that I would be forced to wait for days before I was allowed to leave, but for once the delay was a blessing in disguise. I was still in need of clothing, and so I made use of my time to buy enough material to have a suit and an extra pair of trousers made on my return to Vienna. Piece goods and, in fact, most commodities which were either scarce or unobtainable in Vienna could still be found in Budapest, though prices were high and quality was very low.

One day, as I was walking along Váczi Street with Robert Iglauer, the local I.T.&T. accountant, we passed a black Steyr convertible sedan parked in front of a shop. The wheels and tires had once belonged to a jeep.

"That's the car," I said, turning around to look at it.

"Oh, you're just imagining things," said Iglauer. "There're lots of Steyrs in Budapest."

"Not with jeep wheels and tires," I said. "Let's look at the trunk."

We walked to the rear of the car and confirmed the unmistakable bayonet marks. That was enough for me, but to make doubly certain we also looked inside. The left front doorknob was Hönig's white plastic replacement, and the gearshift knob was the stainless-steel ball that he had fashioned.

Iglauer wanted to call the police, but I decided it would be better to do nothing until I could prove that the car belonged to I.T.&T. Otherwise it might disappear again if we failed to produce the necessary proofs of ownership. The official license plate indicated that the car was being used by an undersecretary of the Ministry of Agriculture. I jotted down the number and went to call on Colonel Stokes, the deputy to General Weems, the chief of the American Military Mission. Colonel Stokes telephoned Vienna and arranged for a sergeant to collect the car's papers from Hans Nissl and bring them down to Budapest in a weapons carrier. When the sergeant arrived with the papers, Stokes drew up a formal claim and presented it to the official in charge of the government's motor pool. The official demurred at first, but was finally constrained to surrender the car, and it was later delivered to me in Vienna. The Hungarians, it developed, had bought the car from the Russians for $2,000 in scarce American currency. As far as I know, General McCreery's car was never recovered.

A few months later the company sent me a black Buick sedan from the United States. Lucile and the boys had meanwhile joined me in Vienna, bringing with them our gray Ford convertible coupé.

Three | The Austro-American Club

By the time my wife and family arrived, in June, 1946, I had acquired a comfortable modern house on Max Emmanuel Strasse in the Währing district of the American sector of Vienna. The house had belonged to a deceased opera singer, whose heirs had sold it to the Österreichische Sparkasse, a savings bank, which had leased it to a Nazi official during the German occupation. During the Russian siege, in April, 1945, the Nazi fled to Germany, leaving all his possessions behind. A Communist physician then moved into the house without permission, apparently expecting the Russians to occupy Währing. As soon as he learned that the Americans would occupy the district, he moved to an empty apartment in the Russian sector, taking with him everything that could possibly be detached. He not only removed all the books, rugs, paintings, and furniture, he also removed the stove and the refrigerator and stripped the house of most of its plumbing and electrical fixtures. He even removed the locks from the doors and cut out several window panes, presumably for the purpose of replacing the broken windows in his new apartment.

The Sparkasse, after much deliberation, agreed to lease the house to me on condition that I should replace all the stolen fixtures and windows and repair the damage that the house had suffered in the siege. It took five months to rehabilitate the house,

but by the time it was ready for occupancy it was one of the
most attractive residences in the American sector of the city.
It was so attractive, in fact, that the Chinese ambassador copied
its landscape garden when he put his own house in order.

I paid the mechanics and gardeners who did the work half
their wages in Austrian shillings and half in CARE packages and
cigarettes valued at the official rate of exchange. This meant
that instead of earning ten cents a day, at the free or black rate
of exchange, they earned $1.35—which was little enough, I admit,
but still far more than most Austrians were earning in 1946.
The shilling, which was officially worth ten cents, was actually
worth but a fortieth of that amount. The discrepancy explained
the widespread use of cigarettes and packaged foods as currency
during the first two years of the quadripartite occupation. One
cigarette was worth one shilling officially, but from fifteen to
twenty shillings on the black market. The value of cigarettes
increased as the value of the shilling declined, and so did the
value of most other commodities, including packaged foods.
Workers who earned twenty-five shillings a day at a time when
the shilling was being sold at four hundred to the dollar naturally
preferred to be paid in cigarettes or food or both, for otherwise
it would have been impossible for them to survive. As conditions
improved, the value of the shilling increased until, by the middle
of 1949, it leveled off at about forty to the dollar on the black
market.

Although it was necessary for most foreign civilians to sell
dollars on the black market, in order to hedge their rising living
expenses, I was fortunate in not having to do so. As the supervisor of Czeija, Nissl's operations, I was entitled to defray all my
living expenses out of I.T.&T.'s local blocked account. I later
enjoyed the same privilege in Prague and Budapest. Thus, when
I was arrested, it was impossible for the Communists to accuse
me of having engaged in illegal currency speculation in any of
the countries in which I had worked.

It is necessary to emphasize this point because the Russians and their stooges, to justify their persecution, customarily accuse their victims, among other things, of having been black marketeers. If the charge happens to be true—and in some cases, I suppose, it has been—the truth is purely coincidental. The purpose of the charge, in every instance, is to blacken the victim's reputation and thus deprive him of public sympathy. I am sorry to say that, in the cases of a good many Americans, our diplomatic representatives have been only too ready to believe the worst. Instead of assuming that our hapless citizens are innocent, and proceeding vigorously to defend them on that assumption, our diplomats have often allowed themselves to be intimidated into assuming a posture of defense—which is precisely the purpose of the smear technique as practiced by its Communist masters. They will continue to smear our citizens, with ever more damaging results, so long as our government's representatives allow themselves to be taken in by this systematic calumny.

Lucile and I enjoyed life in Vienna in spite of our difficulties with the Russians. We went to the ballet and the opera as often as we could, and we attended scores of plays, concerts, and recitals. Yehudi Menuhin came to Vienna to play his violin under American auspices, and so did Jascha Heifetz. I also enjoyed the performances of the Austrian pianist and conductor Herbert von Karajan. Unfortunately for Karajan's career, he had become a protégé of Joseph Göbbels during the war, with the result that he was forbidden to visit the United States. If and when he is ever allowed to do so, I am confident that most American concertgoers will agree that his talents, both as a pianist and a conductor, compare favorably with those of José Iturbi.

Another Viennese performer whom I much admired was Raoul Aslan, whom I saw in a number of plays, including Molière's *Le Malade Imaginaire*. Aslan's brother, Marcel, was second in command of Radio Austria, which represented I.T.&T.'s subsidiary, Mackay Radio.

Although I was new to Vienna, and then only thirty-five years old, I was nevertheless the dean of the postwar American colony. As such, I was asked to become the president of the Austro-American Chamber of Commerce, a position that led to my becoming a vice-president of the Austro-American Society and the honorary chairman of the Austro-American Club.

In the meantime, of my own volition, I had joined the International House and the Jockey Club. The International House, in the Schwarzenberg Palace, was a club for foreign visitors. It operated what was then the best restaurant in Vienna. The Jockey Club, in the Pallavicini Palace, was a venerable organization that had been closed by the Nazis during the war as a "center of Austrian separatism." It was reopened in 1946, but its Austrian members were so poor by then that they had to lower their standards in order to pay their bills. The club's reputation suffered accordingly, and when Carol Reed arrived in Vienna to direct J. Arthur Rank's production of Graham Greene's thriller, *The Third Man*, he caused the Jockey Club to become the scene of two cinematic murders.

The implication was hardly fair to the regular and honorary members, including General Clark. But Vienna was such a Third Man city by then that the club's officers were unable to resist the opportunity thus afforded them to pay off some of its debts. Old Margrave Pallavicini, who still occupied an apartment on the top floor of his ancestral palace, was rather unhappy about the whole affair. But he, too, needed money, and the only way the Jockey Club could pay its back rent was to lease its quarters to the Rank organization for the production of the film.

The Austro-American Chamber of Commerce had also fallen on evil days. Except for the automotive plant at Steyr, the aluminum plant at Ranshofen, and the former Hermann Göring steel works at Linz (which had once belonged to Hedy Lamarr's former husband, Fritz Mandl), there was very little industry in the American zone of Austria. What little industry there was, moreover, was handicapped by a lack of raw materials. About all the Chamber of Commerce could do, therefore, was to encourage the exportation of Austrian costume jewelry, hats, gloves, and leatherwork in order to obtain the wherewithal to import materials and machinery from the United States.

When the aging Viktor Kienböck, the chairman of Czeija, Nissl, retired, I succeeded him as the honorary chairman of the Austro-American Club. The club, like the Austro-American Society, was approved and, in theory, subsidized by the United States government. The purpose of the club was to develop social relations, and of the society to develop cultural relations, between Americans and Austrians.

If either organization had been properly supported by the State Department's Office of Information and Educational Exchange, both might have been able to realize their basic purpose, which was to combat despair, and thereby Communism, by inspiring hope in Austria's relations with the United States. Instead, the two organizations were allowed to founder.

The Austro-American Society, for lack of suitable quarters of its own, was forced to hold its subsidized concerts, recitals, lectures, and art exhibits in the inadequate quarters of the Austro-American Club. As early as 1946 the society had arranged to lease a damaged palace on condition that it pay for its rehabilitation. An architect and a contractor were employed to repair the palace, but the funds that the society expected to receive were not forthcoming, and so the repairs were never completed. The American Army finally paid for the uncompleted repairs, but only after the architect and the contractor had threatened to file suit against the United States government.

The Austro-American Club owed its initial success to the fact that it was able to serve cheap meals prepared from imported food supplied at cost by the American authorities. But later, as the local food situation improved, its membership fell off and the club began to go into debt. I was traveling so much in 1947 and 1948 that I was unable to keep track of its recurrent financial crises. Additional funds were promised, but they failed to materialize, and by 1949 there was nothing to do but declare bankruptcy and dissolve the club. A committee was duly elected to liquidate its assets and pay each of its creditors an equitable percentage of what was due them.

As far as I was concerned, the club ceased to exist when it filed its petition of bankruptcy in April, 1949. On my return from a trip to Budapest the following August, however, I discovered to my chagrin that the club had never been more than formally dissolved. A group of its less reputable members, "to pay off its debts," had secretly leased its quarters, together with what remained of its good name, to a group of gamblers, who proceeded to convert the club into a private casino.

You may gamble all you want in Austria, but only in a public casino owned and operated by the government. It was not surprising, therefore, that the club should have been raided by the police. Sixty-eight persons were arrested, including two former croupiers from the public casino at Baden, in the Russian zone.

The Communists exploited the scandal in such a way as to cause the greatest possible embarrassment to the United States. Along with all but one of the club's former officers, I was publicly absolved of any wrongdoing. The guilty persons freely admitted that the club had been converted into what the Communists called a "gambling hell" without our knowledge. Yet the official newspaper of the Austrian Communist Party, the *Österreichische Volkstimme* (the "Austrian People's Voice"), accused me of having dissolved the club only when it ceased to serve my purpose as a "cover" for smuggling refugees through the Iron Curtain into Austria, with the help, incidentally, of no less a personage than Oskar Helmer, the Socialist Minister of Internal Affairs. Another Communist newspaper, the *Abend* (the "Evening"), after expressing its doubt that the club had ever really been dissolved, went on to accuse me of having used it as a "cover" for my operations as the "chief" of an American "spy ring." When I threatened to sue them for libel, the Austrian Communist papers immediately changed their tone. In the meantime, though, their unfounded charges had been reprinted in the official Communist newspapers of Czechoslovakia, Hungary, and other countries behind the Iron Curtain.

The Austro-American Club, according to the Communists, was obviously a spy center because it was located on the Rathausplatz, and everybody knew that the American Counter-Intelligence Corps maintained an office across the square. It was like saying, as the Communists probably would say, if pressed to do so, that the State Department is a creature of the Standard Oil Company because it maintains a passport office in Rockefeller Center.

I became honorary president of the club only because I considered it my duty, as an American businessman, to take an active part in the civic affairs of a country whose entire future depends on its relations with the United States. If the Communists ever succeed in destroying those relations, which are neither as good nor as bad as they might be, Austria's future will be black indeed.

Four | Lucile and the Russians

I had warned Lucile repeatedly to stay out of the Russian sector of Vienna, but for a long time she refused to take my warnings seriously. One day, against my express instructions, she took a shortcut through the Russian sector from our house in Währing to the Hotel Bristol, in the International sector, where we were to dine with friends and then go to the theater. She was driving the Ford, which bore American license plates and which I had decorated, for reasons of self-protection, with miniature American flags on either front fender. Some Russians in a jeep caught up with her and playfully attempted to force her into the curb. She managed to outmaneuver them until she came to a red traffic signal, where she had to stop. The Russians drew up beside her, shouting amorous remarks in poor German. Lucile ignored them, and when the light changed she drove off as rapidly as she could, but not rapidly enough. This time the Russians in the jeep succeeded in forcing her into the curb. Lucile was so angry that she got out, walked over to the driver of the jeep, and slapped his face. She then returned to the Ford, got in, backed up, circled the jeep, and drove off again toward the Bristol. The Russians were so surprised that they made no further effort to molest her.

I was so angry when Lucile told me what had happened that I refused to let her have the keys to the Ford for several days.

I returned them only after she had promised me faithfully never to enter the Russian sector again.

One Saturday in November, 1946, I was sitting in the living room of our house, listening to the Army-Navy football game as rebroadcast for the benefit of the American forces in Austria by the Army's Blue Danube Network. Lucile came in at a critical moment in the game to tell me that she had seen a face peering through the barred window in the front door.

"It was probably your own reflection," I said impatiently.

"I tell you, I did see a face, and it wasn't my own. It was a man's face."

"Well, don't let it worry you."

I turned back to the radio, trying to catch up with the play I had missed, and Lucile walked out of the room. A moment later she returned to tell me that she had seen the face again and that I would have to do something about it. Rather reluctantly, I called Rudolf Fiala, our houseman, and told him to go out the back door while I went out the front, thinking that between the two of us we ought to be able to catch whoever had been peering into the house.

A Russian soldier ran away from me right into Rudolf's arms. While I searched him, Rudolf questioned him in Russian. I have forgotten his name, but I recall that he was twenty-two years old and came from somewhere in Central Russia. His wallet contained 100,000 shillings. Inside a blue denim sack that he had been carrying were a pair of stolen American officer's shoes. While Rudolf guarded the burglar, using my *Gutentag* (a sort of Flemish shillelagh) to prevent him from escaping, I telephoned the Provost Marshal's office.

In a few minutes four jeeploads of military policemen arrived, followed by a command car bearing the usual four-man international patrol. The Russian member of the patrol, after questioning the prisoner, insisted that he was a Bessarabian deserter with false papers who should be surrendered immediately to the Russian police. The lieutenant in charge of the MP's, however, decided to take him into American custody. The Russian later admitted that he had been responsible for a whole series of burglaries in our neighborhood. Instead of being prosecuted by the Americans, though, he was eventually turned over to the Russians, at their request. What, if anything, happened to him I was never able to learn.

One of Lucile's younger sisters, Wilhelmine Eykens, who was then twenty-three, came to Vienna from Wondelgem to spend a year with us in 1947-48. Lucile, whose birthday falls on March 22, decided to celebrate the occasion by taking Wilhelmine to the Tirolese Alps for a few days of skiing. I put the two sisters on the midnight Arlberg Express, warned them to be careful, and went home to bed.

At three in the morning the train stopped as usual at the bridge across the Enns River, which divides the Russian from the American zone. Two Russian corporals armed with pistols passed through the train examining the passengers' papers. When the steward knocked on the door of their sleeping compartment, Lucile handed out their passports and the "gray passes" that specifically authorized them to cross the Russian zone to and from Innsbruck, which was their destination. One of the corporals told Lucile that she and Wilhelmine would have to leave the train. Lucile asked him why.

"Your papers are not in order."

In vain Lucile explained that their papers had been checked and double-checked in Vienna against just such an eventuality. There was no question, therefore, of their papers not being "in order." The only clue to the corporal's behavior was his statement, "We know you hate us. Hurry up and get dressed."

Lucile and Wilhelmine took as long as they could in dressing so as to prepare themselves for the worst. Lucile hid her jewelry in her underclothing and told Wilhelmine to do the same. The only plan of defense they could think of was for Lucile to pretend that she was pregnant and for Wilhelmine to pretend that she was seriously ill. Wilhelmine's role, in the circumstances, was less difficult than Lucile's. Wilhelmine had always suffered from a weak heart and a queasy stomach, and her frail appearance lent credence to her pretended illness. Neither of the sisters applied any cosmetics, and both arranged their hair and clothing in such a way as to hide as much of their beauty as they could. It was Lucile's hope thereby to minimize the danger of being raped.

When they at last emerged from their compartment, neither the steward nor the Russian corporals would help them with their four pieces of baggage, and so they had to struggle with them alone. It was sleeting outside, and in the darkness there was nothing to be seen except the lighted windows of a nearby shack. A Russian lieutenant, who was apparently in charge of the train's inspection, signaled to the engineer that he was free to depart. The train then crossed the bridge to the American check point on the other side of the Enns.

As soon as the train had gone, the Russian lieutenant and one of the corporals left Lucile and Wilhelmine alone with the other corporal and walked off in the direction of the village of Sankt Valentin, a mile or two away. For half an hour the two sisters were made to stand there in the cold with their backs to the driving sleet. Wilhelmine soon began to shiver so violently that Lucile took off her fur coat and placed it over Wilhelmine's shoulders.

Finally, when the lieutenant failed to return, the corporal escorted them to the shack. Inside the shack were half a dozen soldiers and a young sergeant sitting on wooden boxes around a red hot stove. They had been smoking *mahorka*, a foul-smelling Russian substitute for tobacco, and drinking colorless schnapps out of a common glass jar. The stench was as uninviting as the appearance of the shack and its Russian occupants. The soldiers were so dirty, according to Lucile, that a rich soup, as the Flemings say, could have been made out of their uniforms.

In the beginning the young sergeant and his men were not unkind. Two of them even surrendered their seats, but not until Lucile had suggested that it would be the gentlemanly thing to do. They asked her a lot of questions about the United States, including, she recalls, whether Chicago was as large as New York, and whether it was really true that American workers could afford to own automobiles. Lucile, hoping to keep their minds off other subjects, answered their questions in great detail.

At length the sergeant, whose name was Vassily, poured some more schnapps out of a jug into the common jar and invited Lucile and Wilhelmine to join him in a drink. He grew so angry when they declined that he drained the jar himself. The soldiers drank another jarful between them and then Vassily drank what remained in the jug and threw it out the door. By that time he was drunk enough to broach the subject that Lucile had feared was at the bottom of his mind. She did her best to discourage him, but without success. He took out his pistol and threatened to shoot her if she refused to submit to his embraces. He then ordered the soldiers out of the shack and proceeded to undress.

Fortunately he had been taken in by Wilhelmine's feigned illness. He paid no attention to her until she distracted him by pretending to vomit. Lucile seized the opportunity to beg him to let her take her ailing sister to the local inn. But Vassily suspected that it was merely a trick, and returned to his effort to make love to Lucile, who was holding him at arm's length as he backed her toward the stove. Lucile finally told him that, if he would let them go to the inn, so that Wilhelmine could get some rest, she would admit him to her bedroom in an hour's time.

Vassily was still not sure that it was not a trick, but in the end he accepted her proposition and let them leave the shack.

It was then about seven in the morning. A Vienna train had just crossed the bridge, and the two sisters, without thinking of their baggage, ran up to it and clambered aboard. Before the train left, however, its conductor was called to the shack. He returned to tell them that they would have to leave the train.

There was nothing for them to do, therefore, but to walk to Sankt Valentin, where they roused the manageress of the local telecommunications office and asked to telephone Vienna. The manageress explained that it was against the law for anyone to make a long-distance telephone call without a written permit from the local Russian commander. Lucile explained her predicament, and offered her 300 shillings, but the woman only replied that she would be imprisoned or shot if she violated her instructions. Lucile offered her another 300 shillings to send a telegram to General Keyes, who had succeeded General Clark as the American High Commissioner, stating merely that she was in urgent need of assistance. It was a prevalent belief in Austria, if not a fact, that the Russians were less meticulous in censoring telegrams than they were in censoring long-distance calls. The manageress finally overcame her fears and tapped out the message, which was relayed to me in Vienna within half an hour.

Lucile and Wilhelmine then returned to the Enns Bridge, where they attempted to hide themselves until the next Vienna train arrived. They were soon discovered by the corporal who had guarded them the night before. He was accompanied by two Russian officers wearing the light-blue shoulder boards of the MVD-MGB. One of them asked Lucile to explain what had happened. When she had done so he gave the corporal a tongue-lashing in Russian. He then turned on Lucile and cursed her in German for causing him "so much trouble." He ended his tirade by ordering the two sisters to collect their baggage, take the next train to Vienna, and never let themselves be seen in the Russian zone again.

As usual, the sisters were forced to handle their own baggage, which they brought back to the side of the railroad tracks, and on which they sat until noon, when the next Vienna train arrived. There was still no sign of Vassily. The corporal who had brought the MGB officers stood beside them until they had boarded the train.

The other corporal passed through their car, examining everybody's papers. When he came to the compartment occupied by Lucile and Wilhelmine, he gave them a knowing leer.

"Have a good time last night?" he asked.

By the time they reached Vienna, at four that afternoon, the two sisters were hysterical. I met them at the Westbahnhof with two agents of the Criminal Investigation Division who had been assigned to investigate the case. General Keyes's office, on receiving Lucile's telegram, had telephoned the Russian High Command to demand that she and Wilhelmine be produced immediately. The timely appearance of the MGB men at the Enns Bridge had evidently been the Russians' response. It took Lucile a long time to convince the CID men that she had not actually been raped. But once she had convinced them, they began to lose interest in the case. Attempted rape, they said, was "not serious enough" to justify an international incident.

As Lucile's husband, I thought that the American authorities should at least demand an official apology from the Russians. But though a complaint was lodged at the next meeting of the Four-Power Commission, it was never published, and the nearest the Russians came to apologizing was to announce, as they almost always did in such cases, that "the guilty persons" had been "punished."

Wilhelmine, as the result of her experience, came down with double pneumonia, from which, in spite of the prompt administration of penicillin, she would never fully recover. She remained

with us in Vienna until September, 1948, when she returned to
Wondelgem. Six months later she was dead.

A few weeks after Wilhelmine's departure, I called at the
garage where I had left the Buick to be repaired.

"Want to see Ross's car?" the foreman asked.

I didn't want to, but I did. The front seat was soaked with
blood, and the steering wheel was covered with a sticky mixture
of blood, hair, and brains.

Irving Ross, a New Yorker, had been working in Vienna for
the Economic Cooperation Administration. On his way home
from a party the night before, he and his Yugoslav secretary,
Dana Superina, had been waylaid by three Russians in a jeep.
Miss Superina was beaten up on the spot and left to find her
way to a hospital. Ross was forced to drive out the Baden highway and turn off into a field, where one of his captors bashed in
his head.

The Russian authorities officially blamed Ross's murder on the
usual "DP's," but I have always suspected that he was put to
death as the result of an "administrative decision" on the part of
the MGB. My suspicions were first aroused when the Communist
organ, the *Österreichische Volkstimme*, attempted to link Ross
with the secretary of Oskar Helmer, the Socialist Minister of Internal Affairs. According to the *Volkstimme*, Helmer's secretary
had been supplying false passports to fugitives from behind the
Iron Curtain. But there was no legal way of either proving or
disproving the charge, since the secretary had been removed by
MGB agents from Helmer's official car as she and the minister
stopped at Enns Bridge on their way back to Vienna from Salzburg, in the American zone.

Soon after the secretary's disappearance, and shortly before his
murder, Ross himself was arrested and held for several days in
a Russian kommandatura in Vienna. He is said to have been

warned at the time to stay out of the Russian sector and to desist in his efforts to keep abreast of economic developments in the Russian zone. Following his murder, a Russian police agent called at the headquarters of the Austrian police and removed from its files all references to Ross's unexplained arrest. What his arrest had to do with his murder has yet to be revealed by either the Russian or the American authorities.

Five | Assignment to Prague

So long as the quisling Socialist, Zdenek Fierlinger, was the prime minister of Czechoslovakia, the government endeavored to allay the suspicions of the West by pretending to negotiate "equitable" settlements with the foreign enterprises that had been expropriated in accordance with the nationalization law of 1945.

Soon after the law was passed, Jacob Jammer joined Dick Brown in Prague to initiate negotiations on behalf of I.T.&T.'s expropriated subsidiaries, Kablo and Telegrafia. Together with Standard Electric Doms, the two companies were valued at $5,000,000, Vladimir Brůza, the chief of the metals section of the Ministry of Heavy Industry, appointed a committee to deal with Jammer and Alfred Plocek, the general manager of Standard Doms, our only remaining property. The committee was composed of three men named Fabinger, Rüdinger, and Fried, all of whom had worked for the nationalized Skoda Works at one time or another, and all of whom wore Communist Party emblems in their buttonholes. Whether any or all of them were Communists by conviction is a question that I am not prepared to answer. All I know is that, in dealing with ISEC, they followed the dictates of the Communist Party even when those dictates were diametrically opposed to the national interests of Czechoslovakia. Brůza, their nominal chief, however, was a loyal Czech who did everything he legally could to hamper the Communists' effort to convert

Czechoslovakia into an economic appendage of the Soviet Empire.

By the summer of 1946 a mutually acceptable agreement had been drafted, and Brŭza and Fried followed Brown to New York to present it to Jammer and other executives of I.T.&T. On its acceptance, with a few minor changes, Brŭza signed the agreement in the name of the Czechoslovakian government, as he had been specifically authorized to do. But Fried had been recalled to Prague in the meantime, and when Brŭza returned he discovered that the government had repudiated the agreement at the insistence of the Communist Party.

That fall I was called to Rome, and later to Zurich, to confer with Colonel Behn and other executives regarding the Telecom Plan, an outgrowth of ISEC's efforts to rehabilitate I.T.&T.'s manufacturing subsidiaries in Europe. I.T.&T., at the beginning of the Second World War, was worth about $500,000,000. Eighty per cent of its assets were located in foreign countries, and a third of its foreign assets, representing an investment of approximately $135,000,000, were located in Europe. By the time the war was over, many of these assets had been written off, and the value of those that were still carried on the company's books was far less than what it had been before the war began.

In 1945, when I was sent to Vienna, I.T.&T. was primarily interested in rehabilitating those of its properties that had not been confiscated by the Communist and crypto-Communist governments that were perched like vultures on Europe's ruins. But it soon became evident that the mere rehabilitation of its own properties would not suffice to restore I.T.&T.'s position on the devastated continent. Hence the Telecommunications Plan, or Telecom Plan, as it was known for short.

Telecommunications, or telecom, is simply commercial jargon for wire communications. The idea was for I.T.&T., acting as a consultant to the governments concerned, to suggest ways and means of rehabilitating their telecommunications systems on the basis of short- and long-range programs, the former to cover five, and the latter twenty, years of development work. It was good business for I.T.&T., of course, and it was good business for every government concerned. The Telecom Plan, if accepted, would have expedited the recovery of Europe by expediting the recovery of its wire communications.

Unfortunately, because of left-wing political opposition, and because the governments approached were unwilling to give telecommunications the necessary priority in the task of reconstruction, the plan failed to gain acceptance. Colonel Behn, when I saw him in Rome and Zurich, was bitterly disappointed. But he was even more disappointed by developments in Czechoslovakia than he was by the failure of the Telecom Plan. The Czechoslovakian government, he told me, had offered to renegotiate its agreement with ISEC, and, though he doubted its sincerity, he felt obliged to accept its offer, if only to convince I.T.&T.'s stockholders that everything possible was being done to protect their investments. Brown had rejoined the export department in New York and would not be returning to Prague. There was no point in sending another representative to Prague until the new Communist government headed by Klement Gottwald had demonstrated its willingness to come to terms. Behn informed me, therefore, that I was to assume responsibility for Czechoslovakia as well as Austria. He wanted me to visit Prague as often as I could in order to keep abreast of all developments there affecting I.T.&T.'s position. And he also wanted me to remind the government at every opportunity that I.T.&T. expected to be compensated for its expropriated properties.

Between January, 1947, and August, 1949, I made a total of twenty-three trips to Czechoslovakia. I was accompanied on my first trip by A. Goodwin Cooke, I.T.&T.'s chief European attorney, with whom I would later work in Budapest. Cooke and I spent two weeks in Prague assisting Plocek, the general manager of Standard Doms, in his efforts to resume negotiations. But the government was so reluctant to make any promises, now that the Communists were openly in control of the situation, that Cooke returned to London and I returned to Vienna to await a more propitious atmosphere.

From then on I was never to spend more than two or three days in Prague at any one time. I revisited the city in February and again in March, 1947, and it was on the latter trip that I first met Eugene S. Karpe, the naval attaché of the American Legation in Bucharest. "Fish" Karpe, as he was known, was a heavy, good-natured Southerner, a native of Delhi, Louisiana, who had commanded a destroyer tender in the Pacific during the Second World War. He knew Henry Burrell, the I.T.&T. representative in Bucharest, and Adrian Nanu, the general manager of our Rumanian subsidiary. Karpe was always traveling, as I was, and during the next two years Lucile and I would often entertain him at our house in Vienna. Our friendship was based on a mutual antipathy for Communism and a mutual affection for the Navy.

The task of a naval attaché is the same as that of an air or army attaché—namely, to obtain as much useful information as he can for the service he represents. Karpe was thus an intelligence officer who operated openly with the sufferance of the Rumanian government. The Rumanians, for their part, maintained a naval attaché in Washington whose function was identical to Karpe's. Governments have long exchanged air, naval, and army attachés on the understanding that, in return for diplomatic immunity, they will observe civilized standards of conduct. In other words, they are free to obtain all the information they can so long as they refrain from flouting the laws of the country to which they are accredited.

Contrary to the accusation made against me at my trial in Budapest, I was not one of Karpe's agents. I sympathized wholeheartedly with his subsequent efforts to save the lives of certain Rumanians, and particularly those Rumanians who had worked for I.T.&T. But aside from the assistance I gave them on their arrival in Vienna, I had nothing to do with their escapes. Most of the fugitives, in fact, managed to reach Vienna without any help from anyone. It was easy enough to walk across the Rumanian-Hungarian border, since both countries were enslaved by the same foreign tyranny, and it was not too difficult, for the same reason, to walk across the border separating Hungary from the Russian zone of Austria.

Until the summer of 1948, when mine fields were laid on either side of Hungary's western border, the greatest danger was encountered by those who attempted to cross from Hungary to the British zone of Austria. The borders of Hungary, Yugoslavia, and the British and Russian zones come together in southern Burgenland at a point not far from the city of Graz. And it was to Graz, in the British zone, rather than to Vienna, that most fugitives attempted to find their way. Vienna, after all, was merely an island in the midst of the Russian zone. It was still necessary for fugitives who wished to reach Western Europe to traverse the remainder of the zone—a risky procedure that placed their lives in double jeopardy.

Once a fugitive reached Graz, however, he was as safe as any European could be. This is the reason why so many fugitives tried to bypass Vienna, and why the MGB took greater pains to guard the Burgenland enclave between Hungary and the British zone than any other portion of the Austrian border. It is also the reason why the northwestern portion of Hungary's frontier with Yugoslavia was guarded almost as carefully. The Yugoslav enclave separating Hungary from the British zone is not much wider than the Russian enclave to the north, and after Tito's break with Stalin, in June, 1948, it was probably the less hazardous of the two.

Although most fugitives crossed into Austria on foot, many of them escaped from Hungary in packing boxes or in the trunks of automobiles, often with the help of venal or disaffected Russian officers. Others managed to reach Vienna disguised as peasants, or as chefs or waiters employed in the dining car of the Orient section of the Arlberg Express.

One case with which I was familiar (though I had nothing personally to do with it) involved a cousin of Prince Pál Eszterházy, who was to be arrested with Cardinal Mindszenty the day after Christmas in 1948. A young colonel, as a gesture of friendliness toward the Western Allies, agreed to help the Eszterházys and their two children escape in one of the Russian army trucks that were continually hauling food from Hungary to the Russian sector of Vienna. To judge from the colonel's name, Toshenko, he was a disaffected Ukrainian. One of Toshenko's subordinates, a lieutenant who was also eager to convince the Allies that he was on their side, was placed in charge of the escape.

Unfortunately, neither the driver nor the guard assigned to the truck, to prevent its cargo from being hijacked, shared the views of Colonel Toshenko. In addition to the Eszterházy family, the truck carried two Jewish fugitives who had made the mistake of revealing that, between them, they possessed $80,000 in American currency. Late at night, as they were nearing the Austrian border, the driver suddenly stopped the truck. He and the guard then relieved the Jews of the money they were carrying and buried it in a hole not far from a concrete kilometer post that would serve to identify its hiding place to them when they returned. The truck then proceeded across the border to the first Russian check point, where the driver and the guard denounced the six fugitives to an officer of the MGB.

The fugitives were taken to Baden for a thorough grilling and were then sent back to Budapest. What happened to the Jews I never learned. Eszterházy's cousin, I was told, was severely bastinadoed and then sentenced to twenty years in a labor camp. His wife was put to work as a seamstress in a women's prison colony, and their children were sent to a special training school to be brought up as Communist wards of the state. Colonel Toshenko was subsequently arrested by the MGB.

It was not long afterward that Adrian Nanu and his wife, together with the two Racotta brothers and their wives, escaped from Rumania. Nicolae Racotta, like Nanu, was an employee of the Rumanian subsidiary of I.T.&T. Alexandru Racotta worked for the Rumanian subsidiary of the Shell Oil Company. During the war he had escaped from Rumania to Turkey in a stolen airplane to present the British intelligence corps in Ankara with some valuable German plans.

Sandru, who was six feet seven, was the taller of the two Racotta brothers. Nicky was only six feet six. His wife was almost as tall as he was, but Sandru's wife was only a little over five feet tall. Individually, either of the Racottas would have been conspicuous; with the Nanus and with their wives, one of whom was conspicuously small, it is a miracle that they were never captured.

The Nanus, who separated from the Racottas in Budapest, were later arrested by the Hungarian police. But they pretended to be Americans who had mislaid their papers and lost their way, and somehow the police believed them and let them go. A week later they turned up in Vienna, to be followed a few days afterward by the four Racottas. I helped them all financially and also put them in touch with an Austrian organization that spirited them across the Russian zone to a point from which they were able to continue their journey to France. The Nanus eventually settled in Brazil, the Racottas in Venezuela.

In helping them to reach the New World, I don't feel that I was acting against the interests of mankind. Neither the Nanus nor the Racottas had been guilty of any wrongdoing. Their only crime was to have identified their interests with those of Britain and the United States. If they violated any Rumanian, Hungarian, or Russian laws in making their way to the West, they did so in accordance with Articles 13 and 14 of the Universal Declaration of Human Rights, a document approved by the General Assembly of the United Nations. Moreover, any laws they may have violated were themselves violations of the human rights provisions of the Rumanian and Hungarian peace treaties.

According to the peace treaties, both governments were legally bound "to secure to all persons under [their] jurisdiction, without distinction as to race, sex, language or religion, the enjoyment of human rights and of the fundamental freedoms, including freedom of expression, of press and publication, of religious worship, of political opinion and of public meeting." Each country was further obliged "to set free, irrespective of citizenship and nationality, all persons held in confinement on account of their activities in favor of, or because of their sympathies with, the United Nations or because of their racial origin, and to repeal discriminatory legislation and restrictions imposed thereunder. . . ." Rumania and Hungary, like Bulgaria, moreover, were specifically forbidden in the future to "take any measures or enact any laws which would be incompatible with the purposes set forth in this Article."

Subsequently, in its Universal Declaration of Human Rights, the General Assembly of the United Nations decreed that everyone is entitled to "freedom of movement and residence" and to "leave any country, including his own." Everyone has the further right to "seek and enjoy in other countries asylum from persecution," a right that may be denied only in the case of "prosecutions genuinely arising from non-political crimes or from acts contrary to the purposes and principles of the United Nations."

In defiance of both the United Nations and its treaty of peace with Russia and the Western Allies, however, the Communist government of Hungary convicted one of my codefendants, István Justh, for having sheltered the Racottas during their flight through Hungary. The Reverend Dr. Justh, the provost of Fel-Söörs, a town near Budapest, knew only that the Racottas were on their way to Western Europe. He did not know that their presence in Hungary was illegal. He accordingly invited them to spend a week end with him in the country, and for that one innocent act he was sentenced to ten years in prison.

In the spring of 1947, during one of my early visits to Czecho-slovakia, I drove up to Carlsbad (now Karlovy Vary) with a Czech friend of mine. It was no secret that the uranium mines in nearby Jachymov had become one of Russia's principal sources of atomic raw materials. Neither was there anything secret about my trip. Thousands of people used to drive up to the Erz Mountains, to see what they could see, and I was as curious as the next man. There was no law against traveling through the area until 1948, following the Communist *Putsch*, when foreigners were forbid-den even to visit Carlsbad. After that I couldn't have come within miles of Jachymov, even if I had wanted to.

Nevertheless, I would be charged at my trial in Budapest with having committed "atomic" as well as "economic" and "military" espionage. It was true that, on my return to Vienna, I told certain representatives of our government what little I knew about Jachymov. Would any American interested in the survival of his country have done any less? It is not espionage to pass along to your government any information you happen to acquire in the course of your travels, so long as such information is not illegally acquired. The British have long made a practice of collecting information from their travelers, and so, indeed, have the Rus-sians. Is there any reason why American travelers should be ashamed to keep their government informed of new develop-ments throughout the world? Although I was convicted of hav-ing driven around Jachymov at a time when it was still legal to do so, no evidence was ever presented to prove, or even to sug-gest, that I had violated any laws.

Jachymov, formerly known as Sankt Joachimsthal (Saint Joa-chim's Valley), is one of the oldest mining towns in Northern

Europe. The American dollar, in fact, derives its name from the silver thaler (*Joachimsthaler*) first coined there in 1518. Marie and Pierre Curie isolated radium in 1898 from samples of pitchblende from the same mines, and visitors had long been taking radioactive baths there until forbidden to do so by the Russians.

There was thus little to be learned about Jachymov that wasn't already known before I visited the area in the spring of 1947. Even the fact that the Russians were using political prisoners to mine the ore had long been public knowledge. The only secrets, which I could hardly have obtained without gaining access to the closely guarded office of the mines, involved the quality and quantity of Jachymov's production.

In the fall of 1947, at the invitation of Jaroslav Peske, the chief engineer of the Slovakian telecommunications system, I inspected two radio links that he had erected in the Tatra Mountains. I drove from Vienna to Bratislava, the Slovakian capital, where I joined Peske, Plocek, and an engineer named Kirby who worked for one of our British manufacturing subsidiaries. Peske wanted to know what we thought of his work before he installed additional links in the Beskid Mountains, which, together with the Tatras, form the border separating the Slovakian portion of Czechoslovakia from Poland.

A radio link is a means of connecting an isolated community with an existing wire communications system without going to the expense of erecting a spur leading off from the main cable. There were a number of Slovakian border communities that had never enjoyed telephone service because of the high cost of stringing lines up into the mountains. Radio links, which had been used successfully in Switzerland and Latin America, appeared to be the answer to their problem. So long as traffic is not too heavy, as in the United States, a radio link is often better than a spur.

We spent three days on our inspection trip, in the course of which we found that Peske had every reason to be proud of his work. We advised him wholeheartedly to request permission of the Ministry of Communications to erect the other links that he was contemplating. All of us except Kirby, who returned to London, would be imprisoned within two years. The Communists would seize on the inspection trip as a means of linking my trial in Budapest with Plocek's trial in Prague. Slovakia's radio links, instead of being used to improve communications, were thus used as a pretext for destroying communications between Czechoslovakia and the outside world.

Six | The MAORT Affair

Albert Pinkney, an assistant vice-president of I.T.&T., was sent to Budapest in 1947 to replace Geoffrey Ogilvie, who had been transferred to Madrid at his own request. Pinkney and his wife found the atmosphere in Budapest so disagreeable that within a year he, too, asked to be transferred to a more congenial post. His request was precipitated by the MAORT affair, which marked the beginning of the end of Standard Budapest and its two subsidiaries, Dial and Telefongyár.

Ogilvie, it will be recalled, had lived in the convent of the Sisters of Social Service until he leased the professor's house in Buda. Among the other residents of the convent, which was located on Thököly Avenue in Pest, were two executives of the Standard Oil Company (New Jersey), Paul Ruedemann and George Bannantine. Ruedemann's job, with Bannantine's assistance, was to rehabilitate and protect a New Jersey subsidiary, the Hungarian American Oil Company, which was known as MAORT because of its initials in Hungarian (*Magyar Amerikai Olajpari, R.T.*). Ruedemann, its president, had been directing MAORT's activities since 1934. He had lived in Budapest until 1942, when Hungary was forced to declare war on the side of Germany, and he had returned to Budapest in 1945, following its supposed "liberation" by the Russians.

The Hungarian phase of Ruedemann's career ended abruptly

on the evening of September 18, 1948, when several agents of the
AVH, the Hungarian section of the MGB, invaded the convent
and placed him and Bannantine under arrest. While the two ex-
postulated with the agents, another foreign resident of the convent telephoned to William Cochran, the then counselor of the
American Legation. Cochran said that he would leave his house
immediately and that Ruedemann and Bannantine should do
what they could to delay their arrest until he reached the convent.

The AVH occupied a group of buildings that were then known
collectively as 60 Andrássy Avenue. (The name of the street
was appropriately changed in 1950 to Stalin Avenue.) Andrássy
Avenue, unfortunately, was closer to Thököly Avenue than
Cochran's house in Buda was. Before Cochran could reach the
convent, a little man with a gray mustache, a twisted left shoulder, and a slight limp appeared, and it was he who ordered the
agents to remove Ruedemann and Bannantine by force. Thus,
by the time Cochran appeared, it was beyond his power as a
diplomat to prevent their arrest. They were already in custody
behind the innocuous-looking façade of the main building at
60 Andrássy Avenue, a former palace with sentries at its entrance and incongruous flower boxes in its windows.

I know now exactly what happened to Ruedemann and Bannantine. At the time, however, I could only imagine the psychological torture by means of which they were forced, within five
days, to confess to numerous charges of "sabotage." As soon as
they had signed the desired "confessions," they were uncere-
moniously deported to Austria and warned never to set foot in
Communist Hungary again.

Although I never met either Ruedemann or Bannantine, I remember discussing their case in Vienna with several American
Army officers. All of the officers agreed that, in similar circumstances, they, too, would have "confessed." It was all very well
to be heroic, they said, but there was no point in undergoing

torture unless your government was prepared to protect your legal rights. Given the continuous retreat of our government in the face of Communist barbarism—a retreat that had been broken only by its belated defense of Greece and Turkey—any American who ran afoul of the Russian police, or any of its subdivisions, would inevitably be sacrificed in the interests of preserving a phony peace. The officers with whom I discussed the problem would undoubtedly have spoken differently if they had not been so demoralized by our abandonment of the Chinese Nationalists, our acceptance of the *Putsch* in Czechoslovakia, our toleration of the Berlin blockade, and our subsequent surrender at the Danubian Conference in Belgrade.

The Russians were obviously convinced that they could now do as they pleased everywhere behind the Iron Curtain. Our failure to retaliate against the shameful treatment accorded Ruedemann and Bannantine would merely strengthen that conviction by demonstrating a repugnant truth—namely, that American citizens, for the first time in history, could be persecuted with impunity.

I accordingly told my wife and certain friends in Vienna that, if I were arrested, I would confess to any crime, however ridiculous, in order to avoid being tortured. They were not to be taken in, I said, by any part of my confession. I would purposely do my best to make it seem incredible.

Badly treated though they were, Ruedemann and Bannantine were lucky in comparison with Simon Papp, MAORT's Hungarian general manager, and his two subordinates, Bodog Abel and Béla Binder. Papp was tried and convicted, along with Abel and Binder, for having "sabotaged" the Hungarian economy by refusing to increase MAORT's oil production to meet the unreasonable demands of the Russians. Specifically, he was charged with having refused to drill an excessive number of wells in

MAORT's field near Lispe. Instead of drilling wells closer together, he had insisted on keeping them at least 300 yards apart.

Papp tried in vain to explain to Vilmos Olti, the judge of the "people's court," what everybody connected with the oil business had known for years: While it is true that more wells will produce more oil, over a short period of time, fewer wells will produce more oil in the long run. Too many wells in a given field will quickly exhaust its gas, necessitate pumping, bring in water, and otherwise increase costs and reduce total production. Papp was guilty only of limiting the production of the Lispe field, which had already suffered from the wasteful methods employed by the Germans, to a rate calculated to bring as much oil to the surface as possible. It was at once good business and practical Hungarian patriotism for him to have followed such a policy. By limiting production to the rate best suited to the field's oil and gas reserves, he was extending its life and thereby conserving one of Hungary's few sources of petroleum.

The Russians, however, refused to recognize the validity of such arguments. They wanted Hungary to deliver as much oil as could be taken out of the ground regardless of the damage that would be done to the shrinking Lispe reserves. They also wanted to expropriate MAORT, the company which had discovered and developed the field, in order to remove an important obstacle to the sovietization of Hungary.

It was illegal, under the terms of the peace treaty, for the Hungarian government to expropriate an Allied company without paying full compensation to its owners. Neither the Russians nor their Hungarian stooges were willing to compensate New Jersey Standard for the confiscation of a company that was valued at $25,000,000. In order to have an excuse not to do so, they arrested Ruedemann and Bannantine, extracted their "confessions," expelled them from the country, and then proceeded unlawfully to convict their Hungarian subordinates of conspiring with the United States, which the judge carefully defined as an "enemy," to sabotage the economy of the Hungarian People's Republic. Papp was sentenced to death, Abel to fifteen years, and Binder to four years in prison. Papp's sentence was later commuted, as a demonstration of Communist "humanitarianism," to life imprisonment; Abel's sentence was reduced to ten years, but Binder's four-year sentence was upheld.

MAORT was expropriated without compensation in accordance with an illegal Communist decree that freed Hungary of its treaty obligations in the case of Allied companies whose executives were found to be "enemies of the state." The decree, though it failed to legalize a flagrant violation of Hungary's international obligations, sufficed to becloud the issue sufficiently to suggest, in terms of domestic propaganda, at least, that the government's behavior was justified. MAORT's facilities have since been divided up between MASOVOL and MALAJ, the Hungarian divisions of the Russian producing and refining trusts that now control every oil company in Eastern Europe.

Seven | Assignment to Budapest

In October, 1948, following the expulsion of Ruedemann and Bannantine and the arrest of Papp, Binder, and Abel, Sosthenes Behn telephoned from London to ask me to meet him at the Hotel Vierjahreszeiten in Munich. He was on his way to Budapest, he said, and wanted me to drive him there. Fortunately I had just received the new Buick, which would make the trip a pleasure; otherwise I would have had to struggle with the Steyr, for the Ford was being overhauled. I applied for a Hungarian visa the next morning, obtained it that evening and drove all night in order to meet Behn in Munich the following day.

On our way back to Vienna, where we spent the night, Colonel Behn told me the reason for the trip. Standard Budapest was being forced into bankruptcy in the hope of justifying its expropriation. Pinkney had despaired of coming to terms with the Hungarian government, and Behn had decided to take matters into his own hands. He wanted me to accompany him to Budapest so that I could act as his representative in the event that the government agreed to negotiate a settlement.

We drove to Budapest by way of Czechoslovakia, entering Hungary near the town of Rajka. I was worried about Colonel Behn's visa, which he had obtained in London, but as things turned out it was my own visa that excited the suspicions of the AVH. After waiting almost two hours for Budapest to confirm

by telephone the validity of my visa, we were at last permitted
to proceed. Pinkney met us in the outskirts of Buda. He was
accompanied by Imre Geiger, then the assistant general manager
of Standard Budapest, and Edgar Sanders, who had succeeded
Iglauer as the local I.T.&T. accountant. The three of them
escorted us to the Hotel Szent Gellért, which the Russians had
finally turned back to the Hungarians, and where a suite had
been reserved for Colonel Behn.

Half an hour later we gathered in Behn's suite to hold a meeting that was destined to blight the lives of four of the seven
persons who were present. Those who attended the meeting, in
addition to Behn, Pinkney, Geiger, Sanders, and myself, were
Ernö Lenkei, Standard's aging general manager, and Mrs.
György Zádor, a Hungarian widow, who was then Pinkney's
secretary. It was a private meeting, since it dealt with private
problems, but it was by no means a "secret" meeting, as it was
later to be described at my trial; no effort was made to conceal
the fact that it was being held.

The problems discussed were of no concern to anyone who
was not connected with I.T.&T. Nevertheless, since we were to
be accused of having secretly conspired at the meeting to overthrow the Hungarian People's Republic, I had better mention
some of them here.

Standard Budapest at the time was still recognized as a private company wholly owned by I.T.&T. Telefongyár and Dial,
however, were in an ambiguous position. The government had
appointed official managers for both companies. Legally, though,
neither had been nationalized, since, as subsidiaries of a subsidiary, most of their stock was indirectly held by Americans.

Standard and Telefongyár were being forced to accept government contracts on such inequitable terms that both companies
were losing money. The contracts involved two types of un-
profitable business—rehabilitation orders for the Hungarian government and reparations orders for the Russian government.

Some of the latter, at Russia's request, were being diverted to Rumania and Bulgaria. Earlier, Standard and Telefongyár had been forced to fill reparations orders for the Yugoslav government, but following Tito's break with Stalin these orders were diverted to Russia. At the time of the fateful meeting, Standard and Telefongyár were jointly working on Russian and Hungarian orders totaling 100,000 lines of automatic telephone equipment worth $8,000,000. They had also produced seven radio transmitters, each of 100,000 watts. Four had been shipped to Russia, two to Rumania, and one to Bulgaria.

The Bulgarian transmitter consisted of a 100,000-watt circuit built into a 34,000-watt frame that the Germans had used as a standby station for Radio Sofia during the war. The Bulgarian Communists had asked for an entirely new transmitter, but the Russians had decided that a rebuilt transmitter would be adequate for their limited needs. The engineers of the Hungarian telecommunications system, which controlled Radio Budapest, had accordingly designed a more powerful circuit to fit into the old German frame. Our own engineers had opposed the idea in the conviction that the old frame would be incapable of carrying such a load. But the Hungarians knew better, or thought they did, and insisted that Standard rebuild the transmitter according to their faulty specifications.

As we had feared, the Bulgarians burned out the transmitter within a week. Several of our local engineers were then sent down to Sofia to build another transmitter around a new and larger British frame. The failure was entirely the fault of Hungary's Communist engineers. But since Communists are not supposed to make mistakes, the government blamed Standard for the failure and refused to pay the bill.

Another problem arose from the Russians' habit of continually changing their specifications. Standard and Telefongyár were consequently being forced to rework half-completed orders—a ruinous practice in view of the fact that they were not entitled to renegotiate their contracts to cover the added cost.

On the contrary, both companies were obliged to pay penalties for failing to complete their orders on schedule even though, in almost every instance, the delays were due either to late deliveries of raw materials or last-minute changes of specifications. The Hungarian government's procurement agencies were so inefficient that they were often as much as six months late in supplying us with critical materials. Non-critical materials, on the other hand, were often supplied in such excessive quantities that they presented a serious storage problem.

The working capital of both companies was thus completely frozen. Inasmuch as the government refused to advance more than 25 per cent on each order, regardless of the delays involved, it was often necessary for Standard and Telefongyár to borrow money to meet their payrolls. But since all banks had been nationalized, they had to borrow on the government's terms, which were a flat 12 per cent. They were not permitted, however, to write off their interest payments as a legitimate cost of production.

In the meantime the government had refused to make any payments on Standard's accumulated dollar debt to I.T.&T. The debt, which dated from 1937, exceeded $2,000,000, not counting interest at 6 per cent, which the company was prepared to waive. Neither had the government made any payments for war damages, which exceeded $1,500,000 in florins, even though it was obliged to do so by the peace treaty of 1947.

Standard Budapest, which had always made money before, was permitted, in theory, to earn a net profit of 8 per cent. As a combined result of exorbitant interest charges, frozen capital, unfair penalties, and interference with both management and labor, however, Standard had lost $521,739 in 1947 and more than twice that amount during the first three quarters of 1948. (Its loss for the entire year would total $1,441,465.) It was thus obvious that, unless drastic action was taken, Standard would soon be faced with bankruptcy proceedings; and bankruptcy, we knew, would be tantamount to nationalization.

Behn and Pinkney met the following day with Béla Sulyok, the Undersecretary of Finance. Although I was not present at this meeting, Behn told me as we drove back to Vienna that Sulyok had agreed, on behalf of the government, either to buy Standard or to negotiate a comprehensive commercial agreement that would make it possible for Standard to survive. Sulyok at first attempted to blame Standard's difficulties on "mismanagement," but finally admitted that they were largely a consequence of the economic policies of the Hungarian Communist Party.

Sulyok also attempted, in view of Hungary's dollar shortage, to get Behn to agree to trade Standard Budapest and its interest in Telefongyár and Dial for certain Hungarian assets in Germany and Argentina. Colonel Behn, however, refused to consider selling Standard and its subsidiaries for anything but dollars or liquid assets that could easily be converted into dollars. Hungary's assets in Argentina and the American zone of Germany were anything but liquid. In Argentina they consisted of certain nationalized properties belonging to Hungarian companies that had been nationalized at home. And in the American zone of Germany they consisted of undetermined numbers of machine tools, barges, tugboats, motor vehicles, locomotives, and rolling stock that the Germans had removed from Hungary prior to their surrender. The United States government had agreed to restore such property on condition that Hungary live up to the terms of its peace treaty. But the Hungarian government had violated the peace treaty by expropriating MAORT, the Hungarian American Oil Company, and, in the opinion of most observers, the United States was under no obligation to

restore any of Hungary's assets in the American zone of Germany. The Standard Oil Company (New Jersey), I venture to
suggest, had a better claim to such assets than the Communist
government of Hungary.

A month later Colonel Behn telephoned from London to say
that the Hungarian government had announced its willingness
to negotiate a commercial agreement with ISEC. He was chart-
ering an airplane, he said, and would pick me up at the Vienna
airport on his way to Budapest the next day. The airplane was
a De Havilland Dove. Except for the fact that the Russian guards
at the Budapest airport broke into the locked airplane and stole
two bottles of whisky during our absence, the flight down and
back was uneventful.

Geiger, Sanders, and Mrs. Zádor met us at the airport and
drove us to the Szent Gellért, where Behn and I were given the
same accommodations that we had had before. That afternoon
we met in the colonel's suite to draw up a detailed memorandum
to serve as the basis of the impending negotiations.

The memorandum defined it as the purpose of the commercial
agreement to "clarify and settle all existing differences" between
the Hungarian government and the Standard Electric Company
of Budapest and its subsidiaries. In return for the government's
acceptance of six conditions, ISEC would provide Standard
Budapest with the necessary licenses, patents, and blueprints to
produce, sell, and install certain specified types of telecommunications and other electrical equipment in Hungary and to export such equipment to Rumania, Bulgaria, Yugoslavia, and Russia so long as ISEC made no separate agreements with its subsidiaries, if any, in those countries. ISEC's fee for such services
would be 4 per cent of sales, payable in dollars or in exportable
merchandise.

The six conditions required the Hungarian government (1)
to supply Standard Budapest with raw materials of such quality
and in such quantities as the company needed to fill the orders;

(2) to pay the company promptly for all completed orders; (3) to fix prices at a level high enough to assure Standard Budapest a reasonable profit on every order; (4) to accept full responsibility for any failure of Standard Budapest to fulfill the terms of rehabilitation and reparations orders because of labor difficulties or the lack of raw materials; (5) to grant necessary commercial credits at reasonable rates of interest; and (6) to permit Standard Budapest to pay into a blocked florin account, and to permit ISEC to withdraw from that account, the funds needed to cover ISEC's expenses in Hungary.

The next day Colonel Behn and I presented the memorandum to Béla Sulyok, who agreed to recommend its acceptance to his Communist superiors. This unctuous little man, having survived the Germans, had joined the Communist Party in the hope of surviving the Russians. He lived with his young wife and child in the suburb of Leányfalu, not far from Edgar Sanders, who told us that he had often been amused to observe Sulyok puffing on a cigar and wheeling his baby carriage up and down the street.

Sanders, a tall, bespectacled Englishman, was a cousin of George Sanders, the actor, and a brother of Alexander Sanders, a naturalized American who worked in Berlin for one of our German subsidiaries, Standard Elektrizitäts Gesellschaft. Edgar and Alex, like their cousin George, were born in St. Petersburg, where their father had been a British consular official. (Their uncle, George's father, had been a rope manufacturer.) Sandy, as Edgar was known, had once intended to be a professional dancer, but his German mother had put an end to that ambition and he had become an accountant instead. He spoke excellent German and Russian and some Hungarian. As a captain in the British Army, he had served in North Africa and Italy during the war, and had later been sent to Budapest as a member of the Allied Control Commission. Sandy's principal task at the time had been to locate the graves of British fliers who had perished over Hungary.

Before the war he had worked in London for one of our British subsidiaries, Standard Telephone and Cables. It was only natural, therefore, that he should have been re-employed on leaving the army; and it was no more than natural, given his Hungarian experience, that he should have been assigned to Budapest.

But this was evidently a mistake. The Hungarian Communists, like their Russian mentors, assumed that everyone who had ever been engaged in graves registration was a spy. The fact that Sandy during the war had been attached to MI-5 (Military Intelligence, 5th Section) was also held against him. It was equally a fact, however, that his "intelligence" work had consisted of interviewing German prisoners of war.

Inasmuch as Pinkney had returned to New York for reassignment, Colonel Behn appointed me to act as ISEC's representative in Hungary as well as Austria and Czechoslovakia. He also appointed a three-man committee to represent ISEC in its negotiations with the government: Henry Scudder, now a vice-president of I.T.&T.; Goodwin Cooke, I.T.&T.'s chief European attorney; and myself. Sulyok, in turn, appointed a three-man committee to represent the government: Zoltán Radó, the chief of the Light Electrical Directorate of the Ministry of Heavy Industry; Ödön Gergely, a former sales employee of Standard Budapest, who was now the chief of Elektroimpex, the import-export branch of the Ministries of Foreign Trade and Light Industry; and a man named Tarján, who was in charge of the nationalized enterprises operated by the Ministry of Light Industry.

Before we returned to Vienna, Colonel Behn accepted Lenkei's resignation as general manager of Standard Budapest and appointed Geiger to take his place. Lenkei was unwilling, in view of his advanced age and failing health, to risk arrest and imprisonment in trying to save a company that he felt was doomed. Geiger was by no means eager to succeed him, but he finally agreed to do so in the realization that if he, too, resigned, there would be no chance whatever of saving Standard Budapest.

Geiger was one of the very few Hungarians whom we could trust to defend the company's interests. He was a plump, gentle man with large features and a high forehead. His brown hair had turned white as a result of his experiences during the early days of the Russian occupation. The daughter of one of his best friends had been raped a score of times by Russian soldiers, and Geiger himself had broken his ankle jumping out of a second-story window in an effort, happily successful, to prevent his own daughter from being raped. He had hobbled for blocks to a Russian kommandatura to report that a group of drunken soldiers had assembled in his apartment in the expectation of forcing his daughter to "entertain" them. Fortunately the Russian officer in command was a family man himself. He dispatched a jeepload of policemen to the apartment in time to forestall the raping bee.

Geiger's wife had been living in a state of hysteria ever since, and Geiger himself, as he had every reason to be, was a very frightened man. He was half Jewish and, because he was, he had been demoted during the German occupation from the rank of sales manager to that of junior salesman. Ogilvie had promoted him to the rank of assistant general manager, but in spite or rather because of his promotion, Geiger and his family were in greater danger than before.

Although he and Lenkei were responsible for Standard's operations, neither was permitted to exercise any real authority. Most of their trusted subordinates had been replaced by Communists who refused to take orders from anyone who was not an officer of the party. The Communists were simply not interested in efficient operations. Their purpose at the time was to convert Standard's factory into a dependency of an all-powerful bureaucratic state. Every few days they would bring production to a standstill in order to herd the workers together to listen to "patriotic" speakers praise the Russians and denounce their "enemies," particularly those who happened to be citizens of the United States. Many thousands of dollars' worth of time and materials were wasted in manufacturing miniature telephone sets for presentation to Communist officials as tokens of the workers' compulsory "admiration."

On one occasion, the factory was forced to present a banner to Mátyás Rákosi, alias Roth, the Vice Prime Minister and Secretary General of the Hungarian Communist Party. The Rákosi presentation was especially ludicrous, since Rákosi is by far the most hated of all of Hungary's Communist oppressors. A bald, fat, and extremely ugly man, he is known to his unloving subjects as "Potato Head." Personally I have always thought of him as a cross between a watermelon and a pig.

Rákosi was once the Commissar of Socialized Production in the Béla Kun (Kohn) dictatorship of 1919. Today he is Kun's successor and Stalin's viceroy. He is hated, among other reasons, for his harsh treatment of the workers in nationalized factories. In the spring of 1948, for example, before the right to strike had been suppressed, Rákosi led a convoy of police trucks to the expropriated Manfred Weiss Works on Csepel Island, just south of Budapest. The Weiss plant, which employs some 30,000 workers, is the largest metallurgical enterprise in Hungary. During the war it became a part of the Hermann Göring Works, and since the war it has been known as the Mátyás Rákosi Works. As soon as the helmeted policemen had surrounded the plant, Rákosi and his bodyguards approached the striking workers, who had retreated into a courtyard between two shops. Climbing onto a table, Rákosi then delivered the shortest speech of his career.

"Comrades!" he shouted. "You have five minutes in which to

return to your machines. Anyone who is not working by then will be handed over to the AVH."

Such was the treatment accorded the workers once a factory had been nationalized. Prior to its nationalization, however, as in the case of Standard Budapest, it was the purpose of the Communists to reduce productivity to such a low level that the factory could no longer be operated at a profit.

It was not only futile but dangerous for either Lenkei or Geiger to oppose the Communists openly. Kelemen Domokos, Standard's factory manager, and two of his assistants had been imprisoned for having done so. The charge against them was not that they were anti-Communists—for Domokos, like Geiger, was an involuntary member of the Communist Party—but that they had accepted bribes for giving preferential treatment to certain of Standard's creditors. The charge was patently false and the government had made no effort to press it; it was merely an excuse for holding the three men incommunicado.

The fact that Domokos was of German origin (his real name was Klemens Kraus) made his position doubly difficult. For just as Hungary's Fascists had tended to regard all Jews as Communists, so Hungary's Communists tended to regard all Germans as criminals of war. The AVH chose to pretend that Domokos had changed his name in 1936 in order to conceal his "Fascist inclinations." Actually, like so many Hungarians of German, Jewish, Rumanian, and Slavic origin, Domokos had changed his name in accordance with the prewar "Magyarization" policy carried out by Prime Minister Gyula Gömbös, who had himself been born Julius Gelb. Even Cardinal Mindszenty (Joseph Pehm) was a member of Hungary's German minority, a fact that was to be used against him in the mock trial that would result in his being sentenced to life imprisonment. His successor, Archbishop József Grösz (Gröss), who was to be sentenced to fifteen years' imprisonment, was another Hungarian of German origin. So was László Rajk, the former Minister of Internal Affairs, who was to be hanged for the "crime" of Titoism. The following interchange between Rajk and his judge, Péter Jankó, the president of the "people's court," betrays the inverted racism of the Hungarian Communist regime:

The President: I have one final question for you. What was the name of your father?

Rajk: József, but he is dead.

The President: What was his surname?

Rajk: József Rajk.

The President: That is, József Rajk, as you say. What was your grandfather's name?

Rajk (irritated): My grandfather being of Saxon descent, wrote his name as Reich.

The President: So you say that your grandfather was called Reich. How did it become Rajk? Legally?

Rajk: Legally.

The President: How?

Rajk: I could not give the exact date when it was legalized. In my certificate of baptism it is still spelled with an "á" [pronounced "ah" in Hungarian], that is, Reich became Rájk; anyhow my university papers were made out in the present spelling.

The President: You simply used an "a" [pronounced "aw"], dropping the accent. And this you call legal?

Rajk: (remains silent).

The President: So you know that Rajk [pronounced "Royk"] came from Reich.

Rajk: In this respect I wish to add that I am of Aryan descent, and genuinely, too, because on one side I am Saxon. The Hungarian Aryan law . . .

The President: The question is not whether you are of Aryan or Saxon descent. But look here, this is your birth certificate . . . your father was József Rájk [pronounced "Reich"], his son was László, that is you. If the Minister of [Internal Affairs] had not approved it, you were using this name illegally. . . .*

MAORT, the Standard Oil subsidiary, had been nationalized in a hurry because the Russians had plenty of engineers who were more or less capable of exploiting Hungary's oil fields. But the Russians had few engineers who were even remotely capable of supervising the production of the electrical and electronic devices that the Communists hoped to manufacture in Hungary. Hence the delay in nationalizing Standard Budapest. Hence, too, our efforts to forestall nationalization by means of a mutually acceptable agreement.

Neither side was kidding the other. We knew that we would be expropriated eventually if the Stalinists remained in power. On the other hand, so long as they could not obtain their manufacturing information from other sources, they would have to reckon with ISEC.

It might be a losing game, as Jule Smith believed, but there was still a chance that we could win. We had been forced to play the same game in other countries where totalitarian regimes had come to power, and in most instances we had been successful. Wherever we had operated, we had established communications systems that were second to none. Wherever we had been expropriated, with or without fair compensation, communications had deteriorated to such an extent that, in several countries, we had been invited to return on a consulting basis. Our trump card was the fact that our know-how was unexcelled.

The Hungarian Communists had three trumps to our one. The first was the precedent established when the United States permitted Hungary to expropriate MAORT without compensation in violation of the peace treaty of 1947. In view of this derelic-

* See the blue book, *László Rajk and His Accomplices Before the People's Court*, Budapest, 1949, p. 81.

tion, the Communists realized that they could expropriate Standard Budapest at any time without fear of retaliation.

Their second trump consisted of the fact that Standard Budapest could be driven into bankruptcy at any time, simply by revising rates, prices, and schedules in such a manner as to make it impossible to operate at a profit.

The Communists' third trump was the fact that various European competitors were eager to displace ISEC in spite of the unpromising conditions that prevailed in Hungary. Whereas ISEC, as an American company, had to count its profits and losses in dollars, which were increasingly hard to obtain, our rivals were apparently willing to take their profits, if any, in the form of food and other commodities that were scarce at home.

The game we had been playing was thus rigged in favor of our Communist adversaries. Even so, with $6,000,000 in Hungarian assets at stake, it would have been folly for us to throw in our cards until we had to. There was always the chance that Hungary, in emulation of Yugoslavia, would break its economic ties with Russia. And if it did, we thought, the National Communists would be less reluctant than the Imperial Communists to deal with us on equitable terms.

Colonel Behn, before leaving Budapest, urged Sulyok to do what he could to see that Domokos and his two assistants were released. Until they were, he said, it would be difficult for him to believe that the government was sincere in its desire to negotiate a commercial agreement with ISEC.

Early in December, following my return to Vienna, I read that Viktor Csornoky, the Hungarian ambassador to Egypt and the son-in-law of the former quisling prime minister, Zoltán Tildy, had been convicted of "espionage" and hanged. Cardinal Mindszenty was arrested the day after Christmas, and on January 19, 1949, it was announced that he had "confessed" to having committed "high treason" as an "imperialist agent" of Britain and the United States. Inasmuch as the official newspaper of the Hungarian Communist Party, *Szabad Nép* ("Free People"), had described the Cardinal as "the greatest and most reckless enemy of the Hungarian people, and the agent of its most wicked enemies," I was surprised to learn, on the very day he was said to have "confessed," that the government had accepted our memorandum and was ready to begin immediate negotiations.

I made nine trips to Budapest in the spring of 1949. The first of these trips, in early February, was my fourth visit to the city since the end of the Second World War. Hank Scudder and Goodwin Cooke flew down from London, and my wife and I accompanied them from Vienna to Budapest by train.

On February 8 the Cardinal was sentenced to life imprisonment by Vilmos Olti, the same "people's judge" who had sentenced Papp to death, and who, in little more than a year, would sentence me to fifteen years in prison. Dean Acheson's protest against Hungary's "conscienceless attack upon religious and personal freedom" was summarily rejected. And because the Secretary of State described as "totally false, baseless, and outrageous" the effort to implicate the American Legation in the Cardinal's alleged "crimes," the government, in addition to rejecting his protest, demanded the recall of Selden Chapin, the American minister, and two of his subordinates.

In the meantime, Hungary had been declared a "people's democracy," a condition that was obligingly defined by József Revai, the Minister of People's Culture, as follows: "The development of our democracy is nothing else than a struggle that began with the goal of destroying Fascism, of realizing our national independence, and of steadily executing civic democratic tasks, and which was subsequently transformed into a fight against the big fortunes and then against the whole bourgeoisie—into a fight against capitalism, aiming first at the expulsion of capitalist elements . . . and then at their liquidation."

The weather was so cold, and the atmosphere so hostile, that Lucile returned alone to Vienna within a week. The Geigers wanted to entertain the four of us, but decided at the last minute that it would be too risky to invite Americans to their home. Mrs. Geiger felt that the most she could do, in the circumstances, was to invite Lucile to have coffee and pastry with her at Gerbaud's, a once-fashionable confectionary in Pest. Lucile tried to convince her that it was neither necessary nor wise for the two of them to meet at all. But Mrs. Geiger insisted, and so Lucile met her one afternoon in the lobby of the Szent Gellért.

Mrs. Geiger appeared in an old overcoat with a shawl wrapped around her head in peasant fashion. She explained that it was necessary for her to dress in such a manner so as "not to attract attention," though she could hardly have attracted more attention than to appear in public with Lucile, an obvious foreigner, who was dressed according to the latest American fashion. The two of them, "so as not to attract attention," walked across the rebuilt Ferencz József Bridge and proceeded on foot to Gerbaud's, on Vörösmarty Square. A man paused to stare at them as they entered. Mrs. Geiger wanted to sit in a secluded corner, but Lucile thought it would be more amusing to sit at the window and watch the passers-by. The same man walked up and down outside, staring at them in such an insolent manner that Lucile finally suggested that they call a policeman.

"But he's a policeman himself," said Mrs. Geiger. "He's been following me ever since I left our house."

On a later trip, Cooke and Scudder drove back to Vienna with me in my car while Lucile and the boys returned with Sanders by train. We traveled separately because our "gray passes"—the travel permits entitling us to cross the Russian zone of Austria—required each of us to return to Vienna by the same means of transportation that we had used to come to Budapest.

We had no trouble at the Hungarian border, but at Schwechat, in the outskirts of Vienna, Cooke and I were arrested along with Scudder because the latter's gray pass had expired. We were taken to a suburban kommandatura, where an MGB captain told us to be seated and then disappeared. Under the watchful eyes of a Russian guard armed with a tommy gun, we sat for more than an hour on a long wooden bench occupied by two Russian soldiers and two Russian officers, all of whom were sleeping soundly. The sleeping officer next to me eventually crossed his legs, forcing me to move in order to prevent his dirtying my knee with his boot. I lit a cigarette and, as I did so, an idea occurred to me.

"I wonder how long it would take him to get out of his boots if I gave him a hot foot," I said.

Cooke laughed, but Scudder was annoyed. "None of your tricks," he said. "We're in enough trouble as it is."

He seemed to have forgotten that the cause of our trouble was his failure to renew his gray pass.

"We'll never get out of here," I said, "unless we notify the Provost Marshal's office."

"We can't," said Scudder. "They won't let us."

"I think they will," I said.

It was then about eight in the evening, and we were all tired, hungry, and thirsty. I asked the guard if we might order something to eat. He shook his head. I then asked if we might order something to drink. He called a lieutenant, who told us that there was a *Bierstube* across the street and that, if we wanted to, he would let us order beer. He called an Austrian policeman, to whom I gave a fifty-shilling note on which I had written the telephone number of my secretary, Thilde Kus. I told him to notify Mrs. Kus of our predicament, to bring us six bottles of beer, and to keep the change, which amounted to half of what I had given him. He did as he was told, and within half an hour an American sergeant arrived with an international patrol. The sergeant asked to see the captain. When the latter reappeared, he said that he would release us only if we signed a statement admitting that we had violated Russian security restrictions. The sergeant advised us not to do so. Instead he asked us to give him our passports so that he could prove that we were Americans traveling on legitimate business. We gave him our passports, but he made the mistake of handing them to the Russian captain, who locked them up in the drawer of his desk. The sergeant angrily retired, promising to return with reinforcements after he had reported to the Provost Marshal's office.

An hour later he returned with an American lieutenant, who advised us to sign the statement on condition that we be given our passports and allowed to depart. The captain, having won his victory, accepted the lieutenant's proposition. He let us go after warning us never to reappear in the Russian zone unless our papers were in order.

That was the first and last time that the three of us traveled together. Thereafter at least one of us always remained in Budapest so as not to give the Hungarians an excuse to break off the negotiations. If the AVH objected to our frequent comings and goings, it succeeded admirably in concealing its annoyance. We received our visas and exit permits without delay (except when the Russian colonel was drunk) and, except on one occasion, when Cooke and I tried to cross the border near Hegyeshalom instead of Rajka, we had no trouble with the authorities.

In March, by common assent, we moved from the Szent Gellért to the Astoria, a small hotel on Kossuth Avenue in the commercial section of Pest. The Szent Gellért, in Buda, though it was the city's only remaining first-class hotel, was cold and dreary. Its cuisine was poor and its service was worse. Moreover, it was always thronged with Communist delegations of one sort or another and, after wrangling with Communists all day long, none of us had any desire to share their revelries at night—particularly since those revelries were posited on the eventual downfall of the United States. The Astoria's rooms were dingy, and its service was almost as bad as the Szent Gellért's, but its cuisine was then the best in town. The head waiter, through no fault of his own, was the official caterer to the Russians, and he always saw to it that we were served some delicacy, such as caviar or *pâté de foie gras*, whenever the Russians gave a banquet. His specialty was *filet mignon à la Rossini* (with goose liver and truffles), a dish that was much too heavy but which we found it difficult to resist.

The ISEC office on Nádor Street, where Sanders, Mrs. Zádor, and several clerks were employed, was located in a large apartment that had formerly been occupied in its entirety by a prosperous physician. The physician, who had been nationalized, was no longer prosperous. He now lived in a suite of rooms that had once been his laboratory, next to his waiting room and office, which were reached through separate entrances. Nobody liked the office, but we continued to use it because no other space was available. And Nádor Street was undeniably convenient. It was within easy walking distance of the American Legation, the National Bank, and the Ministry of Heavy Industry, and equidistant from the Standard factory in Buda and the Telefongyár factory in the industrial suburb of New Pest.

It would have been better, even so, to have moved back to the Standard factory, where ISEC had maintained an office before the war. But the old office had been converted to other uses, and to provide us with a new one would have required the use of scarce materials that the government insisted were not available. The fact was that the government was opposed to our moving back to the factory for fear that, if we did, we would be in a better position to combat the Communist sabotage that was driving Standard into bankruptcy.

The office in Nádor Street, moreover, was better suited to the purposes of the AVH. In the room that Ogilvie and Pinkney had used as their private office, and which I now shared with Cooke

and Scudder, was a tile stove that was fed with briquettes from a
dark passageway behind the wall. We frequently heard foot-
steps in the passageway, but never succeeded in determining
who, if anyone, was eavesdropping for the police. It may only
have been the old *Volksdeutsche* charwoman, who had served
the wartime Nazi occupants of the apartment, and whose excessive curiosity was somewhat hampered by her limited knowledge of English.

As far as we could tell, there were no microphones concealed
in the office, though its telephones were certainly tapped. Whenever it was necessary to hold an important conference, therefore,
we usually retired to the Astoria. If the bar was crowded, as it
seldom was, we then retired to one of our rooms upstairs. The
telephones at the Astoria were also tapped, and the walls of our
rooms had been wired for sound; but each of us had borrowed a
radio from the Standard factory, and by turning it on full blast
we could talk safely beneath its protective din.

Imre Geiger often came to see me in my room to tell me of
his troubles while we pretended to listen to Radio Budapest.
One day in April, 1949, an employee of Standard's engineering
department had been arrested, tortured, and forced to sign a
deposition stating that Geiger was "supporting American interests against the interests of the Hungarian state." The man, who
was later released, knew nothing whatever of Geiger's role in
the negotiations. He had simply told the AVH what they had
wanted him to tell them. A few days later a personal friend of
Geiger's, who was not employed by the company, had also been
arrested and subjected to torture. He, too, had been released,
but not until he had deposed that Geiger was an "imperialist
agent" who had joined the Communist Party in order to distract
attention from his "treasonable activities" as a "spy" and "saboteur." The same friend had further deposed that Geiger was

drawing more than his legal salary from Standard Budapest, an assertion intended to imply that Geiger was a paid agent of the American intelligence corps.

It is true that Geiger, along with thousands of other Social Democrats, was technically a member of the Communist Party, which had "merged" with—that is, absorbed—the Hungarian Social Democratic Party in May, 1948. But he had never held a party card, and had failed to dissociate himself from the Communists only on the advice of Pinkney and a representative of the American Legation, both of whom had felt that it would do more harm than good for him to make an issue of the matter. Geiger was assured, when he applied for an American visa in March, 1949, that his involuntary membership in the Communist Party would not be held against him. His position was identical to that of all Hungarian "Communists" who had been "co-opted" from other parties against their will. Edina Dőry, the barmaid at the Astoria, was another involuntary "Communist." She had been forced to join the party in order to obtain a job. Non-Communist Hungarians were not eligible for employment, and unemployed Hungarians starved.

It is also true that Geiger had been drawing more than his legal salary of 3,200 florins a month. But the fact that his legitimate expenses were being defrayed did not mean, as the AVH intended to make it seem, that he was being paid to act as an "imperialist agent" of the United States. It meant only that he was being paid—but not overpaid—to defend the interests of a company for which he had worked for more than twenty years and of which he was now the general manager.

Our negotiations with the government committee headed by Zoltán Radó had meanwhile reached an impasse. It was becoming increasingly evident that the government was holding out for concessions in the form of strategic equipment that I.T.&T. was neither willing nor able to manufacture in Hungary. At one point the discussions became so acrimonious that Scudder protested to Béla Sulyok. He told Sulyok that, unless the government gave some indication of its willingness to give as well as take, I.T.&T. would be forced to call off the negotiations.

If the negotiations collapsed, as they seemed likely to at any moment, Sulyok and Radó would be tempted to blame their failure to get the better of us on persons other than themselves. Since they could not blame it all on the Americans, they would have to blame it partly on one or more Hungarians, and who would make a better scapegoat than Imre Geiger?

Among my papers is a copy of the memorandum I sent to Colonel Behn on my next trip to Vienna:

Geiger [it reads] is in very serious danger. The political police are compiling a dossier accusing him of sabotage and other crimes. They may put him in jail if the negotiations are unsuccessful from the government's point of view. The Communists want all the technical information they can get, and they have submitted . . . a list of impossible requirements. . . .

At the moment, the discussions are revolving around the issue of claims. The claims include those of the telecommunications system as well as those of the reparations administration, and the obvious intent is to assess enough penalties to wipe out the company's debt to ISEC. The committee refuses to accept our defense that late deliveries have been due to lack of raw materials, conflicting priorities, frozen capital, etc.

The three prisoners are still being held over our heads as blackmail, and there has been a veiled threat that if the agreement is not concluded to the government's satisfaction there will be a scandal. . . .

My concluding statement referred to a remark made by Radó, to whom I had complained about Sulyok's procrastination. Sulyok had repeatedly promised to see that justice was done, yet more than six months had gone by and our employees were still in prison.

"Well," said Radó, "the agreement hasn't been signed—"

"And it never will be," I said, "unless Sulyok keeps his promise."

Eight | The Draft Agreement

Early in May, in response to our continued prodding, the AVH released Domokos and his fellow prisoners on condition that they were never to be employed by Standard Budapest again. In a free society it would have been impossible for the police to impose such a condition. But Hungary was not a free society, and we had no choice but to accept the condition, even though it meant that the three men would be unable to earn an honest living so long as the Communists remained in power. To keep them from starving, we granted them each the monthly pension they would have received on retirement for reasons of age. But the pensions were hardly adequate since, without employment cards, they were not entitled to rationed commodities. Thereafter, until the day they were again arrested, they had to buy everything they needed on the black market at many times its rationed price.

Cruel and conditional though it was, the release of the three prisoners seemed to be a good omen. It suggested that the government was prepared to come to terms and, if so, Geiger was in no immediate danger of arrest. If the negotiations failed, everyone concerned would be in danger. On the other hand, if the negotiations were successful, no one would be arrested so long as the government lived up to its side of the bargain.

A bargain was finally struck in the form of the draft agreement that the two committees initialed on May 31, 1949. The agreement, with its schedules and annexes, ran to more than forty pages of legalistic verbiage, but its essentials were as follows:

Standard Budapest would appoint ISEC as its technical consultant in connection with the *commercial* manufacture of telephone substations; telephone switching systems; wire, cable, or radio telephone transmission systems; telegraph substation apparatus; telegraph switching systems; wire, cable, or radio telegraph transmission systems; radio broadcasting systems, including studio sound and television equipment and cable or radio links for sound and television broadcasting; cable or radio television transmission systems; sound and television broadcasting systems; sound and television home receivers; wired sound distribution systems; *instrument approach systems;* public address systems; power supplies for any of the foregoing; toll cables; power cables; train dispatching and interlock systems; and train describer equipment (a sort of ticker apparatus). ISEC would also advise and consult with Standard Budapest in the construction and remodeling of factory buildings, the procurement and installation of machinery, the modernization of manufacturing techniques, the fabrication of jigs, tools, and dies, the procurement and application of raw materials, and the training of personnel.

ISEC would also furnish Standard Budapest with all technical information available to ISEC concerning *standardized products* —that is, *products regularly manufactured by those I.T.&T. subsidiaries participating in the agreement.* It was understood, however, that ISEC would *not* be obliged to design exclusively for Standard Budapest *new or special types of products,* or to conduct *special research or development work,* except on such terms as might be agreed upon for such co-operation. ISEC, at the request of the Hungarian government, and at the Hungarian government's expense, would permit *a reasonable number* of Standard employees *acceptable to* ISEC to visit factories operated by or associated with ISEC for the purpose of inspection and of receiving instruction in planning, engineering, manufacturing, or testing products *within the scope of this agreement and to the extent that access is not prohibited by the authorities.*

In return for these and other services, the Hungarian government would recognize Standard Budapest as a wholly owned subsidiary of I.T.&T.; would refrain from nationalizing Standard Budapest and its subsidiaries so long as the agreement remained in force; would guarantee Standard Budapest's dollar indebtedness to ISEC; and would enable Standard Budapest to pay ISEC an annual service fee equivalent to 4 per cent of sales in dollars. The Hungarian government also agreed to pay Standard Budapest's war damages and to revise its priorities, interest rates, and penalties to the extent necessary to make it possible for the company to earn an annual profit of 8 per cent within the structure of Hungary's controlled economy.

The italicized phrases indicate the strategic aspects of the agreement. Although ISEC agreed to enable Standard Budapest to manufacture instrument approach systems for Iron Curtain airports, it restricted such equipment to "standardized products . . . regularly manufactured," and specifically exempted itself from any obligation to design "new or special types of products" —meaning radar and other such devices—or to conduct "special research or development work" leading to their manufacture by Standard Budapest. We agreed to permit Hungarian engineers to study our manufacturing techniques in other countries, but we reserved the right to select the engineers and restrict their studies to manufactures "within the scope of this agreement" and in so far as such studies were not "prohibited by the authorities."

What it all meant was that, in return for guaranteeing the survival of Standard Budapest, Telefongyár, and Dial, the Hungarian Communists wanted us to give them all the technical information they desired; and we had agreed to do so up to but not beyond the point where our information might jeopardize the military security of the United States and its allies. There were so many escape clauses in the agreement that I saw no reason for the United States government to withhold its approval. As John MacCormac, the Vienna correspondent of the New York *Times,* described it, the draft agreement, "on its face," at least, "was the best that any Western firm [had] obtained in Hungary" since the Communists seized power.

Nicholas Nyaradi, a former Minister of Finance who left Hungary before I arrived, has lately volunteered the misinformation that Standard Budapest, *under my supervision,* was "forced" by the Communists to produce for Russia "the jamming devices which are used to muffle the Voice of America." * Dr. Nyaradi's statement is totally untrue. No jamming devices of any description were manufactured by Standard Budapest prior to its expropriation.

After the prisoners had been released, and I knew that we would soon be initialing the draft agreement, I invited Lucile and our two sons, Bob and Bill, to come down to Budapest to spend the rest of my stay with me in the new hotel that had been opened on Margaret Island. The Grand Hotel Palatinus, as it was called, had replaced an older hotel of the same name that had been destroyed by bombs. It ought to have been a pleasant place in which to live and, geographically speaking, it was. Margaret Island is a landscaped park, linked by a newly reconstructed bridge with Buda and Pest, in the middle of the Danube. The Hotel Palatinus, however, turned out to be as unpleasant as the Szent Gellért, and for the very same reasons. It was full of visiting Communists celebrating what they hoped would be the eventual downfall of the United States.

It was also full of what the Communists call *agents provo-*

* See *My Ringside Seat in Moscow,* New York, 1952, pp. 143-144.

cateurs. A waiter who never waited on us used to approach our table in the dining room to apologize for the poor food and service. It was only a question of time, he said, before the Communists would be overthrown. The underground was patiently awaiting military assistance from the United States. Did we think it would arrive soon, and was our government prepared to intervene in order to assure the success of the counter-revolution?

I had to warn Lucile repeatedly not to let him trick her into saying something that could be used against us. I was only partially successful, though, because she was always ready to say exactly what she thought of the Communists to anyone who would listen. She refused to believe that the waiter was what I thought he was until the day she joined the boys in the hotel's swimming pool. The waiter, who hadn't expected her, had gone swimming too, in an effort to catch Bob and Bill in a damaging conversation.

A display of flags in the lobby of the Palatinus surrounded a banner announcing the Second World Youth and Student Festival that was to be held in Budapest in August. It was perhaps unintentional that the American flag was upside down, and the manager put it right side up as soon as the boys called his attention to the error. But we were made to feel so unwelcome throughout our stay that, after ten days, Lucile returned to Vienna with Bob and Bill and I moved back to the Astoria.

Among the other guests at the Palatinus while we were there were an advance delegation of "American students," who looked like no American students that I had ever seen. They all wore glasses and dungarees, which they never changed, and spoke in such a loud tone of voice that even some of the Hungarian Communists were annoyed. In August they were joined by 200 other Americans, mostly of the same sort, who were housed in a former convent decorated with a red-and-white banner reading, literally, in English: "DECAY THE IMPERIALISTS, THE WAR INSTIGATORS, AND THEIR BASE AGENTS!"

I left Budapest in early June, and returned again in early August, but I had no opportunity to observe the festivities in the City Park. I learned from members of the American Legation, however, that the American students' exhibit, so called, was confined to pictures of lynchings, slums, and other "typical" aspects of life in the United States. Leaflets in four languages were distributed on behalf of Henry Wallace's Progressive Party. One of them read: "In a time of developing economic crisis, the few of us lucky enough to land jobs face declining wages, insecure seniority, speed-up, and campaigns of terror and sabotage against our unions. But the greater part of our young people have no jobs at all, and walk the streets in search of employment." Among the many posters on display was one designed to convince the beholder that, whereas Russia was spending more and more on its educational facilities, and less and less on its military establishment, the United States was doing just the opposite.

Actually, as I was in a position to know, Russia and its satellites were sacrificing everything in a single-minded effort to overtake the lead of the United States in the production of modern weapons. It was largely for this reason, in fact, that the United States government was so reluctant to approve the draft agreement.

After my return to Vienna in June, I received the following telegram from Geiger:

TELEGRAPHED SCUDDER AS FOLLOWS: RADÓ AIRMAILED TO YOU AS PER COPY JUST RECEIVED FOLLOWING LETTER THIS MORNING. I QUOTE:

"YOUR LAST VISIT IN BUDAPEST TO ISTVÁN KOSSA THE MINISTER OF HEAVY INDUSTRY UNDOUBTEDLY CONVINCED YOU OF HIS INTENTION TO PROMOTE THE FURTHER DEVELOPMENT OF STANDARD BUDAPEST IN EVERY WAY. I HOPE YOU WERE ABLE TO CONVEY THIS IMPRESSION

TO ISEC'S DIRECTORS. I AM PLEASED TO INFORM YOU THAT THE DRAFT AGREEMENT HAS BEEN SUBMITTED TO ALL INTERESTED MEMBERS OF THE CABINET. ALTHOUGH NO FORMAL DISCUSSION HAS YET TAKEN PLACE I HAVE BEEN AUTHORIZED TO ADVISE YOU THAT THE GOVERNMENT OF HUNGARY IS PREPARED TO APPROVE THE AGREEMENT SUBJECT TO A SINGLE MODIFICATION OF THE FIRST SENTENCES OF PARAGRAPHS SEVEN AND EIGHT AS FOLLOWS:

SEVEN, THE HUNGARIAN GOVERNMENT HEREBY ASSURES TO STANDARD BUDAPEST EFFECTIVE CONTROL OF DIAL AND TO THIS END CONFIRMS THE EXEMPTION OF DIAL FROM NATIONALIZATION FOR THE DURATION OF THIS AGREEMENT. EIGHT, THE HUNGARIAN GOVERNMENT HEREBY ASSURES TO STANDARD BUDAPEST EFFECTIVE CONTROL OF TELEFONGYÁR AND TO THIS END HEREBY CONFIRMS THE EXEMPTION OF TELEFONGYÁR FROM NATIONALIZATION FOR THE DURATION OF THIS AGREEMENT.

I WOULD APPRECIATE YOUR SUBMITTING THE DRAFT AGREEMENT AS MODIFIED TO YOUR DIRECTORS. IF THEY APPROVE THE MODIFICATION THE AGREEMENT MAY THEN BE CONSIDERED RATIFIED BY THE GOVERNMENT OF HUNGARY. I HOPE YOUR DIRECTORS WILL RATIFY THE AGREEMENT AS MODIFIED IN THE NEAR FUTURE AND I AWAIT YOUR CONFIRMATION THEREOF SO THAT I MAY TAKE APPROPRIATE ACTION."

The directors of ISEC, on behalf of I.T.&T., accepted the modification, which merely substituted the adjective "effective" for the adjective "complete" before the noun "control." It was impossible for them to ratify the agreement, however, until it had been approved by the United States government. Copies of the agreement were accordingly submitted to the State Department, which in turn submitted them to an interdepartmental committee representing interested civilian and military agencies. Such scrutiny was necessary in view of the restrictions imposed on strategic exports (including technical information) to the countries behind the Iron Curtain.

If the United States government had been as quick to make up its mind as the Hungarian government, I might never have been arrested and this book might never have been written. But Washington, for reasons that I was unable to understand, decided to procrastinate. Washington's procrastination forced ISEC to procrastinate in turn, and ISEC's procrastination aroused the suspicion of Budapest. For five months ISEC had been complaining of the Hungarians' lack of sincerity; now the shoe was on the other foot, and the Hungarians did their best to make it pinch.

On July 6, after a month of stalling, I received the following cable in Vienna from Hank Scudder in New York:

MEETING OF DIRECTORS TO CONSIDER AGREEMENT HAD TO BE POST-PONED BECAUSE NECESSARY CLEARANCE FROM GOVERNMENT AUTHORITIES NOT YET RECEIVED. MAKING EVERY EFFORT TO ACCELERATE ACTION BY AUTHORITIES AND HAVE BEEN ASSURED OF EARLY DECISION. PROMPT ACTION WILL BE TAKEN BY BOARD OF DIRECTORS IMMEDIATELY DECISION IS RECEIVED FROM GOVERNMENT. PLEASE ADVISE GEIGER THAT NEXT BOARD MEETING IS JULY THIRTEENTH WHEN WE EXPECT ACTION TO BE TAKEN.

Early in August, after a trip to Prague, I returned to Budapest in an effort to placate an implacable Communist regime. Sanders as well as Geiger, I discovered, was now being shadowed by the AVH. Both men were apparently suspected of having had something to do with the delay in ratifying the agreement. Actually, they knew nothing whatever about the cause of the delay, since I had decided not to tell them. For their part, they suspected that the Hungarian government had been secretly negotiating with one or another of our European competitors. Representatives of L. M. Ericcson, a Swedish company; Simens-Halske, a German company; and Philips of Eindhoven, a Dutch company, had recently visited Budapest. It was too much to believe that their visits were accidental; it was reasonable to suppose, therefore, that they were hoping to take our place in the event that we were ousted from Hungary.

A few hours after my return to Vienna, I received a telegram from Belgrade informing me that Sanders' employment permit had been canceled; that he was no longer allowed to withdraw funds from ISEC's blocked account; and that neither he nor Geiger were permitted to visit the Standard factory except in the presence of a Communist escort.

In the absence of Colonel Behn, who was visiting Western Europe, I cabled as follows to Sir Francis Brake, the managing director of Creed and Company, of Croydon, and the vice-president in charge of ISEC's European operations:

HAVE RETURNED WITHOUT INCIDENT FROM BUDAPEST WHERE I DID EVERYTHING POSSIBLE TO ALLAY NERVOUSNESS. WILL ADVISE IN GREATER DETAIL BY LETTER. FOLLOWING RECEIVED FROM BUDAPEST VIA BELGRADE [and here I quoted the telegram]. INASMUCH AS NISSL AND I INTEND TO VISIT BELGRADE IN SEPTEMBER [in connection with Czeija, Nissl's effort to export telephone equipment to Yugoslavia] SUGGEST ARRANGING FOR SANDERS TO MEET US THERE TO ACQUAINT US WITH BUDAPEST SITUATION WHEREUPON WILL REPORT FOR YOUR CONSIDERATION.

Sir Francis, however, vetoed my suggestion for fear of involving Yugoslavia in our difficulties with Hungary. I then sent the following telegram to Scudder, who was then in Rome:

WOULD APPRECIATE YOUR TELEPHONING ME AT HOME AS I WANT TO DISCUSS CABLE I SENT TO BRAKE TODAY FOLLOWING HIS REJECTION OF MY SUGGESTION THAT SANDERS MEET ME IN BELGRADE TO DISCUSS DETERIORATING SITUATION IN BUDAPEST. I QUOTE: "RECENT TRIP REVEALED THAT GOVERNMENT PEOPLE ARE VERY UNEASY. FACTORY PROGRAM AND REFINANCING HELD UP PENDING AGREEMENT. FROM INFORMATION RECEIVED ASSUME ISEC IS WILLING TO RATIFY PROVIDED WASHINGTON APPROVES. HAVE OPPORTUNITY TO PRESENT

PROBLEM TO CERTAIN OFFICIAL VISITORS HERE. DO YOU APPROVE
MY PROVIDING THEM WITH DETAILED MEMORANDUM STRESSING
URGENCY OF SITUATION?"

Goodwin Cooke, in Brake's absence from London, authorized
me to provide the visitors from Washington with the memorandum that I had suggested. I explained that, unless the agreement was promptly approved, Standard Budapest and its subsidiaries would probably be expropriated and that Sanders,
Geiger, and other local employees would probably be arrested
and tried for sabotage. I reiterated that the information with
which we intended to supply the Hungarians was limited to
"standardized" equipment already available to the Russians from
other sources. It was true that we proposed to equip Iron Curtain
airports with instrument approach systems and other navigational
aids, but it was not true that such equipment would involve
military secrets. The draft agreement in no way obliged us to
manufacture electronic computers, radar, or other devices of
prime military importance. I concluded, therefore, that it was
more to the interests of the United States for an American company to supply Hungary with technical information than for a
foreign company to do so. I even offered to fly to Washington
to state our case in person. But my presence was not considered
necessary, and a few days later I received the following cable
from General Harrison, the president of I.T.&T. and the chairman of ISEC's board of directors, in New York:

REFERENCE YOUR MESSAGE VIA SCUDDER: DESIRABLE YOU GO TO
BUDAPEST AND STAY THERE FOR NEXT SEVERAL WEEKS IF NECESSARY
TO KEEP THINGS TRANQUIL PENDING ACTION HERE ON PROPOSED
AGREEMENT WHICH WE USING EVERY ENDEAVOR TO EXPEDITE.

I telegraphed Geiger on August 10 to have Sanders apply for
a Hungarian visa in my name. When a week passed and nothing
happened, I again telegraphed Geiger, who replied that my visa

would be granted on or about the 24th. On the 29th, when my visa had still not been granted, I telegraphed Geiger (for the benefit of the AVH): PLEASE EXPEDITE VISA AS I HAVE IMPORTANT COMMUNICATION FOR MINISTRY OF HEAVY INDUSTRY.

On the 31st, Colonel Behn telegraphed from Paris: UNDERSTAND YOU STILL AWAITING VISA. I AM SURPRISED AT DELAY AND URGE YOU ARRANGE TO GO TO BUDAPEST AS SOON AS POSSIBLE.

Two weeks elapsed before Geiger was able to inform me indirectly why my visa was being withheld. As I telegraphed to Colonel Behn:

HAVE BEEN REPEATEDLY PROMISED BY HUNGARIAN LEGATION IN VIENNA AND BY OUR PEOPLE IN BUDAPEST THAT VISA WOULD BE GRANTED WITHOUT DELAY. LATEST DATE MENTIONED IS SEPTEMBER NINETEENTH. INVESTIGATION REVEALS THAT DESPITE RADÓ'S AND SULYOK'S EFFORTS CABINET HAS ORDERED VISA WITHHELD PENDING OUTCOME OF OTHER NEGOTIATIONS. UNDERSTAND ERICCSON SIEMENS OR PHILIPS PREPARED TO SIGN AGREEMENT SIMILAR TO OURS. HAVE NOT BEEN ABLE TO CONFIRM THIS INFORMATION BUT WILL MAKE THOROUGH INVESTIGATION ON REACHING BUDAPEST.

Noel Field, a former American diplomat who had worked for the League of Nations and the Unitarian Service Committee, a relief organization, had been abducted by the MGB in Prague on May 12, 1949. His wife Herta, who had gone to Prague to investigate his plight, was herself abducted on August 26, four days after she had gone to the Prague airport to meet Noel's brother Hermann, who had expected to arrive on an airplane from Warsaw. Hermann was abducted in Warsaw on August 22, the day he had expected to arrive in Prague. On September 11, Erika Wallach, a German protégée of Noel's, flew from Paris to Berlin to confer with Leo Bauer, a Communist friend who had promised to help her to arrange for the Fields' release. But Bauer himself was under arrest, it seems, and Erika was abducted a few hours after her arrival in Berlin.

On the same day, in Budapest, László Rajk and seven co-defendants were indicted on charges of conspiring to overthrow the "democratic order" in Hungary in association with numerous Yugoslav, British, and American "imperialist agents." Although it was widely believed in the United States that Noel Field had been a Russian agent, he was accused, in the Rajk trial, of having been an American agent employed by Allen W. Dulles of the Office of Strategic Services. In the meantime I had been accused myself in the Communist press of having used the Austro-American Club in Vienna as a blind for an "international spy ring." It was small comfort to know that the charge was false. The indictment of Rajk, the Minister of Foreign, and earlier of Internal, Affairs, was equally false. Yet Rajk, a fanatical Communist, had confessed to a weird assortment of "crimes against the state." He was condemned to death on September 24 and hanged on October 15, a month before I was arrested.

I received my visa the day before Rajk was condemned. It took me several more days to obtain the gray pass I needed in order to cross the Russian zone of Austria en route to Hungary. In the meantime, Alfred Plocek had telegraphed to say that my presence was urgently required in Prague in connection with the long-delayed settlement that we were still negotiating with the Communists in Czechoslovakia. I flew to Prague on the 25th and flew back to Vienna on the 28th. On the 29th, after receiving my gray pass from the Russians, I informed Colonel Behn that I would leave for Budapest the following day. Behn replied as follows:

WILL TRY TO REACH YOU BY TELEPHONE BEFORE YOUR DEPARTURE. IN CASE I FAIL TO DO SO YOU WILL ADVISE THE HUNGARIAN AUTHORITIES THAT OWING TO SUMMER VACATION PERIOD IN THE UNITED STATES IT HAS NOT BEEN POSSIBLE TO TAKE FINAL ACTION

ON THE AGREEMENT AND YOU WILL OF COURSE TRY TO MAINTAIN
OUR POSITION IN EVERY WAY POSSIBLE.

In other words, I was to keep stalling until Washington, in
its own good time, decided whether or not to permit ISEC to
ratify the agreement. Lucile, whose feminine intuition had been
working overtime, was convinced that my trip to Budapest would
end in disaster. She begged me to ask Colonel Behn to let me
remain in Vienna until Washington came to a decision. I shared
her fear that I would be entering a trap if I returned to Budapest, but I was even more afraid of being thought a coward if I
failed to carry out my orders. Sanders and Geiger were in greater
danger than I was, and it was my duty, I thought, to share the
danger with them.

A few days earlier, in fact, Sandy had smuggled out a letter
in which he told me that "our friend" (meaning Geiger) had
been given

a second secretary to watch over him. . . . I am afraid that he
sees the handwriting on the wall and, agreement or not, is convinced
that he can serve no useful purpose in remaining here any longer. . . .
My impression of the whole situation is that the bubble is likely to
burst at any moment. As far as I can make out, the authorities, after
waiting for over three months for news from New York, have decided that the agreement has been disapproved and that the company
is only playing for time.

As you know, I am no longer permitted to enter the factory, except
under guard, and I am no longer permitted to draw any funds from
the blocked account. This is not a hysterical report. I have simply
tried to put down the facts so that you will know how things have
deteriorated since your last visit. I intended to come to Vienna to
make a personal report but, having failed to obtain an exit permit,
I have decided to write. Please don't think that I am being molested
in any way. Apart from my pecuniary position and *agents provocateurs,* I'm all right. Though I'm not exactly kicking, I'm still hobbling
on one leg.

I was full of forebodings as I drove to Budapest on September 30. Geiger, I feared, would surely be arrested, and Sanders and I would probably be arrested, if the agreement was disapproved. I accordingly arranged for Lucile to telephone, if she learned that the agreement had been approved, to say that she and her sister Pia, who had come to live with us in June, would like to visit me in Budapest. This would mean that all was well. If Lucile learned that the agreement had been disapproved, however, she was to telephone to say that I should go to London "to pick up the signed agreement." (By referring to the "signed agreement," I hoped, it would be possible to allay the suspicions of the official eavesdropper who would be listening in to our conversation.) For my part, if I felt that I was in imminent danger of arrest, I was to telephone Lucile to ask, "Has Colonel Behn returned to London?" This would mean that she was to have London telephone to say that I was expected to "pick up the signed agreement."

It was my eleventh trip to Budapest since the end of the Second World War. On all but three occasions, when I had either flown or gone by train, I had driven to Budapest by way of Czechoslovakia and the border town of Rajka. Diplomatic travelers usually avoided Czechoslovakia by entering and leaving Hungary through the border town of Hegyeshalom. The Hegyeshalom route, they said, took only five hours in comparison with the six hours it took to make the trip by way of Rajka. Moreover, by entering and leaving Hungary directly, it was possible to avoid the inconvenience of the double customs inspection involved in crossing the Czechoslovakian enclave south of Bratislava.

Cooke and I had attempted to return to Vienna by way of Hegyeshalom in March. Unfortunately, instead of canceling Cooke's latest visa on his entry, the border authorities had canceled one of his earlier visas twice. Although it was an understandable mistake, and one that not infrequently occurred in

Europe, the authorities at Hegyeshalom chose to find his papers "not in order." He was told to return to Budapest to obtain a document certifying that he had entered Hungary legally. It was already dusk and, rather than return to Budapest, we turned off on a side road and drove up to Rajka in the hope that the authorities there would be more lenient. But they took the same view as their colleagues in Hegyeshalom, and so there was nothing to do but return to Budapest. The manager of the Astoria telephoned a friend of his who was an official of the AVH. The AVH official telephoned the authorities in Rajka to order them to let Cooke pass without any further difficulties. We then drove back to Rajka and crossed the border without incident, but it was dawn by the time we reached Vienna.

Now I decided to try the Hegyeshalom route again. But I was so distracted that I took the wrong turning at a town called Prellenkirchen in the Russian zone of Austria. By the time I had found my way back to the highway the sun was already setting, and for fear of losing my way again, I drove into Czechoslovakia and re-entered Hungary, as usual, through Rajka. My forebodings were not allayed by the fact that, in driving through a village, I had inadvertently killed a dog that had run out in front of my car. It seemed to me, in my perturbed state of mind, to be an evil omen.

Nine | Hide and Seek

Soon after returning to Budapest, I discovered that I, too, was being shadowed. I had been shadowed before on several occasions, but never to the extent that I was being shadowed now. One pair of agents trailed me during the day. In the evening they were relieved by a second pair whose job was to observe my nocturnal movements. A third pair took over as soon as I went to bed. They stood watch in the corridor outside my room at the Astoria, and as soon as I left the hotel in the morning, followed by the first pair of agents, they would go through my belongings to see if I had acquired or disposed of any papers since the day before.

One morning I sprinkled talcum powder on my papers as a test. After blowing off the surplus powder—in the bathtub, where I hoped it would not be noticed—I locked the papers up in one of my suitcases, handling them with the backs of my hands in order not to touch them with my fingers. On my return from work that evening, I opened the suitcase, scooped up the papers —again with the backs of my hands—and examined their upper surfaces. The fingerprints on the thin coatings of talc were unmistakable.

Sanders, in his British way, had chosen to make a joke of the fact that he was under suspicion. He went out of his way to behave as "mysteriously" as possible in order to dismay his shadows.

For lack of anything better to do, I decided to follow his example. Lucile was planning a Hallowe'en party for Bob and Bill, and she had asked me to send her a pair of false beards so that the boys could dress up as pirates. For some reason, false beards were unobtainable in Vienna. They were plentiful enough in Budapest, however, and I had bought a pair which I eventually sent up to Vienna with a friend who was returning by automobile.

One day I hooked one of the beards on my vest, buttoned up my jacket, and went down to the bar to meet Jule Smith, with whom I was having lunch. In the mirror behind the bar I saw my shadows take seats at a table near the entrance from the lobby. I told Smith what I was about to do, and then called a waiter.

"Those people in the doorway want a drink," I said.

As the waiter went over to their table, I bent down, unbuttoned my jacket, and hooked the beard over my ears. I then walked out to the men's room, bowing in the direction of my shadows. The look on their faces was so funny that even the waiters and Edina Dőry, the barmaid, laughed, though it was dangerous for them to have done so.

One evening I had the cloakroom attendant take my hat and gabardine topcoat out to the Buick, which I had parked on Kossuth Avenue not far from the hotel. I then left the bar through the restaurant, which had a separate entrance opening onto the street. It was more than an hour before my discomfited shadows, who had been waiting for me in the lobby, overtook me in the Anna Bar, on the Danube Embankment, near the ruins of the Hotel Dunapalota. I often visited the Anna Bar to listen to its guitarist, a nationalized doctor of medicine, who was forced to work as an entertainer after hours in order to support his family.

After several days of such nonsense, I protested to Béla Sulyok, the Undersecretary of Finance. The oily Sulyok, who was most apologetic, promised to see to it that the AVH behaved itself in the future. Like so many of Sulyok's promises, however, nothing ever came of this one. The shadowing continued, twenty-four hours a day. All that I gained from my audience with Sulyok was permission to make a final withdrawal of 50,000 florins from ISEC's blocked account with the National Bank. This sum would be enough to keep the office going until the end of November. By then, Sulyok intimated, the agreement would either have been ratified or we would have no further need for funds.

My answer to his veiled threat was to protest to Zoltán Radó at the Ministry of Heavy Industry. Radó, a dark, taciturn man, had fled to England during the war and had joined the Communist Party on his return to Hungary in 1945. He was by no means friendly, but I liked him better than Sulyok, whom I would have disliked even if he had not been a Communist. Radó expressed his regrets, but told me that there was nothing he could do to prevent my being treated as if I were a criminal. He hinted, however, that the AVH would behave differently as soon as the agreement was ratified. But time was growing short, he said, and the agreement was becoming "less and less interesting" to his superiors with every week that passed. Unless it was soon ratified, it would be necessary for the Ministry of Heavy Industry to make "other arrangements."

I knew exactly what he meant. Though he denied it, of course, Radó had been negotiating with Philips of Eindhoven behind my back. Communist bureaucrats must always be, or seem to be, successful. Failure, whether real or imagined, is a crime. The state, based as it is on the "infallible" teachings of Marx, Lenin, and Stalin, is never wrong. Every difficulty is always the fault of "treacherous" officials. Radó's only hope, therefore, in the event that our agreement was disapproved, was to obtain from one of our competitors an agreement that would be at least as satisfactory; and I was told that Philips was prepared to concede more than either of the others.

The State Department had been skeptical about our negotiations from the start. As Jule Smith explained the department's attitude, we could forestall expropriation only by supplying the Hungarians—and thereby the Russians—with information that they could not otherwise obtain. I liked Smith, a sandy-haired Texan who was partial to pipes and tweeds, but I disagreed with the State Department and I said so.

I tried to explain that the officers of I.T.&T. were loyal American citizens. We were Americans, I said, before we were businessmen. If we didn't come to terms with the Hungarians, Philips or some other company would; and a foreign company would be under no obligation to consult with the United States government. But Smith was not convinced. He refused to believe that Philips was in any position to negotiate an agreement with Hungary. And even if it were, he said, the United States could always intervene, on the basis of the North Atlantic Treaty, to prevent Philips from supplying Hungary with unauthorized information.

In order to convince Smith that he was wrong, I obtained from a certain official at the Ministry of Heavy Industry—not Radó—a copy of what purported to be the draft agreement with Philips. In so doing, I laid myself open, perhaps, to charges of "unethical conduct." But it was not "espionage." The purported agreement with Philips was a commercial, not a military, document. It constituted evidence, moreover, that the Hungarians had never intended to live up to their agreement with ISEC.

I won my argument with Smith on November 11, the day I showed him the aforementioned document. The Hungarians represented to me that Philips had agreed to it, but Philips denies this and I accept Philips' word that it was either a fake document or the Hungarians' proposal. I am glad to know that Philips

succeeded in outsmarting the Hungarians. The fact remains, however, that the Hungarians hoped to constrain Philips, or some
other foreign company, to supervise the production of cathode-
ray tubes, used in radar as well as television, and microwave
"peanut" tubes used in ultra-high-frequency radar circuits.

I had no way of knowing that the draft of the agreement I
showed to Smith was not authentic, and I am indebted to Philips
for later setting me right in the matter. All I knew at the time
was that, if the draft were signed, ISEC would be out and Philips
would be in—though not for long, of course, for on December 28,
1949, the nationalization law was amended by decree to include
all foreign as well as domestic enterprises employing more than
ten persons. As of that date, the sovietization of Hungary was
complete. In addition to MAORT, Philips, Standard Electric,
Telefongyár, and Dial, the following foreign companies were
confiscated: Brown, Boveri, a Swiss electrical concern; Buda-
kalász, a French textile mill; the Anglo-Saxon Oil Company, a
subsidiary of Shell; the First Hungarian Thread Company, a
subsidiary of J. & P. Coats, Ltd.; the Hungarian Rubber Goods
Company, a subsidiary of Dunlop; and the British-Hungarian
Jute Company.

After reading the purported draft of the Philips agreement,
Smith showed me a paraphrase of a coded message that he had
just received from the American Embassy in London. The Embassy reported that ISEC's agreement had at long last been
disapproved.

While I was debating whether or not to attempt to leave Hungary legally, I learned that Imre Geiger had already fled. He had
left Budapest on an afternoon train to Györ. There he had boarded
a night train to Pinnye, near the Austrian border, where two men
disguised as peasants were to have met his party and led it safely
across the mountains.

Geiger had fled with his wife, daughter, and three other persons, including Edina Dőry, the barmaid at the Astoria. Edina's father, a wealthy landowner, had been expropriated. Her sister Ilona had married George S. Kovach, a former lieutenant colonel with the American Military Mission in Budapest, and had gone to the United States to live. Edina had not been so lucky. After joining the Communist Party, she had been put to work at the Astoria bar, where she earned $3.47 a week, plus tips. Every holiday, in order to hold her job, she had been forced to march in a Communist parade. She had also been forced to kick back 10 per cent of her meager wages to pay for her union dues and a compulsory subscription to a Communist newspaper.

I played golf as usual that week end, and as usual I was not alone. Buda's only course, which belonged to the nationalized Magyar Golf Club, had been reduced from eighteen to nine holes in order to provide members of the Communist Party with a "park of culture and rest" in imitation of Moscow's. A miniature steam railroad, eight miles long, encircled the entire course. The railroad was operated by youngsters who wore uniforms, sold tickets, and operated their single train on schedule. A "workers' café" had been erected opposite the main station at the edge of what was now the ninth fairway. My shadows, as usual, sat on the terrace of the café as they waited for me to complete my solitary game. Golf was officially regarded as a "reactionary" pastime, and the club's Hungarian membership had consequently dwindled to a dozen impoverished representatives of the old regime, who were stoically awaiting the day when they would be sent away to concentration camps. So as not to embarrass them, I always played alone or with other foreigners. Five greens could be seen from where my shadows sat, and I waved to them from each one to prove that I had not escaped. It would have been difficult to escape in any event; the caddy had been warned that he would be held responsible for my return to the clubhouse.

Geiger, it seemed, had decided to escape as soon as he learned that Radó and Gergely had been arrested on November 3. (Tar-ján, the third member of the government's negotiating committee, was not arrested until later.) It was ironic but true that Geiger, if he had wanted to, could have left Hungary legally. He had been given a passport and an exit permit entitling him to visit Turkey on company business. But he was naturally unwilling to leave his wife and daughter behind as hostages, and so, instead of arranging for them to escape separately, as he should have done, he attempted to escape with them in a party of six. It was a foolish thing to do, and doubly foolish for the Geigers to have driven to the station, loaded down with baggage, in their automobile. Its abandonment merely served to warn the AVH of their intentions.

On Tuesday, November 15, Mrs. Zádor, the secretary I had inherited from Pinkney, received an anonymous telephone call informing her that Geiger and his party had been arrested. Geiger's mother-in-law telephoned that afternoon to say that she, too, had received an anonymous telephone call to the same effect. She added that a certain shyster lawyer had offered to procure Geiger's release if I would pay him the equivalent of $6,000 in florins. Fearing a trap, I suggested that it would be better to wait until Geiger's arrest had been officially announced before we attempted to procure his release.

If Geiger had really been captured while attempting to escape, he would probably be forced to confess to "crimes" that would implicate everyone, including myself, who had been involved in ISEC's abortive negotiations with the government. When I telephoned Lucile in Vienna that evening, I therefore gave her the prearranged signal: *"Has Colonel Behn returned to London?"*

It was Wednesday, I recall, when Mrs. Zádor asked me to help her to escape from Hungary too. I did my best to convince her that I had no means of helping anyone to escape.

London telephoned that evening to confirm the "signing" of the disapproved agreement. I announced, for the benefit of the AVH, that I would drive to Vienna on Friday, the 18th, fly to London on Saturday, the 19th, and return to Budapest, "with the signed agreement," early the following week. It would take me until Thursday evening to obtain my exit permit from the Ministry of Internal Affairs.

I had still not decided whether I should risk trying to leave Hungary legally or whether I, too, should try to escape. If I escaped, of course, I would be playing into the hands of the AVH. The mere fact of my flight would be presented as evidence of sufficient "guilt" to justify the confiscation of Standard Budapest. On the other hand, if I were arrested while trying to leave Hungary legally, I would probably be held incommunicado until I confessed to sabotaging the planned economy, after which the company would be expropriated as a matter of course.

It was my plan, if I escaped, to retire to a certain monastery in southern Hungary long enough to grow a beard. Then, disguised as a monk, I intended to make my way to Belgrade. The Serbian border of Yugoslavia, I knew, was not as closely guarded on the Hungarian side as the Croatian border, which joined the Russian and British zones of Austria. I hopefully assumed that the Titoists, having just received the first of a series of grants from the United States, would not deprive me of my liberty.

At the last minute I decided to attempt to leave Hungary legally. Thursday night, after receiving my exit permit, I attended a formal dinner party at which Geoffrey Wallinger, the British minister, was present. Wallinger told me that he would be driving to Vienna by way of Hegyeshalom at eight-twenty the next morning. Lieutenant Colonel John T. Hoyne, an assistant army attaché of the American Legation, would be driving to Vienna by the same route at nine. It occurred to me that, if I drove to Vienna at eight-forty, bracketed between Wallinger and Hoyne, both of whom had diplomatic immunity, the AVH might not arrest me. And even if its agents did arrest me, I thought, Wallinger or

Hoyne or both could be counted on to raise an alarm on their arrival in Vienna.

What I was most afraid of was being arrested secretly. If my arrest were promptly reported, I hoped, the American Legation would take immediate steps to procure my release. Otherwise I would be held incommunicado until I had been forced to confess to whatever crimes of which it pleased the AVH to find me guilty. The worst that would happen to me, I thought, would be what had happened to Ruedemann and Bannantine of MAORT. It did not occur to me that I would be charged with espionage as well as sabotage, tried and convicted, and then held as a hostage for seventeen months until I was ransomed by the United States government.

Ten | The Trap Closes

At eight o'clock the next morning, November 18, 1949, I said good-by to Sanders and Mrs. Zádor, who had called at the Astoria to see me off. Sandy was still hoping to obtain his exit permit. Mrs. Zádor, on my advice, had given up any thought of attempting to escape. She asked me if it would be all right for Ferencz to drive me to the border. Ferencz, or Feri, as he was known for short, was the office chauffeur. He had told Mrs. Zádor that he wanted to visit his brother, who lived in a village not far from Hegyeshalom. It was strange, I thought, that Feri had never mentioned his brother before, but I could think of no excuse for denying his request.

Feri was a sallow young man with a thin black mustache. Inasmuch as he spoke neither English nor German, I had to converse with him in sign language because of my scant knowledge of Hungarian.

On our way out of Pest, I stopped at the American Legation to confirm the arrangements I had made with Colonel Hoyne. As an afterthought, I asked him to take my briefcase to Vienna with him. It contained no papers of any great importance, but I wanted to avoid every possible difficulty at the border. I also checked my golf bag and an extra suitcase with the legation's porter in the hope of lending credence to my supposed intention of returning to Budapest the following week. I assumed that the porter worked

for the AVH. If he reported that I had left some baggage at the
legation, I thought, the AVH might change its mind if it had already decided to arrest me.

Feri and I left the legation promptly at eight-forty. Hoyne
promised to follow twenty minutes later. It was a drizzly morning and the asphalt was slippery, but there was no good reason
for Feri to drive as slowly as he did. It took us three hours and
five minutes to complete a trip that seldom took longer than two
hours and a half. If Hoyne had left Budapest when he said he
would, he ought to have been right behind us. But there was no
sign of him when we paused in the outskirts of Hegyeshalom at
eleven forty-five.

Despite my protests, Feri stubbornly insisted on driving me the
remaining distance to the border station. It was only a mile or so,
but a light rain had begun to fall, and I feared that he would be
drenched if he walked back to Hegyeshalom. As things developed,
however, there was no need for my concern on Feri's behalf; he
had no intention of getting wet.

The gates were down at the railroad crossing between Hegyeshalom and the border station. As we halted, two AVH guards
armed with tommy guns approached the Buick. One of them
asked to see my passport. Instead of examining the page on which
my exit permit was stamped, he merely looked at page two, bearing the official request of "All whom it may concern to permit
safely and freely to pass, and in case of need to give all lawful
aid and protection to ROBERT A. VOGELER, a citizen of the United
States," and page four, bearing my photograph and signature.
Nodding, he handed the passport back to me. The other guard
had meanwhile raised the crossing gates. He then climbed into
the front of the car with Feri, and his companion climbed in
beside me in the rear.

We drove up to the temporary wooden shed that housed the
border authorities. Inside were six or eight guards, instead of the
usual two or three whom I was used to seeing in Rajka, and half

a dozen AVH men in civilian clothes. An AVH major was sitting behind a desk.

Feigning a sense of calm that I was unable to feel, I handed the major my passport, wallet, and currency-control slip. My wallet contained $2,000, varying amounts of British, Austrian, and Czechoslovakian currency, and 500 florins. (It was illegal to leave Hungary with more than that amount, and so I had left my remaining 7,500 florins with Sanders, from whom they would be seized at the time of his arrest.)

"Empty your pockets," said the major.

One by one I placed my possessions on his desk—my two cigarette lighters, a large one with a wind guard and a smaller one for indoor use; my gold Sheaffer pen-and-pencil set; and the platinum pocket watch that I had forgotten to leave in Vienna.

"Hold out your hands," said the major, and as I did so he felt my wrist.

"Give me your other watch," he said.

I took it off and laid it on his desk, wondering what he would make of the fact that I had been carrying two watches and two lighters. I recalled that Lucile's sister, Pia Eykens, had laughed at my habit of acquiring two and three examples of almost every gadget, and I was glad that I had left my third cigarette lighter in Vienna. My wrist watch was an inexpensive chromium object that I wore when traveling in Russian-occupied territory. I was glad that I had at least remembered to leave my gold wrist watch in Vienna.

"Take off your ring," said the major.

Fortunately, I had also left my only valuable ring in Vienna. The one that I had been wearing was merely my class ring from the Massachusetts Institute of Technology.

The major put everything, including my passport, into a large brown envelope. I asked him why. He told me that my papers were not in order and that we would have to go to the kommandatura, which was located in the Hegyeshalom railroad sta-

tion. The shamefaced Feri drove us over in the Buick. The station was a buff-colored stucco building with a red tile roof. At one
end was the Russian kommandatura, and at the other end the
Hungarian. The latter was full of AVH guards, all heavily armed;
the floor was covered with mud. The major delivered me and the
envelope containing my possessions to a lieutenant colonel, who
told me that I would have to return to Budapest.

"Why? Am I under arrest?"

"You'll find out in Budapest."

"May I telephone the American Legation?"

"No. Please go into the next room."

There a pair of guards ordered me to strip. They examined my
clothing piece by piece, inspecting every seam. They laughed as
they removed the miniature American flag from my buttonhole
and tossed it onto a table. After confiscating my belt, handkerchief, tie, and shoelaces, they ordered me to dress.

On being escorted back to the lieutenant colonel, I asked him
again, though my status was obvious, if I was under arrest.

"It won't do any good to ask questions," he said, "because I'm
not permitted to answer. Please be seated and keep your hands
on your knees."

He motioned me to a chair in a corner. As I sat down, two
guards took up positions on either side of me, reminding me at
intervals to keep my hands on my knees. At that time the members of the AVH wore traditional Hungarian army uniforms with
red patches on their shoulders. Before long the red shoulder
patches would be replaced with blue shoulder boards, and Sam
Browne belts would be worn over their khaki blouses, as the
AVH, little by little, adopted the uniform of the Russian MGB.

It was then twelve-thirty, but there was still no indication that
Hoyne had reached the border station. I felt confident, however,
that when he finally arrived he would inquire as to why my name
was not listed in the register of arrivals and departures lying open
on the major's desk. If he were told that I was being held at the
kommandatura, he would probably come to look for me. If not,

he would drive on to Vienna, where he could be counted on, I thought, to report my disappearance to the American authorities.

Assuming that Hoyne had been delayed an hour, and that it took him three hours to drive up from Budapest, he would reach the border station not later than one o'clock. Assuming that the major refused to tell him where I was being held, he would drive on to Vienna. It seldom took more than an hour, I had been told, to reach Vienna from the Hegyeshalom border station. Even assuming that Hoyne were further delayed, and that the trip took an hour and a half, he would still have time to report my disappearance by two-thirty. It would take another half-hour, perhaps, to get through to the American Legation in Budapest by telephone. It would then be three o'clock. The legation would still have time to determine what had happened.

The next day was Saturday, the 19th, and the legation would be closed for normal business. But the disappearance of an American citizen would be taken seriously enough, I thought, to justify assigning a skeleton staff to week-end duty. If I could only hold out long enough, it might just be possible to effect my release before I had been forced to confess to crimes that I had not committed.

Ruedemann and Bannantine, of course, had been forced to "confess" before they were released, and they had been able to notify the legation at the very moment of their arrest. I recalled what I had said in Vienna about confessing to any crime, however ridiculous, to avoid being tortured. But now, as I thought things over, I changed my mind. I had long opposed the appeasement of Russia, and the time had come for me to practice what I had preached. I had no idea what sort of torture would be applied in my case, but I resolved to resist it for at least ten days, if I could, in order to encourage the State Department to take a strong position.

Two agents in civilian clothes arrived at three to take me back to Budapest. One of them, a major, as I later discovered, was a

bald, stocky man with a hoarse voice; the other, who turned out
to be a captain, was taller and younger—an evil-looking man
with a broken nose and a scraggly blond mustache. They led me
outside to a black Mosely sedan, driven by a chauffeur, and made
me sit between them in the rear. Warning me to keep my hands
on my knees, they took out automatic pistols which they rested
in their laps.

Feri was standing at attention beside my Buick sedan, which
was still parked in front of the kommandatura. I asked my captors
about the baggage and the gabardine topcoat and black Homburg
hat that I had left inside. They told me that everything, including
the car, would be brought back to Budapest later on.

As we drove away, I waved to Feri, but he failed to return my
salutation. I would never see him again.

My captors pulled down a black curtain which they hooked
to the back of the driver's seat. The purpose of the drawn curtain, I gathered, was to prevent oncoming motorists from seeing
who was inside.

My captors and I exchanged but a very few words on our way
back to Budapest. The major spoke nothing but Hungarian. The
captain, who spoke a little German, refused to tell me where I was
being taken. Later he asked me with a grin if I still had the false
beards. I told him that I had long since sent them to my sons in
Vienna.

"Das ist besser," he said, resuming his silence.

The black curtains on the rear and side windows were not low-
ered until we reached the outskirts of Buda, where occasional
pedestrians might have been able to peer inside. It was already
dark, but the curtains were translucent, and I could tell from
the reflection of the street lights against certain public buildings
exactly where we were going.

Crossing the Danube into Pest, we followed the Leopold and
Theresa rings (now known by other names) as far as the Octagon,
once renamed in honor of Hitler and now renamed in honor of

Stalin. We turned left at Stalin Square and drove two blocks, turning left into Csengery Street and then right into a driveway. The Mosely paused long enough for two steel doors to be opened and then it moved forward and stopped. The steel doors closed behind us with a sound that I shall never forget. We were inside a small garage—the prisoners' entrance at 60 Andrássy Avenue, now called 60 Stalin Avenue.

The elderly major with the hoarse voice led me through another steel door into a dimly lighted antechamber full of guards. Two of the guards led us up a dark, winding stairway. The captain with the broken nose and the blond mustache followed at my heels. Two more guards, as I remember, brought up the rear.

The higher we climbed the darker it became. It was difficult for me to keep my shoes on without laces, and between the third and fourth landings I happened to stumble, whereupon the captain gave me a violent shove. For six hours I had been struggling to control my emotions; now I was filled with sudden anger. I turned around and hit the captain a glancing blow on the cheek. He immediately replied by hitting me over the right temple with his drawn automatic. At that moment the major took me by the tops of my trousers and dragged me up the remaining stairs.

On the fourth and top landing was another steel door, which swung open as we arrived. I was led through several rooms into an inner office, where my captors left me in the care of two other agents in civilian clothes. Presently my captors returned, and the four of them, together with the four guards, escorted me along a corridor and then down a broad wire-enclosed stairway to the second floor. I was led through another series of rooms into another inner office, elegantly furnished with overstuffed chairs, sofas, and Oriental rugs.

To my left as I entered was a small blond man seated behind a desk. The wall behind him was blank. To his right, at a smaller desk, sat a mousy-looking woman with a pimpled face. On the wall beside her was a bookcase and, above it, a portrait of Lenin in a visored cap. To the left of the blond man's desk was a dark red sofa, and on the wall behind it a portrait of "Potato Head" Rákosi, the Communist viceroy of Hungary.

Beyond Rákosi's portrait was a closed door. At the other end of the room were two casement windows with drawn red curtains. On the wall between them, facing the blond man at the desk, was a portrait of Stalin in his generalissimo's uniform. Beneath Stalin's portrait was another dark red sofa, and on either side of it, drawn out from the wall, were two matching overstuffed chairs.

Immediately in front of the desk was a plain wooden chair in which I was told to sit. As I did so, the blond man adjusted the chromium reflector of his desk lamp so that it shone straight into my eyes. My head ached from the blow I had received, and in the glare my right eye began to water. Presently it closed altogether, and I had to squint at my inquisitor, for such he proved to be, out of my left eye, which also began to water. My two captors left with two of the guards. The other two men in civilian clothes sat behind me in the overstuffed chairs. The other two guards stood watch at the door through which we had entered.

"Good evening," said the blond man in English.

"Good evening," I said. "Am I under arrest?"

The blond man turned inquiringly to the mousy woman, who translated my question into Hungarian. "Good evening," it seemed, had exhausted his knowledge of English.

"You speak German, no?" said the woman.

"*Bin ich verhaftet?*" I asked again. "Am I under arrest?"

"You're being held for questioning," she translated.

"Why?"

They ignored my question.

"May I telephone the American Legation?"

"It's too late now," the blond man said. "The legation will be closed. Perhaps, when we have finished, you will be allowed to telephone. In the meantime I have some questions to ask you."

My eyes were watering so badly that I had to wipe them every now and then with the back of my hand. I hoped that the blond man would focus his lamp in another direction. Every time I moved my head, however, he readjusted the lamp so that it shone straight into my watering eyes. No. 1, as I shall call him, was the first of my two inquisitors. Although I never learned his name, I later saw him in the uniform of a lieutenant colonel. The woman, his secretary, referred to him merely as "the colonel"—"*Herr Oberst.*"

"Why did you come to Hungary?" he asked.

"I came to Hungary at the invitation of your government to negotiate a commercial agreement on behalf of the International Standard Electric Corporation of New York."

No. 1's voice, which had been almost genial up to now, became suddenly harsh, but the woman translated tonelessly:

"Here we will drop all pretense. I want you to tell me the real reason why you came to Hungary."

"That was the real reason."

"We won't get anywhere if you lie. You'll learn soon enough that we have methods to obtain the truth."

"I have told the truth," I said.

No. 1 smiled as if he were dealing with a retarded child. He passed me a crude Manila package of Hungarian cigarettes—Olympias—and a wooden box of Swedish safety matches.

"Smoke as much as you like," he said, "because we're going to be here for a long, long time."

A guard came in with a tray on which were two glasses of black coffee. It was strong, heavily sweetened Italian coffee, made in an *espresso* machine. I drink it with relish, for I had eaten nothing since breakfast, and it was now seven-thirty. I could tell the time by glancing at No. 1's wrist watch whenever he moved his left hand into the reflection from the lamp.

"Why did you come to Hungary?" he repeated.

"I've already told you," I said. "I came to Hungary to negotiate an agreement with your government."

"As you know," said No. 1, "Zoltán Radó was arrested two weeks ago. Imre Geiger and his party were arrested last week while trying to escape from Hungary with your knowledge and assistance. They and the others whom we have arrested have accused you of directing their espionage and sabotage activities."

Until that moment I had expected merely to be accused of sabotage—a Communist crime so vague and all-embracing that it has no legal meaning. Espionage, however, was something else again. If Geiger and Radó had indeed confessed to "espionage" as well as "sabotage," and if they had blamed me for their "crimes," it meant that I would not be allowed to get off as easily as Ruedemann and Bannantine. Is was thus imperative for me to hold out until the legation procured my release, for if I confessed to "espionage" I would almost certainly be sentenced to a long term of imprisonment.

It is impossible for me to recall exactly what was said in the course of my "preliminary investigation," as it was called, but I shall do my best to reconstruct the interrogation exactly as it evolved, without adding or deleting anything of consequence.

"Well?" said No. 1.

"I know nothing about espionage or sabotage," I said. "I am an American businessman who came to Hungary in a purely commercial capacity. But now that you have accused me of espionage, I demand that you let me communicate with my legation."

"You'll be allowed to communicate with your legation when we see fit. In the meantime you'd better answer my questions truthfully. Now, for the last time, what were you really doing in Hungary?"

I spoke for ten minutes without interruption while No. 1's secretary took notes in shorthand. I mentioned, in general terms, almost everything that I had done. I failed to mention, of course, the fact that I had obtained a copy of the government's draft of the agreement it wanted to sign with Philips. Neither did I attempt to deny the assistance that I was supposed to have given Geiger and the others who had wanted to escape from Hungary. It was a crime, I knew, in the Communists' eyes, for anyone to have co-operated with the underground railroad. But, in my opinion, it was not a crime in the eyes of God or, indeed, of the United Nations. None of the would-be fugitives was guilty of any wrong-doing. All of them would have been free to leave their country legally if the Communists had not seized power, with the help of the Russians, in violation of the Hungarian peace treaty.

I had spoken in German. As the secretary translated my remarks into Hungarian, No. 1 began to make unpleasant faces, glancing first at her and then at me, as if he could not believe his ears.

"Lies, lies, lies," I can still hear him saying. "Everything you tell me is a lie."

He then began to dictate to his secretary in Hungarian. When he had finished, she read his speech back to me in German. It was a systematic distortion of everything I had said. What it amounted to was a confession that my work for I.T.&T. had merely been a "cover" for my "real" activities as an intelligence officer of the United States Army, Navy, and Air Force, and that my "real" assignment in Hungary had been to obtain state secrets by unlaw-ful methods and to sabotage the planned economy. It was then that I lost my temper.

"I'm not going to answer any more questions," I said, "if you insist on twisting everything I say. You're apparently not interested in the truth. You're apparently interested only in tricking me into admitting your ridiculous accusations."

No. 1 stared at me quizzically for a moment and then nodded to the two agents who were sitting on the sofa behind me. I heard them rise and then I felt their hands on my shoulders as they yanked me out of my chair. They dragged me through the door next to Rákosi's portrait into a large bathroom that was surpris-ingly dirty in comparison with No. 1's immaculate office. In one

corner was a tub full of cold water. The agents made me strip and
then they grabbed me by my arms and legs and threw me struggling into the tub. Laughing and shouting in Hungarian, they
ducked me up and down, holding my head under water for such
long intervals that I was choking and gasping for breath when
they finally let me go.

"Have you cooled off now?" asked No. 1 as they sat me in
the chair again before his desk. I had been forced to dress without drying myself and I was clammy with cold. But in some
ways I felt better than I had before. My head was throbbing
and I felt nauseated, but the ducking in cold water had renewed
my determination to resist.

"That's only one method we have of treating hot tempers,"
said No. 1, as he readjusted the desk lamp so that it shone into
my eyes. "I warn you not to lose your temper again, or we'll have
to try a more drastic method."

"I want to speak to my legation," I said.

"You're foolish if you think your legation can do anything to
help you. The day when Americans received special consideration in Hungary is over. You're a prisoner of a sovereign state, a
people's republic, an ally of the great Soviet Union, whose leaders are determined to punish everyone who breaks its laws. I
advise you to forget about the American Legation and to attend
to the business at hand, which is to answer my questions truthfully and completely."

And then it began again, the same questions and the same
answers, and the same mock incredulity on No. 1's part that I
should be so foolish as to expect him to believe my "lies."

"Here's a pencil and some paper," he said at last. "I'm going
to leave you alone with your conscience. While I'm gone, I want
you to write me the true story of your treacherous and antipopular activities in Hungary."

"Antipopular" was the word he used. I don't pretend to know what it means. Among his other favorite words were "diversionary," "obstructionist," and "provocative." I could only assume that they added up to "sabotage," which I knew meant anything of which the Communists disapproved. "Espionage" apparently consisted of the acquisition of any information, by whatever means, that the Communists would have preferred not to publicize.

It was then a little after eleven, according to No. 1's wrist watch. As he and his secretary left the office, the two agents who had been sitting behind me moved over to the sofa beneath Rákosi's ugly visage. The two guards at the door were relieved by two replacements, who stood beside me as I wrote—exactly what I had already said. A little later I was served another glass of coffee.

Every now and then I was permitted to visit the toilet in the corridor beyond the outer office. I was accompanied on each visit by both agents and both guards. There was never any toilet paper. Once, when I needed some, one of the guards brought me two sheets of the paper on which I was supposed to write what No. 1 called my "autobiography." I crumpled them and was about to use the first sheet when the guard tapped me on the shoulder. He made signs to indicate that I should tear each sheet into four pieces in the interests of conservation.

No. 1 and his secretary returned at three, when both the agents and the guards were simultaneously relieved. One of the fresh guards placed in front of me a tray with another glass of coffee and two small sandwiches on it. The sandwiches were really appetizers, of the sort served in Budapest's *espresso* bars, to go with coffee and brandy or *barack,* the native apricot schnapps. They consisted of thin slices of ham and cheese between small buttered rolls. I munched them greedily as the secretary read aloud in Hungarian what I had written in German.

"No," said No. 1 when she had finished. "This will never do. All you've written is a pack of lies."

He then told the secretary to read me the text of a typescript in German, which had evidently been prepared while they were out of the office. Every now and then she would stop to ask, in reference to a given statement, "Is that true?"

I would reply yes or no, depending on what she had said. Usually it would be a distortion of the truth, and I would say, "Yes, that's true, but not the way you've stated it."

One example I recall was the statement, "I attended a military school and was trained as a professional officer." It was true, of course, that I had attended the Peekskill Military Academy, and it was likewise true that I had attended the United States Naval Academy at Annapolis. As every American knows, however, many young men attend private military academies without becoming professional army officers. And in my case, even though I attended the Naval Academy for two and a half years, I had not even become a professional Navy officer, much less a professional Army officer. Professional Army officers are trained at West Point, not at Annapolis; but the AVH, as will presently be seen, was determined to make me an Annapolis colonel, and nothing I said or wrote sufficed to correct—or perhaps I should say "divert" or "obstruct"—its misapprehension.

"Under prevailing conditions," I had written, "it was impossible for Standard Budapest to operate at a profit, which is why we wanted to modify the unfair penalties that were being imposed by the Hungarian government."

This statement, as distorted by No. 1, was read back to me as follows: "We were eager to sign the agreement in order to charge exorbitant prices and thus destroy the popular benefits of the Three-Year Plan."

I pointed out that all we wanted to do was to make a profit, or at least break even, so as not to be forced into bankruptcy and thus provide the government with an excuse for confiscating Standard Budapest.

"Aha," said No. 1. "What you mean to say is that you wanted corrupt government officials like Radó to play your game and thus give you a legal excuse for sabotage. You wanted to make the Hungarian people pay for your inefficiency. We fixed fair prices, but you wanted to increase them in order to form an imperialist monopoly."

Once, I remember, No. 1 asked me if I had ever gone to Vienna with Cooke or Scudder, leaving one or the other alone in Budapest. I told him that I had. He then asked me if it wasn't possible, while I was absent, for either Cooke or Scudder to have bribed Radó. I agreed that it was possible, but insisted that it wasn't probable, since neither of them would have had any desire to bribe Radó.

"But you admit that it was possible."

"Yes, I admit that it was possible."

"For Scudder or Cooke to have done so in your absence?"

"Yes, it was possible, but—"

"And for you to have done so in their absence?"

"Yes, but—"

"But it wasn't Scudder, and it wasn't Cooke. It was you, wasn't it?"

"No, it wasn't. Nobody bribed Radó."

"But you did. We know you did because Radó has already confessed that you did."

"He couldn't have confessed to something that didn't happen."

"Oh, so you think we don't know what happened? Well, for your information, Radó has confessed to many things that are a lot worse than taking bribes. He has confessed to selling you state secrets. Do you deny that he did?"

"Yes, I do."

"Well, you won't, for very long, because we're going to confront you with your fellow criminals as soon as they're physically able to appear."

It was daylight when the second session ended. I knew it was daylight only because the office had become so stuffy that No. 1

asked his secretary to open a window. In so doing, she had to
pull back one of the curtains and raise a blind between its inner
and outer panes. The inner pane, I noticed, was of frosted glass.

No. 1 and his secretary again left the office. For the next four
hours I was made to write, and then No. 1 and the secretary
returned for another four hours of grilling.

Such was the routine that was followed for sixty-five hours,
from seven on Friday night until noon on Monday, November
21. Every four hours No. 1 and his secretary would leave the
office, and for the next four hours I would have to write. The
agents who watched me were relieved at eight-hour intervals;
the guards at the door, at four-hour intervals, coinciding with
the arrivals and departures of No. 1.

I was the only one who got no rest. Every time the guards
were changed, I was given another glass of coffee. I was also
given all the cigarettes that I could smoke. Except for the two
small sandwiches, however, I was given nothing to eat until
Monday afternoon. The desk lamp was trained on my eyes
throughout the entire period of the "preliminary investigation,"
and I only once saw the light of day.

By Saturday afternoon I was ravenously hungry, but whenever
I mentioned food No. 1 replied, "Only after you've signed a
full confession."

Although I did not know it at the time, the typescript that No.
1's secretary had read to me was the first of more than twenty
"confessions" that I would be asked to sign. I refused to sign it,
and I likewise refused to sign the second, third, and fourth
"confessions" that No. 1 prepared.

Gradually, as my fatigue increased, my hunger lessened. Late
on Saturday night, I remember, I fell out of my chair from sheer
exhaustion. The agents picked me up, emptied a pitcher of water

over my head, and gave me a vigorous shaking. Thereafter, every time I began to lose consciousness, they would douse me with water and shake me until I felt that my head was falling off.

By Sunday I was suffering from hallucinations, some of which were extraordinarily vivid. On one occasion Lucile appeared in the office and begged me to return to Vienna. I could even smell her perfume.

"But can't you see I'm under arrest?"

"Please come home, Bob; the boys are asking for you."

Such was the conversation that was going on in my head when I was again shaken back into reality.

"Here," No. 1 was saying, "just sign this and you'll be given a nice, comfortable bed."

It was yet another typed confession. A new personality was struggling to take command of my body, a personality that was prepared to do everything that No. 1 suggested. But my old personality—or perhaps it was merely the instinct of self-preservation—still held its ground.

"You're distorting everything I've written," I remember saying. "It's against the law to make a man incriminate himself. I demand the right of counsel."

"All right," said No. 1. "If you don't want to sign, we can always use other methods."

"I'll sign what I've written because it's the truth, but I won't sign what you've written because it's a lie."

"Watch your tongue," said No. 1, "or we'll have to cool you off again."

He then resumed the interrogation, repeating the same questions again and again, in the hope of tricking me into giving him contradictory answers. I struggled against fatigue, pains in every part of my body, and a growing lightheadedness, to repeat exactly what I had already said. Whenever No. 1 seemed on the verge of tricking me into contradicting my previous testimony, I would disentangle myself by saying, "All right, let's review the whole

question." And then I would start all over again from the very
beginning.

What happened to Hoyne? I often wondered. *And what's become of the American Legation? Why don't they get me out of
here?*

And the thought kept running through my mind, *You can't do
this to an American.* And then I would laugh hysterically, thinking of the old chestnut about the indignant citizen saying, "You
can't do this to me," and the gangster's stereotyped reply, "Oh,
yeah?"

It was an unequal struggle, and in the end I succumbed, for
No. 1 had been able to refresh himself with food and drink and
rest at four-hour intervals, while I had been kept hungry and
awake with coffee and cigarettes. Sometimes the coffee tasted as
if it had been spiked with brandy, and sometimes the cigarettes
tasted as if they had been perfumed. But perhaps these were
merely olfactory manifestations of my visual hallucinations.

I was familiar with actedron, a drug that I had taken voluntarily on occasion, and particularly when I had had to do a lot
of work at night. Egbert Kus, my Vienna physician and the husband of my secretary, had told me that actedron was more effective and less injurious than Benzedrine. It corresponded, he said,
to pervitin, the "superman" drug that was used so freely by German officers during the Second World War. I knew nothing about
scopolamine and mescaline, the other drugs that were said to
have been used to extract Cardinal Mindszenty's incredible confession, except that the former, in combination with morphine,
produces twilight sleep, and the latter, hallucinations and schizophrenia.

Whether any or all of these drugs were administered in the
course of my own inquisition I am unable to say. My second inquisitor would later insist that drugs were superfluous in view of
the "more effective" methods used by the AVH. Perhaps, in my
case, he was telling the truth. I was given pills only once, and

no injections at all. I doubt that anything was administered while I was asleep, and though I occasionally suspected that I was being given something in my food and drink, I was never able to taste it. All I know is that, with or without the use of drugs, I resisted for seventy-one days. And by then, as I shall explain, I had been reduced to such a state of despondency that I was ready to confess to anything.

The toxins of fatigue are enough in themselves, I suspect, to account for my partial breakdown at the hands of No. 1. Shortly before noon on Monday, November 21, 1949, I agreed to sign the fifth of the "confessions" that he placed before me. It was so much less incriminating than the other four, which I had refused to sign, that it seemed to me, in my weakened state, to be hardly a confession at all. It was merely a summary of my true statements distorted in such a way as to make it seem that I had contributed, as I.T.&T.'s representative in Budapest, to certain unspecified acts of "sabotage" affecting Hungary's Three-Year Plan.

After sixty-five hours of interrogation, I was drunk with fatigue, hunger, cigarettes, coffee, and whatever it was, if anything, with which my coffee had been spiked. But I was not so drunk that I signed the fourteen pages of my "confession" in my normal handwriting. No. 1, however, was not deceived. He compared my signature with that in my passport, and, seeing that they were not the same, he ordered his secretary to retype the entire confession. He then told me to sign each of the fourteen pages exactly as I had signed my passport. There was no alternative but to submit to further grilling, and so I did as I was told.

A guard brought in one of my suitcases, and No. 1 told me to change my dirty shirt. I was then taken up to a small room on the fourth floor. There I was shaved in a plain chair with my arms folded behind my back. Two guards stood on either side of me to prevent my seizing the barber's razor. Presently No. 1 and two of the agents appeared, and, together with the two guards, they escorted me down the main wire-enclosed stairway to the second floor.

We passed through a mirrored vestibule into a large anteroom full of uniformed officers. No. 1 and his subordinates clicked their heels and bowed. A major announced that *"a tábornok"* ("the general") was expecting us. We were then ushered into an elaborate inner office.

The general, a small dark man, was seated behind a desk covered with silver knickknacks, including a miniature horse and flamingo, an inkstand, a cigarette box, a lighter, and several ashtrays. He was dressed in a dark gray suit that matched his cropped gray hair and gray mustache. His heavy-lidded eyes, which were also gray, gave his face a vaguely Oriental cast. His hands had been freshly manicured, and his heavy jowls had been freshly shaved and powdered. His left shoulder, I noticed, was lower than his right.

Like No. 1's office, its floor was covered with Oriental rugs, but unlike No. 1's office, from which the daylight had been excluded, the general's office was bright and sunny. I was seated in a plain chair before the general's desk. Staggered out from the desk on either side of me were two rows of red leather easy chairs. In three of them sat men whom I had never seen before but who would be present at most of my subsequent audiences with the general. One of them was the general's deputy, an enormously fat colonel with a row of Russian medals on his chest. He was the only man in uniform. Next to the colonel sat a dark pudgy man with two missing fingers. He wore a brown shirt with a blue serge suit, and would later prove to be a major of the MGB, the foreign division of the Russian political police. The third man was a Hungarian civilian who turned out to be the assistant state prosecutor. No. 1 and his subordinates sat in the remaining chairs.

Behind and to the right of the general's desk was an interoffice switchboard. In other circumstances, I might have been amused by the way the general crossed his wires as he attempted to receive his incoming calls. Several times in the course of the first audience he seemed on the point of asking me to tell him how the apparatus worked. But I made no effort to help him, even though the switchboard had obviously been manufactured by Standard Budapest, and he continued to muff his calls by flicking the wrong keys in response to the flashing lights. The fat colonel stared at his chief in bewilderment.

On the wall behind the general's desk was a portrait of Mátyás Rákosi. On the opposite wall were twin portraits of Lenin and Stalin in wooden frames embossed with the great seal of the USSR.

"How are you feeling?" the general asked me through his deputy, who acted as his interpreter, as soon as he had ceased to fiddle with the switchboard.

"Very tired," I said.

He offered me a cigarette from his silver box and passed me his silver lighter. Unlike the cigarettes that No. 1 had been feeding me, the general's cigarettes were British, not Hungarian; the one I smoked was a Player.

The general then began a little speech, the sense of which, as nearly as I can remember it, was as follows:

"You've now been our prisoner for three days, and I suppose you're wondering whether any inquiries have been made about your case. So far, we haven't been asked a single question by the American Legation, even though your diplomatic representatives know as well as you do why you were arrested and where you are being held. No government, and least of all a capitalist government, likes to be embarrassed when one of its spies is caught. You are therefore completely in our power, and you can look only to us for your salvation.

"The lieutenant colonel," and here he glanced toward No. 1, "has been very patient with you, but it seems that you are not yet ready to tell the truth. You have admitted only a small part of your hostile activities against the Hungarian People's Republic. There is a great deal more that you will have to tell us, and the sooner you do so the better. We have methods to loosen people's tongues, and we shall not hesitate to use them if we have to.

"But I have decided to give you another chance to make a clean breast of things, and I advise you to take advantage of it. It may be the last chance you have. We realize," and here I recall his exact phraseology, "that you are but an actor in the drama that is now unfolding (*das Spiel der sich jetzt entwichelt*), and we are less interested in punishing you, Robert Vogeler, than we are in demonstrating the mean and predatory nature of American imperialism. We intend to demonstrate that Hungary, though a small country, can no longer be exploited by the United States. Your future treatment will depend on your willingness to cooperate with us in the fulfillment of our task."

It was not until 'seventeen months later, just before I was released from prison, that I learned who the general was. He was Benö Ausspitz, alias Gábor Péter, the former tailor who was now (at least nominally) the chief of the AVH. The original Gábor Péter, an appointee and presumably a friend of László Rajk's, was rumored to have committed suicide prior to the latter's trial—which perhaps accounts for the fact that few, if any, photographs of the present Gábor Péter exist.

When Péter had finished, I was led up a back stairway that was not protected by the usual wire grille. It occurred to me that I could commit suicide, if I wanted to, by vaulting into the stair well. My plight was apparently hopeless. I suspected, though I couldn't prove, that Péter had been lying when he said that no inquiries had been made by the American Legation. But it now seemed evident that, regardless of the legation's efforts on my behalf, I was to be cast as the villain of a "drama," as Péter called it, designed to eliminate the last remnants of American prestige in Hungary. Images of the Rajk and Mindszenty trials flashed through my mind. If a man with the spiritual resources of Cardinal Mindszenty had been unable to foil the unholy inquisition, how, I wondered, was a mere businessman to do so?

As Daniel Webster once remarked, "There is no refuge from confession but suicide; and suicide is confession." Suicide, however, would be less degrading than the ultimate "confession" demanded by the AVH.

As we neared the fourth floor, I gripped the bannister with my hands and was just throwing my legs over when I was tackled by the agent behind me. The two guards then caught me by either arm and dragged me into the little room where I had earlier been shaved. One of the agents called a doctor. He was a large man in a white smock, whose appearance, voice, and manner reminded me of the actor Sidney Greenstreet.

"You won't be any good to us if you kill yourself," he said. "We want you to live, so that you can help us to demonstrate your guilt."

With the help of the two guards he made me take some pills—luminol, I suppose—and before I had time to regret my unsuccessful suicide I was fast asleep. It was the first sleep that I had had in seventy-eight hours.

After my release from prison, I learned that the Ministry of Internal Affairs, on November 22, 1949, had issued the following communiqué:

Imre Geiger, general manager of the Standard Electric Company, attempted to cross the border illegally and has been arrested. During his examination he confessed that he had conducted espionage and sabotage activities.

Because of the confession of Imre Geiger and other evidence, the state authorities have taken into custody Robert Vogeler, American, and Edgar Sanders, Briton, who, during their examination, confessed in detail their sabotage and other hostile activities against the Hungarian People's Republic.

I was of course unaware at the time that Sandy had even been arrested. Neither was I aware of the arrest of Mrs. Zádor and the others with whom I would soon be confronted. I was still hoping, though without much conviction, that the American Legation would somehow effect my liberation before it was too late.

After my release from prison I also learned, to my surprise, that Colonel Hoyne had failed to report my disappearance. Hoyne, on reaching Vienna, had gone to the room he held at the Hotel Bristol, where he changed into civilian clothes. On his way out he left my briefcase with the hall porter, asking him to deliver it to my wife. Lucile at that very moment was sitting at a table in the Bristol's dining room with Captains Quinby and Wallis and their wives, but the porter, perhaps thinking that Hoyne had already spoken to her, failed to call his attention to her presence.

Spotswood Quinby, the chief of our naval forces in Austria, had been recalled to the United States. He was a good friend of mine and, knowing that I was expected to return from Budapest early that afternoon, he had invited us to lunch at the Bristol with him and his successor, Bert Wallis, and their wives. Lucile had left word with her sister Pia that I was to join them as soon as I came home. She had explained that they would wait until two o'clock before having lunch.

When I failed to appear at two, they lunched alone, and at three-fifteen they left the hotel separately. The porter handed Lucile my briefcase, saying that a Colonel Hoyne had left it for her, and Lucile, thinking that I had arrived too late to join the luncheon party, rushed home to greet me. She and Hoyne had never met, and she was unaware, of course, that I had asked him to report my disappearance if I failed to cross the border ahead of him.

Lucile and Pia dined alone with the boys that evening, each doing her best to pretend that there was no cause for alarm. When I had still not appeared at nine, Lucile telephoned the

Astoria in Budapest. At eleven, when the call came through, the
Astoria's night clerk told her that, as far as he knew, I had left
Budapest soon after eight that morning and should have reached
Vienna not later than two in the afternoon.

Lucile then telephoned the Bristol and asked for Colonel
Hoyne. On being told that he had left the hotel around three,
and had not yet returned, she telephoned the Counter-Intelligence Corps. It was not until four the next morning that the
CIC, after canvassing all the night clubs in Vienna, succeeded
in locating Hoyne. His explanation of his failure to report my
disappearance was that he had been an hour late in crossing the
border, and was in such a hurry that he made no effort to determine whether or not I had crossed ahead of him. He assumed
that I had, since there was no sign of my Buick or any other
evidence (aside from the register of arrivals and departures) that
I had been arrested.

Lucile had meanwhile telephoned the American Legation in
Budapest. She explained the situation to the young secretary on
night duty and asked him to request the minister to make a
prompt investigation. She then telephoned Hank Scudder in
London to ask him to alert New York and Washington.

It was not until late Saturday morning that Nathaniel P. Davis,
the American minister, was received by Gyula Kállai, the Hungarian Minister of Foreign Affairs. Kállai assured Davis that he
had no knowledge of my whereabouts. Nothing more happened
until Monday afternoon, when Kállai, in response to several
telephone calls, informed Davis that the police, after making a
thorough investigation, had failed to find any trace of me. It
was only on Tuesday, when Davis again called in person at the
Ministry of Foreign Affairs, that Kállai admitted that I had indeed been arrested. He attempted to justify my arrest on the
ground that I had already confessed to "espionage and sabotage,"
but Davis apparently protested so vigorously that the word
"espionage" was deleted from the communiqué that was issued
a few hours later.

As Davis himself recalled, in an official note delivered to Kállai on December 20:

I reiterated my Government's grave concern . . . and expressed dissatisfaction with the statement of the Hungarian police authorities. . . . I further stated that . . . I must insist upon the right of American consular officers to visit [Mr. Vogeler] in order that they might satisfy themselves as to his welfare and the protection of his right to competent legal counsel of his own choice. While disclaiming authority in the matter, you replied that you would take up my request with the competent authorities and would inform me in the matter as soon as possible.

Since November 22, the Legation has been in touch with the Ministry of Foreign Affairs once or twice daily, and on two further occasions, November 29 and December 14, respectively, I personally called on Undersecretary Berei and yourself to renew my long-standing requests for an explanation of the charges against Mr. Vogeler and an opportunity for American consular officials to visit him. As you are well aware, the Hungarian Government has neither taken any action nor made any satisfactory response to these repeated representations. It is also pertinent to recall in this connection that, having sought for many days an interview with Deputy Prime Minister Rákosi and subsequently, on December 1, having received assurances from the Ministry of Foreign Affairs that an appointment with Mr. Rákosi would be arranged for the week of December 4, I was eventually informed on December 12 that he was on vacation and would not return for several weeks.

This is the record of inaction, evasions, and bad faith on the part of the Hungarian authorities in the case of Mr. Vogeler. . . .

[It] has served only to confirm my Government in the conclusion that the charges against Mr. Vogeler are wholly false and that the Hungarian Government is motivated by ulterior purposes. . . . The secretive proceedings of the police in the circumstances can only raise doubts as to the treatment which Mr. Vogeler has received during his detention. Such treatment must be considered, according to prevailing concepts of justice in civilized countries, as arbitrary and inhumane, and as a clear denial of justice. . . .

Eleven | The Tortures of the Damned

Three hours after being put to sleep, I was shaken into wakefulness and told to dress. A glass of black coffee and two small sandwiches—identical to those that I had eaten sixty-one hours earlier—had been left for me on a table. As soon as I had eaten the sandwiches and drunk the coffee, No. 1 and the major with the hoarse voice, together with four guards and two other agents, led me down the main stairway to an office on the first floor.

A tall man with blue-black jowls was seated at a desk piled high with legal documents tied together with string. He was Gyula Alapi—the state prosecutor, as I later learned—the man who had concocted the case against Cardinal Mindszenty and who, among other things, was the chief of the Control Bureau of the Hungarian Communist Party. Also present were Alapi's assistant, whom I had earlier seen in Péter's office, and a male secretary—an albino who spoke English with what I took to be a West Indian accent.

I sat in the usual plain chair before his desk while Alapi read aloud from an official document in a high-pitched, nasal voice. When he had finished reading in Hungarian, his assistant read aloud from a translation of the same document in German. According to the penal code of the Hungarian People's Republic, it seemed, it was illegal to hold a prisoner for more than seventy-two hours without preferring charges. I thought of Kelemen

Domokos and the other two employees of Standard Budapest who had been held for seven months in the absence of any charges—but they were Hungarians who didn't count, apparently, whereas I was a foreigner, an American, whose case had to be handled with punctilio. On the face of the "evidence," Alapi said, he was satisfied that I was guilty of numerous "crimes against the state." It would therefore be entirely "legal" to hold me incommunicado for another thirty days.

When I at first refused to countersign the document, Alapi's assistant explained that my signature would not be an admission of guilt but merely an indication that I understood that I could be legally held for another thirty days of questioning. Of course, he said, it might not be necessary to hold me that long; the document merely empowered the authorities to do so. I asked for permission to consult a lawyer, but he said that a lawyer would not be necessary, since it was merely a "formality." I also asked for permission to consult the American Legation, but the assistant prosecutor said that such permission could not be granted until after the "preliminaries" had been completed.

He finally persuaded me that there was nothing to be gained by persisting in my refusal, and so I signed the document. It was still November 21. The same little farce would be repeated on December 21 and again on January 21. By February 21, it would be unnecessary to repeat the farce, for I would have been convicted and sentenced to fifteen years in prison.

After I had signed the document, I was led back to the little room on the fourth floor, given some "supper"—consisting of tea and a chunk of black bread—and then put to bed and allowed to sleep as best I could with four guards watching over me. Three hours later I was again awakened. One of the guards brought me another glass of coffee. He then gave me a pencil and some paper and told me to proceed with my "autobiography." No. 1 had prepared for me a long list of questions. I wrote until eleven that night, when I was again taken before No. 1 for another four hours of grilling.

This was to be my life for the next ten days. Most of my time was spent in answering No. 1's interminable lists of questions, each concerned with one phase or another of my alleged activities as an "agent" of the Army and Navy intelligence services and also of the FBI. Inasmuch as I was deprived of food and sleep until I had answered every set of questions, my only recourse was to make my answers as ridiculous as I possibly could. Once, when No. 1 asked me to describe Sosthenes Behn's "confederates," I wrote an imaginative essay about such sinister American "capitalists" as Abner Yokum and Senator Claghorn. Again, when No. 1 asked me to describe my "superiors" in the FBI, I discussed at length the careers of Richard Tracy and Clark Kent, with whom my sons, who were avid readers of comic books, were on familiar terms even in Vienna.

For four days I was quartered in the little room on the fourth floor. Then I was moved downstairs to a large windowless room on the second floor, next to a room in which other prisoners, women as well as men, were tortured every night. Their screams were obviously calculated to drive me to distraction.

The electric lights were never turned off and I was never left alone. The guards were always present. During waking hours, they made me sit at a desk and continue working on my "autobiography." During sleeping hours, they made me lie on a daybed with my face exposed to the light. I was never allowed to sleep for more than three hours at a time.

I was now fed three times a day, but henceforth my "coffee" would be ersatz. My breakfast consisted of black bread and watery "coffee," lunch of black bread and watery "soup," supper of black bread and ersatz "tea" and an occasional chunk of sausage. Although I rapidly lost weight, I suffered more from lack of cleanliness than I did from lack of nourishment. I was not shaved again until December 17—one month after my arrest—when I was allowed to take my first shower bath. Thereafter I was shaved and showered every Saturday morning. In the meantime, though I was allowed to visit a toilet periodically, I was seldom allowed to wash; and even then I had to do so quickly, without soap and without a towel, at a wash basin in the corridor.

It soon became evident that the guards were under orders not to let me see or be seen by the other prisoners at 60 Stalin Avenue. Hence their reluctance to let me wash, for the only available basin was located in the corridor, along which I could hear people walking at all hours of the day and night. The guards were also under orders, I gathered, not to identify themselves or their superiors to me in any way. Hence, instead of using each other's names, or calling each other *"Bajtárs"* (pronounced "bóy-tarsh," and meaning "comrade"), they called each other "Bandi." The word is pronounced in Hungarian as if it were spelled "Bondy," which is almost the way the French pronounce the word "bandit," and which is what I first thought it meant. Actually, as I later learned, it is the Hungarian diminutive of Andrew. The address of the AVH at the time was still 60 Andrássy Avenue or, in English, 60 Andrews Avenue. It was for this reason, I suppose, that the merry-andrews who guarded the prisoners chose to call each other Andy.

The Andies, or Bandis, who kept watch over me used to while away the hours playing chess, a game that Stalin has long been attempting to present to the world as a peculiarly Russian pastime. My Bandis were not very good at the game, as I could tell from watching them, but it appeared to be the duty of all good Stalinists to play it.

I take no particular pride in my own game, which I learned as a child from my paternal grandfather, but I am well grounded in both its theory and its practice. I often played chess with the late Lieutenant Commander Robert Gallagher, who was a classmate of mine at the Naval Academy and later at MIT, where he studied naval construction. (Gallagher, I remember, once described Pearl Harbor to me as "the worst port imaginable for a concentration of ships." He always said that, if he were a Japanese admiral, Pearl Harbor would be the first on his list of targets in the event of war with the United States.) We continued to play chess together when he was on duty at the Brooklyn Navy Yard in 1940 and I was working for Cornell-Dubilier. Poor Gallagher died on Corregidor in 1942.

Once, when I was watching the Bandis at play, one of them looked up and said to me in German, "In Russia, everybody plays chess. The Russians are the greatest chess players in the world." And then, to show off his Communist learning, he mentioned several "Russian" champions, including Samuel Reshevsky, a naturalized American who, in spite of his Russian name, had been born in Poland.

On the wall of my room was a Russian poster depicting a godlike Stalin beaming on an endless procession of deliriously happy workers, peasants, and children. On the opposite wall was a slogan in Hungarian: *"Egyesült, Erös, Boldog!"* ("United, Strong, Happy!").

Sometimes the agonized screams that emerged from the next room were more than I could bear in silence. But whenever I protested the guards warned me to keep quiet. In the beginning they had treated me with distant contempt. Now they baited me at every opportunity.

One night, while the torture was going on, I was seized with an urgent desire to visit the toilet. All but one of the guards laughed at my predicament. I was told that I would have to wait until the prisoners in the next room had been removed. One of the guards finally went out to investigate, and when he returned he said, "Now you can go." He and another guard led me out into the corridor just as a line of stumbling prisoners were being led out of the room next door. One of the prisoners was a middle-aged man with a terribly swollen face. His shirt front was covered with blood. I had no time to observe any more because the two guards swung me around and made me stand with my face to the wall until the prisoners were out of sight. This "accidental" encounter, I suppose, was calculated to weaken my resistance.

Only one of the guards showed any sympathy for my plight, and for obvious reasons I shall not describe him here. One night, as I was writing my autobiography, the other guards left him alone with me while they went into the next room to observe the nightly torture. The friendly guard offered me a cigarette and lit one for himself.

"In America," he said, "it's not like this, eh?"

Presently, in the next room, the screams began. The friendly guard winced and looked at me with a troubled expression on his face.

"I suppose that will soon be happening to me," I said.

"No," he said, shaking his head. "Only primitive people are beaten. Educated people are treated differently."

I would soon learn what he meant. On the evening of November 30 (I remember the date because it was my younger son's eighth birthday) I was taken to see No. 1 for the last time. My autobiography, which now totaled several hundred pages, was piled up on his desk. With a melodramatic gesture he swept it into his wastebasket.

"Rubbish," he said. "You've written nothing but rubbish. You'll now be given an opportunity to reconsider your folly."

A guard brought me my gabardine topcoat, and I was led out through a courtyard into another group of buildings. Along the wall of a former movie house, once called the Orpheum, were several lean-tos. In one of them I was registered at a desk and then ordered to strip. Two guards again examined my clothing.

The only thing they found that had previously been overlooked was the metal clasp that held the tops of my trousers together. They ripped it off. They also ripped the heel pads out of my lace-less shoes and confiscated my shirt, socks, and underwear.

After I had dressed, I was led through another lean-to into the former movie house, which was full of makeshift cells. After being frisked once again, I was led down a rickety wooden stair-way to another prison beneath the courtyard. At every turning stood a uniformed guard who shouted *"Megy vissza!"* as we passed. I soon learned that the phrase meant "Coming back!" Every time a prisoner was led down into the dungeon the same shout was repeated until he had been sequestered in his cell. *"Megy ki!"* (Coming out!) was similarly shouted whenever a prisoner was led upstairs. It was against the rules, apparently, for prisoners to confront each other while entering or leaving the dungeon.

My cell was in a far corner beneath the foundations of the Orpheum. It was a cold, damp, airless cubicle that measured nine feet by six. Its only furniture was a bunk made of angle iron and wooden slats, the legs of which were firmly cemented into the floor. There was a blanket but no mattress, and I had to sleep on the slats, which were raised at the end opposite the cell door to form an angle of forty-five degrees. The cell stank of a combination of germicide and dirty human bodies but, surpris-ingly, it was free of vermin.

Its door, which was of solid steel, contained a square peep-hole covered with a loose steel plate. Ten times every hour, day and night, a guard would walk by, swinging back the plates and peering into every cell. Above the door, in a thick glass recep-tacle, was an electric light that was never turned off.

Every now and then the guards would call out a number, whereupon the occupant of the corresponding cell would be led upstairs to the accompaniment of shouts of *"Megy ki!"* The high-est number I ever heard shouted was thirty-nine, from which fact I concluded that there were forty cells in the dungeon. The number of my own cell was nineteen, I gathered, for whenever "Eighteen" was shouted the guards removed the woman who occupied the cell next to mine.

I could tell that she was a woman because of the sound her heels made as she paced the floor. Was she Edina Dőry, perhaps, or Mrs. Zádor? I never knew, because we never saw each other, and it was impossible for us to communicate through the thick stone wall that separated our cells.

Silence was the rule of the dungeon. Whenever anyone cried out, the guards would proceed to his cell to administer a beating. We were fed three times a day, and were allowed to visit the lavatory, one by one, after each meal. There were no spoons, and we had to eat what little was shoved into us with our hands. The lavatory consisted of a toilet and three water faucets over an inclined wooden trough, where we had to wash ourselves and clean the mess kits in which we were served our food. A single clean towel was hung on the lavatory wall every other day. It was so dirty by the time I was taken to the lavatory that I never used it. Every morning, after the invariable black bread and ersatz "coffee," each prisoner was given a bucket of cold water and a dirty rag with which to wash the floor of his cell. The rest of the time there was nothing to do but pace the floor or lie on our wooden bunks. Usually it was too cold to sleep, and so we paced, or rather shuffled (for most of us were men), in our laceless shoes. The muffled sound of the male shuffling, punctuated by the sound of the clicking wooden heels of the two or three women prisoners, was indescribably sad. But it was less unpleasant than the regular clanging of the steel plates as the guard on observation duty went from cell to cell, peering in at their occupants.

The woman in the cell next to mine was frequently taken upstairs for questioning. So were most of the other prisoners, some of whom were so badly hurt that they had to be carried back to their cells. Because of the difficulty they had in walking, I began to suspect that several of them had been bastinadoed, and indeed it was not long before I learned that this Oriental torment was the AVH's favorite method of extracting confessions from certain types of prisoners. The ones who had been bastinadoed, of course, were unable to do any shuffling. They merely lay on their bunks and whimpered—until the guards came in and slugged them into silence. Then all that could be heard was the spasmodic sound of their breathing.

I was confined in the dungeon without being questioned for a full ten days, which I counted by scratching marks with my finger nails on the moldly wall of my cell. Then I was taken upstairs and back into the main building to a large room full of prisoners, women as well as men, each seated with his hands on his knees in a plain chair facing the wall. I sat in the same position for several hours before I was taken out to meet my second inquisitor.

No. 2, as I shall call him, was also a lieutenant colonel. Unlike No. 1, who always wore civilian clothes, he often wore his uniform. He was a short, dark man with a sagging left shoulder and a slightly twisted face. Although he was a sloppy dresser, and wore no mustache, he so closely resembled "the general" whom I later identified as Gábor Péter that I suspect that, on certain occasions, he acted as Péter's double. The only photograph I have seen that looks at all like Péter (and I have seen a number of fakes) looks more like the man I knew as No. 2. The photograph shows him wearing a thin mustache—far thinner than Péter's mustache—and one that No. 2 could have grown in a matter of days. Without the mustache, I would swear that the man presented as Péter is really No. 2. The photograph, moreover, shows him wearing an ill-fitting suit of a sort that No. 2

occasionally wore but that Péter, I am sure, would never have worn, given his professional knowledge of men's suitings.

No. 2's English consisted of exactly two phrases—"How are you?" and "See you later!"—with which he never failed to receive and dismiss me in the course of more than a hundred interrogations. He was a chain smoker of cigarettes, which he inserted into quill-and-cardboard holders. He never used the same holder twice, and wherever he went he carried two boxes with him, one containing cigarettes and the other containing holders.

Although his name was never mentioned in my presence, No. 2 was a good deal more communicative than No. 1, who had failed, I gathered, to produce the necessary change in my personality. No. 2 was a veteran Communist who had himself spent seven years in prison, and he referred to everyone, except his victims, as *"Bajtárs"* ("Comrade"). For all I know, he may have been József Balázs, a lieutenant colonel of the AVH who is believed to have been one of Cardinal Mindszenty's inquisitors. Whoever he was, No. 2 often boasted of the part he had played in extracting the Cardinal's confession, and he assured me, at the very outset, that he expected to have no difficulty in extracting mine, even though it took him several weeks to do so.

"Before I've finished," he said, "we'll know everything there is to know about you."

I remarked that, if he wanted to know any more than he already knew, he would have to make it up, because I had told his predecessor everything there was to know, and then some.

"You told him nothing but lies," said No. 2. "What you're going to tell me is the truth."

"I've already told the truth."

"Not the truth I want to hear. If Mindszenty told me what I wanted him to tell me, so will you. Make no mistake about it. Even if Jesus Christ were sitting in your chair, He'd tell me everything I wanted Him to."

One of No. 2's first acts was to take me to see the general—Gábor Péter—again. I was shocked at the sight of myself as we passed through the mirrored vestibule. I looked like a stumble-bum. My eyes were bleary, my hair was matted, and my face was covered with a three weeks' growth of beard. I normally weighed 170, but I doubt that I then weighed more than 120. My filthy clothing looked as if it had been made for a much larger man. Having been deprived of my shirt and underwear, I had become accustomed to wearing the collar of my jacket turned up. I had also become accustomed to holding the collar closed with my left hand while I held up my sagging trousers with my right.

"Have you been cold?" asked Péter with mock solicitude, as I sat in the chair before his desk.

"Yes."

"You seem to have lost some weight. Don't you like our food?"

I made no reply.

"I want to help you," he continued in the same mocking tone of voice. "Is there anything you'd like?"

I told him that I would like to take a bath, and to shave or be shaved, and that I would also like to be given back my shirt, socks, and underwear. (These requests, to my surprise, were subsequently granted.)

"You didn't heed my warning," Péter said. "But you know now that we can make life very unpleasant for you, if we must. Now that you've had time to think things over, what is your decision?"

"I can't confess to crimes I haven't committed," I said.

Péter smiled. "We've now arrested eighty people," he continued, "each of whom has identified you as the leader of his spy ring. You have no choice but to confess. We realize, of course, that if you do, and you return to the United States, you'll probably be sent to the electric chair."

He paused to gauge the effect of his absurd remark. Although I made no comment, he was apparently satisfied that he had frightened me.

"We are prepared to help you," he said, "if you help us. There are several possibilities. You can work as an engineer in Hungary or, if you prefer, in Czechoslovakia, or even in the Soviet Union. There are all sorts of jobs that we can give you to do. We can also arrange for you to be reunited with your wife and family. We'll even exchange you for some Communist Vogeler, if you like, and send you to any neutral country you select."

I wondered what Péter meant. Could it be that I was being held as a hostage for Valentin Gubitchev, the Russian spy who had been arrested with Judith Coplon in New York? If so, perhaps my plight was not as hopeless as I thought. Perhaps negotiations were even now in progress to exchange me for Gubitchev. I was disillusioned, however, by Péter's subsequent remarks.

"In any event," he said, "you'll have to go on trial in Hungary. We have enough witnesses against you to condemn you to death. But you may have to be sent to Czechoslovakia for a second trial. I've just been informed that Alfred Plocek and several others of your agents have been arrested in Prague."

Plocek and his associates had been planning to escape to the American zone of Austria. But they had waited too long, apparently, and were now to be punished for the crime of attempting to maintain normal commercial relations with the United States. Vladimir Brůza was the only one of my Czechoslovakian acquaintances who managed to avoid arrest. He fled to Austria in the fall of 1948 and eventually made his way to Holland, where he is now publishing a highly informative weekly newsletter devoted to events in Czechoslovakia. The State Department has yet to be convinced, however, that he deserves to be granted an American visa.

Instead of being taken back to the dungeon after Péter had dismissed me, I was placed in a windowless cell in the Orpheum. This time I was to have a cellmate. He was a dark, heavy man, dressed in filthy gray flannels, a ragged sweater, and a British sports jacket that was out at the elbows. His laceless shoes were badly worn around the outer edges and he walked with a painful limp.

"Cseresnyés Sándor," he said, holding out his hand. He gave me his last name first, in the Hungarian manner, and pronounced it as if it were spelled "Chéreshnyesh."

"Vogeler Robert," I said, shaking his hand.

The cell was a large one, measuring twenty by fifteen feet, and, as Cseresnyés told me later, the Gestapo had once confined as many as eighteen prisoners in it at a time. There were marks in the longer walls where rows of triple-deck bunks had once been affixed. The AVH had removed the extra tiers as a precautionary measure. Too many of its prisoners, Cseresnyés explained, had thrown themselves head first off the upper tiers before they had completed their "confessions." He proved his point by indicating a number of blood stains on the concrete floor.

A few days later, for reasons best known to our jailers, we were transferred to a smaller cell, measuring ten by eight feet, which we were to share until the day I was sentenced to fifteen years in prison. The new cell, the fifth of nine in our particular block, contained two bunks with an unpainted wooden table between them and two unpainted wooden chairs facing the table. As in the dungeon, the furniture had been cemented into the floor. The cell door, which was made of steel bars, was covered from the outside with a white sheet hung like a shower curtain on sliding steel rings. In the absence of a window, the door was our only source of ventilation. A guard slid back the sheet to observe us once every fifteen minutes. The sheet made an unpleasant metallic sound, but it was not as unpleasant as the sound of the steel plates being swung back from the peepholes every six minutes in the dungeon. Neither was it as unpleasant as the sound made by the warrant officer who roused me several times each night by running his key back and forth across the bars.

"*Aufstehen!*" he would shout. "*Mach schnell!*" ("Get up! Make it snappy!")

Every time he thus awakened me, to take me out for further questioning, I was horrified to discover where I was. It was like a serial nightmare in reverse. Sleep was my only release, and it was severely rationed. Until I agreed to sign a "full confession," I was never once allowed to sleep a whole night through. The result was a sort of schizophrenia. At times, I could actually "see" myself struggling to get out of my bunk before the warrant officer came in and began to shake me. It was as if my mind were separate from my body. The fact that the electric light was never turned off contributed to the illusion.

It was so cold in the cell that I seldom removed my clothes. I wore my gabardine topcoat during waking hours and, while sleeping, used it as an extra blanket. Cseresnyés, who had no topcoat, slept in his sweater, and used his jacket as an extra blanket.

My shirt, socks, and underwear, as Péter had promised, were eventually returned, but until I completed my "confession" they were never changed. I washed them as best I could while taking my weekly shower. My shirt and underwear lasted for several months, but my socks wore out in a matter of weeks. The heels and the toes were the first to go, but I prolonged their life by wearing the legs as feet and wrapping the ribbing over my toes. The socks were good ones, of British lisle, which my father had sent me for my thirty-eighth birthday in September, 1949.

Next to a certain guard, who delighted in stepping on my heels as he led me to the toilet, the warrant officer was the most unpleasant of my jailers. Cseresnyés and I were each given five cigarettes a day, but to light them we had to call the guard, who held his match so far away that we had to stick our chins through the bars of the door. The same guard sometimes kept me waiting thirty or forty minutes before he opened the door to take me out to the toilet. He apparently hoped thereby to make me dirty my trousers, but, if that was his purpose, I managed to defeat it by anticipating my needs to such an extent that I always reached the toilet in time. The guard suffered from chronic catarrh, and used to blow his nose with his thumb and forefinger and wipe it with his sleeve. Another man whom I particularly disliked was an agent who often led me up to No. 2's office. He took great pleasure in twisting my arm, as if to prevent me from trying to escape, and he was always bumping my leg in an effort to make me trip.

Cseresnyés was surprised to learn that I was an American. "I didn't know we'd begun to arrest Americans," he said, switching from German to English, which he spoke with a Cockney accent. "How long have you been in our little sanitorium?"

"Twenty-two days."

"Oh, that isn't long. I've been here 199 days. Tomorrow will be my 200th anniversary."

I asked him his name again.

"Sándor Cseresnyés," he said. "But you can call me Alex. My real name's Alexander Kirschner. I changed it into Hungarian back in the thirties, when everybody was supposed to be a super-patriotic Magyar."

Kirschner, in German, means "Cherry Grower." Cseresnyés, he said, was as close as he had been able to come to Kirschner in Hungarian.

"But I suppose you've heard of me. My name was in all the papers."

When I confessed that I was unaware of his identity, Alex insisted on telling me the story of his life.

Twelve | My Cellmate, Alex

Alex had been born in a village in Transylvania, a younger son of poor German peasants. His family had been so poor, he said, that he had never slept in a bed until he came to Budapest at the age of sixteen. In Budapest he had worked nights and studied by day at the university, where he soon transferred his spiritual allegiance from the Catholic Church to the Communist International. He later worked as a copy editor on various Hungarian newspapers.

In 1937, at the age of twenty-two, he was secretly recruited to fight in Spain as a member of the Rákosi Battalion of the International Brigades. The Comintern's recruiting office, which was then located in Vienna, was headed by a man named Josef Babitch, alias Josip Broz, who would later emerge as Marshal Tito, the dictator of Yugoslavia. The political commissar of the Rákosi Battalion was another Hungarian of German origin named László Rajk, whose protégé Alex soon became. His admiration of Rajk approached hero worship after the latter was severely wounded in combat.

In 1938, following the withdrawal from Spain of the International Brigades, Alex, along with Rajk and other survivors of the Rákosi Battalion, was confined in various internment camps in southern France. After the French surrender, the inmates of the camps were given their choice between working for the

Germans or working for the French. Rajk chose to work for the Germans in the hope, which he eventually realized, of returning to Hungary to reorganize the local Communist Party. Alex, however, chose to work for the French, and was accordingly shipped to North Africa, along with thousands of Spaniards, to build the Trans-Sahara Railroad.

Following the Anglo-American invasion, in the fall of 1942, he was liberated and recruited into the British Army. He had grown up speaking Hungarian, Rumanian, and German, and had since learned Spanish and French. He now learned English, and before long he was sent to Bari, in Italy, where he became a radio monitor for the Psychological Warfare Branch of the British Eighth Army. He received a commendation, he told me, for being the first monitor to report the capitulation of Bucharest. He had meanwhile married a Yugoslav girl, a *partizanka* attached to Tito's military mission in Bari.

At the close of the war his wife was sent back to Yugoslavia and Alex, who was now a sergeant, was sent to Klagenfurt, in Austria. Eventually he learned that his wife had fallen in love with a Yugoslav officer. He requested and was granted leave, he said, to visit his wife in Yugoslavia, but he failed to recapture her affection. They were divorced before Alex returned to Austria four months later.

What else he did in the course of his visit to Yugoslavia he never told me. As a Communist in the British Army, however, he had performed a number of valuable services for Tito, in return for which he had received two Yugoslav decorations.

Rajk, in the meantime, had returned to Hungary to become, in due course, its Minister of Internal Affairs. As such he was responsible for all police operations and particularly those calculated to terrorize everyone who opposed the sovietization of Hungary. Alex sent him his congratulations, and Rajk, in reply, promised him a responsible job with his ministry as soon as he returned. But Alex was in no hurry, first because he had acquired an Austrian mistress of whom he was very fond and, second, because he still had a year to serve in the British Army.

In 1947, after completing his first four years of service, he was given his choice of being demobilized or enlisting for another four years, at the end of which time he would be entitled to British citizenship. Alex was tempted to re-enlist and become a Briton, but he finally decided to return to Hungary and join the government. Rajk rewarded his old comrade from Spain by making him his information officer. He also obtained two Hungarian decorations for Alex to go with the two decorations that he had received from Tito.

For two years Alex thrived as a junior Communist bureaucrat. He married a Hungarian girl, who bore him a baby daughter, and moved into a requisitioned apartment on Kis József Street in Pest. In his spare time he wrote two books, one about his experiences in Spain, the other about his experiences in Italy. His salary at the Ministry of Internal Affairs was 2,200 florins a month, whose purchasing power was enhanced by his privilege, as a government official, of buying food and clothing at greatly reduced prices. He earned enough money from his books to buy new furniture for his requisitioned apartment, in which he lived rent free, and had enough left over to buy a handsome baby carriage for his daughter. In short, he lived much as any young paterfamilias might have lived before the Communists seized power.

Following Tito's excommunication from the Cominform, Rajk was appointed Minister of Foreign Affairs and replaced as Minister of Internal Affairs by János Kádár, a Stalinist who had lived in Russia during the war. Alex, however, remained at his post. It never occurred to him, in spite of Moscow's hysterical denunciations of Titoism and all its works, that Rajk and his friends —and particularly those who had served with him in Spain—

would be made to serve as the Kremlin's principal Hungarian scapegoats.

And then, at eleven o'clock, on the night of May 25, 1949, came the dreaded knock on his door. He and his wife were reading in bed, Alex said, when the knocking began. His wife followed him to the door and hid behind him as he admitted two agents of the AVH, who entered the living room with drawn pistols.

"Where's your gun?" said one of the agents, frisking Alex but hesitating to frisk his wife, since both of them were in their night clothes.

"In the dresser in the bedroom," Alex said.

The agents motioned him to lead the way. As soon as they had pocketed Alex's pistol, they ordered him to dress. His wife began to cry, but the agents told her not to worry, that he was merely wanted for questioning. Alex had often wondered what the AVH's victims thought about as they were being arrested. Now he knew. He thought of his wife, but he thought of his little daughter most of all, and wondered what would become of her if he failed to reappear. His last memory of the outside world, which he often mentioned to me, was of his daughter waving to him from her crib as he was led out of the bedroom and the apartment that he and his wife had shared so cozily at the expense of other victims of the AVH.

At 60 Stalin Avenue he was told that he had been arrested on charges of treason, and his inquisitor warned him that, if he wanted to save his life, he would have to tell him everything he knew of Rajk's "plot" to overthrow Rákosi and make himself the head of a "Titoist" government in Hungary.

Alex's experiences during the next three weeks were not very different from mine—several days of sleepless interrogation, followed by a partial confession, then a respite in a room next to a torture chamber and, finally, confinement in the dungeon. His cell was No. 27. It was "one of the bad cells," Alex said, because it was flooded with water after every rain.

On his release from the dungeon, instead of being sent to the
Orpheum, he was immediately subjected to torture. Whenever
he failed to give the answers that were expected of him, a canvas
bag was tied over his head. The bag was lined with cheesecloth
pockets containing freshly grated horseradish. Horseradish fumes
(butyl sulfocyanide) produce an effect similar to one of the tear
gases, brombenzylcyanide. They tickle so much they make you
laugh; then you begin to cry; finally you choke and lose consciousness altogether.

I had first heard of the horseradish treatment from my Austrian
chauffeur, Rudolf Hönig, who said that the Gestapo had used it
in Czechoslovakia. Baron Emmanuel von Stillfried, the former
chief of the Austrian gendarmerie, confirmed Hönig's story. Stillfried told me that the horseradish treatment had been used on
him when he was a prisoner at Dachau. Instead of tying a bag
over his head, however, his German inquisitors had merely
stuffed bits of horseradish up his nose.

Once, Alex said, he was forced to watch the torture of his assistant. The man was tied naked to four hooks in the floor. A
plumber's friend was then applied to his genitals. He was ruptured before he agreed to make what the AVH called a "full
confession."

Whereas Rajk himself was forced to confess that, in addition
to being a Trotskyist, he had also been a Spanish, French, German, Yugoslav, British, and American spy, Alex was merely
forced to confess that he had been a British spy—the liaison man,
in fact, between the British intelligence corps and Rajk's "clique"
of "spies and traitors" in Hungary. He resisted as long as he
could, but then, one night, he was forced to lie on his stomach
on the floor of his inquisitor's office. Two agents sat on him to
prevent him from moving while a third beat his feet and ankles
with a rubber truncheon until he chewed the rug and vomited
from the pain. The treatment was repeated nightly for a week,
whereupon he broke down completely and agreed to tell the lies

that were necessary to convict Rajk and his codefendants of treason, subversion, and espionage.

Alex took off his shoes and socks and pulled up his trousers. Six months after the act, his feet and ankles were still covered with the ugly hemorrhagic patches left by the rubber truncheon with which he had been bastinadoed.

"My peasant origin was against me," he said. "I didn't come from a cultured family."

It was some time before I understood what he meant. But gradually, in answer to my questions, he managed to explain the difference in the treatment accorded "cultured" and "uncultured" prisoners. The Russian police had learned from experience that most "uncultured" prisoners were of little value to the prosecution in court. They forgot their lines, for one thing, and they were so obviously incapable of having committed the crimes to which they confessed that they often excited the sympathy of the audience. Moreover, from the Communist point of view, it was propagandistically undesirable to convict workers and peasants of being "enemies" of a "people's" state. It was better to use them merely as witnesses against "cultured" prisoners whose imaginary crimes could be blamed, in Marxist fashion, on their economic and social background.

Since few "uncultured" prisoners were ever called upon to recite their confessions in public, their physical appearance was unimportant. They could therefore be tortured with impunity. If they were crippled or killed in the process, it made little difference, since no one would ever be the wiser.

"Cultured" prisoners, however, and particularly those who were selected to be the principal defendants, had to be handled with care. It was risky to torture them physically. Too many of them died without confessing, and those who survived too often showed the scars of the treatment they had received. Physical torture was usually eschewed, therefore, in favor of psychological torture. It was a slower process, but its effects were likely to be more satisfactory. Almost all "cultured" prisoners would confess in the end if they were properly conditioned. Threatening their loved ones, Alex said, was the most effective means of extracting their confessions. The important thing was to excite their imagination and thus drive them to distraction. If hostages were unavailable, the same results could be achieved more slowly by subjecting them to prolonged lack of sleep, malnutrition, excessive stimulation, and solitary confinement.

"Uncultured" people, on the other hand, were much less susceptible to suggestion. Their imagination was often so undeveloped that they could resist psychological torture indefinitely. The prescribed treatment in Hungary, therefore, was the bastinado. It was as painful a torment as has ever been devised, yet one that seldom causes death or permanent disability. If the bastinado failed to produce the desired results, the "water cure" was then applied. The water cure, as Alex explained it, was a cold-water enema prolonged to the point of death. It ruptured the intestines as effectively as Mussolini's castor oil.

Alex told me that he knew of only one cultured person who had ever been subjected to physical torture by the AVH. He was Prince Pál Eszterházy, one of Cardinal Mindszenty's codefendants, who had been tied naked to a hook in the ceiling and beaten with rubber truncheons in the Cardinal's presence. The purpose of the torture, in Eszterházy's case, was to undermine the Cardinal's will to resist.

Confrontations, Alex added, often served the same purpose. Even though your confronter had not been physically tortured, his broken spirit, combined with his emaciation, served to convince you that it was hopeless to prolong your own resistance. Timing, of course, was important. You were usually not confronted until your inquisitor felt that you were on the verge of surrender.

As soon as Alex had been broken with the bastinado, he was used in confronting Rajk, who groveled before his inquisitor like a beaten dog. "I don't believe he even knew who I was," said Alex sadly. "He was beyond all human feeling."

It was difficult for me to share Alex's sympathy for László Rajk. Kádár's predecessor as the Minister of Internal Affairs had been responsible for treating thousands of innocent victims exactly as he himself was treated by his former subordinates. He was the victim of a terror that he himself had introduced. Although his trial was a hoax, and his judges as guilty as he was, he was guilty, nevertheless, of greater crimes than those of which he was convicted.

"Was László executed?" Alex asked.

"According to your government," I said, "he was hanged on October 15."

Alex began to cry. Then, as he often did in moments of great despondency, he knelt before a cross that he had scratched in the wall and prayed in Latin to the Virgin Mary. In the same wall, not far from Alex's cross, some earlier prisoner had scratched the following inscription: "MY DARLING. I LOVE YOU. I SHALL DIE BUT I AM INNOCENT."

Once I asked Alex how he had been able to square his Catholicism with the persecution of Cardinal Mindszenty.

"I was a Communist then," he said. "I had ceased to be a Catholic. It wasn't until after I was tortured that I began to believe in God again."

He was silent for a moment, and then he said, "But anyhow, the Cardinal was persecuted for his politics, not for his religion."

"I don't see that it makes any difference."

"No, I suppose you're right. I was as guilty as any of the others."

He asked me if the Vatican had retaliated in any way. I told him that the Pope had excommunicated every Catholic involved in the Cardinal's persecution.

"Were any names mentioned?"

"Not that I remember. It seemed to be a blanket excommunication."

Alex was shocked to realize that he himself had probably been excommunicated.

"How could I have been so stupid as to return to Hungary?" he said. "I was once an honest Communist. Now I'm less than nothing. I've been deprived of everything—my family, my liberty, even my religion—for serving a cause that I now know was false."

I asked him, as politely as I could, why it had taken him so long to come to that conclusion.

"You people on the outside," he said, "will never understand. It's a question of belief. As a Communist, I was ready to accept any injustice so long as it furthered the cause—a cause that I thought would eventually justify its own injustices by putting an end to injustice altogether. At the time I didn't realize that one injustice leads to another."

Thirteen | How They Broke Me Down

I spent sixty-nine days in the same cell with Alex Kirschner, alias Sándor Cseresnyés, and I got to know him rather well. In return for testifying against his friend and protector László Rajk, he told me, he hoped to get off with seven years in a concentration camp. I have no doubt, though he always denied it, that he had been promised another year or two off in return for assisting in the extraction of my confession.

"You'd better confess," he said. "If I were you, I'd tell them anything they want to hear. Nobody will blame you. The whole world knows by now how the Communists obtain their confessions."

"But I haven't got anything to confess."

"Say you bribed some government official. Name somebody you don't like. Say you gave him $5,000. That ought to help."

"But I didn't bribe anybody."

"What if you didn't? They want you to say you did."

"But I can't denounce innocent people."

"Hah!" said Alex. "That's a good one. 'I can't denounce innocent people.' Don't you realize they're all denouncing you? It doesn't make any difference. Everybody's expected to denounce everybody else."

I began to understand. For days No. 2 had been trying to get me to name the members of my non-existent "spy ring." If Alex was trying to help him, I had better set him straight.

173

"I'm not going to name any names," I said.

"All right, don't name names. But give them some details that they can develop."

"What do you mean by that?"

"Tell them about the sabotage in your factory."

"But there wasn't any sabotage—at least not on the company's part."

"What if there wasn't? All the AVH wants is a plausible case. Don't you understand? You've got to be guilty of something. You can't be tried unless you're guilty. And unless you're tried, you can't be released."

And so it went. Alex and No. 2 worked on me by turns, in their different ways, but I was still determined to resist.

On the night of December 15, after an hour's grilling, No. 2 said that he was going to invite a friend of mine to join us. My "friend" turned out to be Zoltán Radó, the former head of the Light Electrical Directorate of the Ministry of Heavy Industry. Radó shuffled into the office, clicked his heels, bowed like a mechanical doll in the direction of No. 2, turned, clicked his heels again, and bowed in my direction. Then he straightened up and stood at attention, swaying slightly as he fixed his gaze on the ceiling. His cheeks were hollow, his bearded face was filthy, and there were dark circles under his eyes.

"Is this the leader of your spy ring?" said No. 2, nodding in my direction.

Radó said that I was. He then began a rehearsed speech. I knew it was rehearsed because every now and then he would hesitate as he groped for the ensuing line. The essence of his testimony was that I had paid him to give me information regarding Hungary's trade agreements with foreign countries. He said that I had told him that ISEC had no intention of signing an agreement with the government. The negotiations, from beginning to end, had merely been an excuse for espionage. When he had finished, No. 2 showed him a sheaf of papers and said, "Is this your confession?"

"Yes."

No. 2 nodded, and Radó was led out of the office.

"You see?" said No. 2. "Radó has confessed that you were the leader of his spy ring. And he is only one of eighty people who have signed the same confession. Is there any reason why you should persist in your absurd denials of guilt?"

No. 2 smiled as his poker-faced interpreter repeated his question, and he roared with laughter as the interpreter repeated my reply:

"I am innocent."

"Bring in the next one," said No. 2. Presently Ödön Gergely was led into the office. Gergely, it will be recalled, had been a member of the government's negotiating committee. He was a slippery character whom I had always disliked, and my dislike for him was in no way diminished by what he now had to say. As Radó had done, he clicked his heels and bowed mechanically to both of us in turn. He then raced through his testimony as if he could hardly wait to get it off his chest. He said that he had resigned from Standard Budapest and become the head of Electroimpex in order to be in a better position to provide me with information concerning the export-import situation, the nature of the electrical equipment involved, and the prices paid and received. He also said that I had paid him, as a member of the negotiating committee, to obtain an agreement that would be favorable to ISEC.

When Gergely had been taken away, No. 2 smiled and said, "You see? It's now two against one."

"Their lies cancel out."

"How so?"

"Radó said that I didn't want an agreement. Gergely said that I'd paid him to get a better agreement."

No. 2, for once, seemed rather disconcerted. But he quickly recovered his composure.

"The explanation," he said, "is really very simple. You were playing a double game. You were using Gergely to cover your relations with Radó."

It was by means of such logic that No. 2 gradually convinced me of the futility of attempting to defend myself by pointing out the discrepancies in the faked confessions of the others.

The next night I was confronted by a man whom I failed to recognize until he was well into his speech. On the last Saturday in October, a few days before his escape, Geiger had come to see me at the Astoria. It was such a pleasant afternoon that, instead of talking to him in my room, I suggested that we go for a ride in my car. Feri drove us across the river into Buda and up the hill known as Táborhegy, or Encampment Mountain, where he circled through the residential area and then started back toward Pest. I suggested that we stop somewhere for a glass of wine, and Geiger, who was badly in need of a drink, said that he knew of a pleasant little tavern near the bottom of the hill.

The only other guests were seated at the end of a glassed-in terrace. We took a table at the opposite end, nearest the bar, so as not to be overheard. Geiger, who was more than usually pessimistic, wanted me to appeal to New York once again to transfer him to some other country—any country, he said, where he and his wife and daughter could live without being hounded by the police.

It was an odd little tavern, full of stuffed birds and squirrels and other small game, and the wine, as I recall, was not too bad. It resembled a light Moselle. The proprietor, who had lived for years in the United States, interrupted our conversation every few minutes to tell me how sorry he was that he had ever returned to Hungary. He had once been a waiter, or so he said, in Bookbinder's Restaurant in Philadelphia. By the time the war was over, he and his wife had saved enough money to return and buy a tavern with which to support their declining years. But it had all been a great mistake. Hungary was no longer the pleasant country it used to be, the Russians were running everything, and he would sooner or later be expropriated if, indeed, he wasn't arrested by the police. I made no comment for fear that he might be an *agent provocateur*.

This was the man who was now testifying against me. A few weeks earlier, when he had talked to me in his tavern, he had been a plump little man in his early fifties. Now he looked at least seventy years old. He had lost so much weight that his dirty jacket fell away from his shoulders in deep folds.

Yes, he said, staring at the floor and speaking in German, he had known me well. I had often visited his tavern to confer with my various agents. He himself was an agent of the FBI. Just before leaving Philadelphia to return to Budapest, he said, the *Geheim Polizei*—and that was the very phrase he used—the *Geheim Polizei,* the secret police, had approached him and arranged for him to convert his tavern, when he bought it, into a *Spiononenlokal*—a rendezvous for spies.

Was it Feri, I wondered, *who had reported our visit to the tavern?*

Three more prisoners confronted me the following night—Mrs. Zádor, László Kozma, and Geza Sándor. Kozma testified that I had paid him to provide me with drawings of the equipment that Standard Budapest had been manufacturing for the government. Sándor, an accountant, testified that I had paid him to buy materials for which Standard had no need. Mrs. Zádor testified that I had paid her to keep track of "union" activities and, also, that I had instructed her to destroy my files.

Their charges were absurd. I knew what the factory was manufacturing and therefore had no need to "buy" our own drawings from Kozma, who was one of our engineers. Sándor had nothing

whatever to do with the purchasing department. And Mrs. Zádor
was the last person I would have asked to tell me about the
activities of the government's so-called "union," which was not a
union at all but merely the labor section of the AVH. I had destroyed my own papers, and I had kept track of the AVH's labor
activities by other means, as I had every right to do. The factory,
after all, belonged to I.T.&T.

I was then interrogated by two Russian inquisitors who attempted, without success, to force me to admit that I had reported regularly on Russian troop movements in Eastern Europe.
A Czechoslovakian inquisitor attempted, also without success, to
force me to admit that my "real" purpose in visiting his country
had been to obtain secret information regarding uranium production.

On December 20 I was informed that Israel Jacobson, of the
American Joint Distribution Committee, a Jewish relief organization, had also been arrested on charges of espionage. No. 2 showed
me a document purporting to be Jacobson's "confession," in which
he admitted having been a member of my "spy ring." Jacobson
also stated that I had paid him several thousand dollars in return
for smuggling certain persons out of Hungary. I had never even
met the man, though he had once been pointed out to me, and I
denied that I had ever had any dealings with him.

When No. 2 asked me to describe him, I said that Jacobson
was a "gray-haired man, partly bald, with a light complexion."
Actually, as I recalled, he was a dark young man with curly brown
hair. No. 2 then showed me an album of photographs, asking me
to identify the persons they depicted. Jacobson's photograph was
among them, but I quickly passed it over, pointing to several
photographs of persons I had never seen and admitting falsely
that I might have known them. Long afterward I learned that the
Hungarians released Jacobson ten days after his arrest without
preferring any charges.

While I was parrying No. 2's questions about Jacobson and the

activities of the JDC, he suddenly asked me to tell him what I
knew about Noel Field and the Unitarian Service Committee. All
I knew, I said, was that Field and his family had disappeared in
Czechoslovakia. As for the Unitarian Service Committee, I had no
reason to believe that it was anything but a relief organization.

"What about the Baptists?" said No. 2. "They also have a spy
ring in Hungary."

"Everybody seems to be a spy," I said, "as far as you're concerned."

"You ought to know," said No. 2, without losing his temper.
"You're one of the key men."

Christmas was celebrated at 60 Stalin Avenue by giving us less
food than usual. Our normal midday meal consisted of potatoes
or turnips, with paprika sauce, and watery ersatz "coffee." On
Christmas, as a reminder that Christ had been displaced in Hungary by the Antichrist of Moscow, our lunch consisted of black
bread and water.

On New Year's Eve, which was celebrated normally, the prison
guards made so much noise that it was difficult for us to sleep. At
midnight, as the bells of a nearby church began to toll, I lay in my
bunk and thought of my wife and children and the way I had celebrated the end of the preceding year. My mother, who had been
visiting us in Vienna, was about to return to New York, and
Lucile and I had decided to combine our New Year celebration
with a farewell party in her honor. (I was doubly glad that we
had, for my mother died soon afterward.) Our guests at the party
included Captain and Mrs. Robert Ruske, the Nissls, and a number of other friends. Bob Ruske was a member of our military
forces in Austria with whom I had often played golf.

I told Alex about the phony golf tournament that Ruske and I
had won in Klagenfurt. We had been selected to represent the
Americans in Austria against the British, the French, and the Aus-

trians themselves. The Russians, however, chose to turn us back
at Semmering Pass, and so we had to drive to Klagenfurt by way
of Linz and Salzburg—a devious route that was at least three times
as long. I was driving the Ford, which broke down at Linz, and I
had to telephone to have the Steyr sent up from Vienna. On arriving in Klagenfurt, many hours late, we discovered that the
tournament had been held the week before and had been won, as
expected, by the British. USFA had mistaken the date. As a joke,
therefore, and not thinking of the consequences, we sent a telegram saying that we had won the tournament. It was too late
when we returned to Vienna to cancel the banquet that was held
in our honor. All we could do was to give a later party of our own
at which we confessed the hoax and awarded each other appropriate prizes—a dead golf ball and a tin cup.

Alex reciprocated by telling me in great detail about the various
women he had known, including his Austrian mistress in Klagenfurt. Once, he said, they had risen at dawn to go swimming naked
in the Wörtersee, after which experience his mistress cooked him
an omelet containing no fewer than a dozen eggs.

I was never certain which of the two bodily pleasures Alex
missed the more. He missed them both far more than I was to
miss them, and he was unable to avoid discussing either for very
long. Sometimes, as when he told me of all the evaporated milk
he had drunk as a soldier in the British Army, I had to beg him to
keep quiet. It nauseated me even to think of evaporated milk.
And though I was as curious as he was about the identity of the
one female prisoner in the Orpheum, I was often annoyed by
Alex's efforts to reconstruct her in his imagination. Every day or
two, when he had tired of telling me about the women of his
memory, he would resume his work on our sister prisoner, taking
her apart and putting her back together again, piece by piece. Depending on his whim, she was either short or tall, fat or slender,
blonde or brunette, but she was invariably both beautiful and
brazen. Once, when I suggested that sex and food were not the
only pleasures in life, Alex accused me of being a hypocrite.

"Look who's talking," he said. "Maybe you're afraid our friend's Edina Dőry."

"And what if she is?"

"Wasn't she your mistress?"

I seldom lost my temper with Alex, but this time I did. No. 2 had been trying very hard to trick me into admitting the same thing, apparently in the hope of adding spice to my confession.

Christmas and New Year's came and went; Jacobson was released; Standard Budapest and all other foreign companies were confiscated by decree; and on January 3, after prohibiting private travel to Hungary, the State Department instructed Nathaniel Davis to deliver the following note to Gyula Kállai:

The Government of Hungary has clearly failed . . . to live up to its obligations under the Treaty of Friendship, Commerce and Consular Rights between the United States and Hungary and to the accepted standards of international practice in regard to the right of consular officers to extend protection to nationals of their country. This right is in no way limited by the fact that a United States national may be accused of violating Hungarian law or detained on such charges or by the nature of the accusations leveled against him. Indeed it is precisely in the case of those nationals who are accused of crime . . . that the exercise of the consular right is most urgently required. Yet the Hungarian Government has for more than forty days denied all access to Mr. Vogeler. Another American citizen, Mr. Israel Jacobson, was, moreover, held incommunicado for nearly two weeks by the Hungarian police and has now been expelled from Hungary without the charges against him having been officially made known to me. . . .

The Hungarian Government, in its note of December 24, accuses Mr. Vogeler of "espionage and sabotage" and arbitrarily states that Mr. Vogeler is guilty of these charges even before he is afforded any sort of public hearing or judicial examination. The question arises whether it is now accepted judicial procedure in Hungary that the police shall draw up the charges, produce a "confession" and hand down the verdict, before a case is even brought before a court of law.

The United States Government states categorically that it cannot
recognize as just or in any way conclusive . . . such arbitrary judgment by the police or any subsequent action which . . . merely en-
dorses a verdict of guilty announced *a priori* by the police authorities. . . .

Apparently it has become increasingly inconvenient to the Government of Hungary that the Hungarian people should have contact
with representatives of the free world. It suits its purpose, moreover,
that these contacts should be severed in a manner which represents
quite normal and necessary business practices as "espionage and
sabotage." Under these circumstances, in which any United States
businessman or relief administrator in Hungary may be subject to
arbitrary arrest and imprisonment, the United States Government has
found it necessary to refuse to permit private American citizens henceforth to travel in Hungary.

In view, moreover, of the serious restrictions placed by the Hungarian Government on the exercise of consular rights . . . the Government of the United States finds it inappropriate to continue to permit the maintenance of separate consular establishments in Cleveland,
Ohio, and New York City.

I am accordingly instructed by my government to inform you that
recognition . . . is withdrawn and that the consular establishments
in New York and Cleveland are required to close on or before 12
o'clock midnight, January 15, 1950. . . .

Weak as it was, the note would have strengthened my determination to resist if I had been permitted to learn of its delivery.
From the beginning to the end of my 527 days of imprisonment,
however, I was held in ignorance as well as isolation. I soon
learned the full and bitter meaning of the word "incommunicado."
Although I was still holding out, my will to resist, in the absence
of any outside aid or encouragement, was gradually being sapped.
My autobiography now totaled more than a thousand pages. No.
2 continued to badger me until, in the hope of avoiding major admissions, I made a number of minor admissions, each of which he
then used to make me admit a little more.

"You'll have to confess in the end," said Alex, "so why wait any longer? Every day of resistance means another month in prison."

On the seventy-first day I surrendered to despair. This was on January 27, 1950. For seventy days, in spite of growing doubts, I had nourished the hope that the American Legation would somehow be able to procure my release. No. 2, however, insisted that I had been abandoned. In the beginning I knew that he was lying, but toward the end I began to wonder.

Convinced at last that I had indeed been abandoned, I told No. 2 that I would sign anything if he would only cease his merciless inquisition. I had lost count of the confessions that he had already prepared for me, and which I had refused to sign, but, together with No. 1's five confessions, they numbered well over twenty.

No. 2, with my help, now prepared a superconfession that ran to more than sixty pages. This time, instead of attempting to minimize my "crimes," I attempted to multiply them to such an extent that no one but a Communist or a fellow-traveler could possibly believe that I was guilty. In this endeavor I was apparently successful, for, as my friends were able to demonstrate, I confessed at my subsequent trial to more than 200 acts that I couldn't possibly have committed.

Parts of my confession were so patently false that they were not even referred to at my trial. If they had been, J. Edgar Hoover might have been surprised to learn that five of his "principal assistants" bore the same names as the members of the basketball team that I had coached when I was working for Kellogg in Chicago. Mr. Hoover undoubtedly has a number of Murphys working for him, but I doubt that even he could identify the "Robert Murphy" to whom I said that I had "reported" when I was supposedly working for the FBI myself. The only Murphy I knew in Chicago was Kellogg's elderly night watchman, and his first name wasn't Robert.

No. 2 apparently realized that he was being kidded, but for some reason he never complained. Perhaps he didn't care, so long as I gave him a "full" confession.

Fourteen | The Rehearsal of My Trial

Early in February, 1950, our diet suddenly improved. Alex and I were now served meat and potatoes twice a day. The portions were so large that I could seldom finish mine, but Alex was such a chow hound that he always cleaned up both our mess kits. Our improved standard of living, he said, was a sure sign that I was soon to go on trial. Emaciated defendants made bad propaganda. It was the practice of the AVH, therefore, to fatten them up like sacrificial lambs.

In December I had been confronted by Radó, Gergely, the tavernkeeper, Kozma, Sándor, and Mrs. Zádor. I was now confronted for the first time by Geiger, Sanders, and Edina Dőry and, for the second time, by Radó, Gergely, and Mrs. Zádor. No. 2 explained that the first confrontations had been "informal."

Geiger looked ten years older than when I had seen him last. His drawn face was the color of ashes as he rattled off his testimony in a singsong voice without once looking in my direction. He accused me, among other things, of having ordered him to sabotage Russian reparations orders by substituting aluminum bronze for phosphorous bronze in automatic telephone equipment. This time, instead of denying such charges, I admitted them, in the hope that engineers, at least, would be able to appreciate their absurdity.

During the Second World War the Germans had used aluminum bronze as a substitute for phosphorous bronze, which they could not obtain, and we had continued to use it after the war. If we had waited until phosphorous bronze became available again, a large percentage of our Russian reparations orders would never have been delivered, in which event I would probably have been accused of sabotaging production by refusing to use aluminum bronze. The fact is that aluminum bronze is equal or superior to phosphorous bronze in every sense but that of hardness, and it is arguable whether hardness is the most desirable quality in an alloy used in telephone equipment. Most of I.T.&T.'s European subsidiaries were using aluminum bronze instead of phosphorous bronze, and the Hungarian government, which had been unable to provide us with phosphorous bronze, had requested Standard Budapest to follow suit.

Edina Dőry, who appeared in lounging pajamas, seemed to have suffered less than any of my other confronters. She was thinner than she had been, and her face was not made up, but otherwise she seemed to be in fair physical condition. In a hesitant voice, she testified that she had seen me coding and decoding messages at the Hotel Astoria, a charge that I readily admitted, since I knew that everyone familiar with life in a Communist country would know that it was false. Hungary's censorship required that all my incoming and outgoing messages be sent in clear.

Sanders, who was nearsighted, had been deprived of his glasses —presumably to prevent him from slashing his wrists—and he could not have seen me very well even if he had looked in my direction, which he was careful not to do. His face was gaunt and his hair was noticeably grayer, but otherwise he seemed to be in better shape than Geiger. He accused me in English of having sent him to the town of Szombathély to report on the Russian garrison there. The charge was demonstrably false, since he said that I had ordered him to visit Szombathély a week before I returned to Budapest on September 30, 1949.

Radó, Gergely, and Mrs. Zádor repeated the statements that they had made before. The apparent purpose of these formal confrontations was to make sure that our respective falsehoods jibed. Stenographic notes were taken, and we were each required to sign a transcript of the proceedings. The confrontations took place in the presence of the codefendant's inquisitor and his staff. In each case the inquisitor was a different man. Sanders' inquisitor, for example, was my own first inquisitor, No. 1, whose more luxurious office had now been taken over by No. 2.

On the night that Sanders and I were confronted, a third person was present in addition to Nos. 1 and 2 and their subordinates. She was a dark, well-dressed woman, who spoke fluent American English with an Eastern European accent. Her task, I gathered, was to provide the British and American Communist parties with suitable arguments to justify our persecution.

Mrs. X, as I shall call her, had brought No. 2 a copy of a book by Ferdinand Lundberg called *America's Sixty Families*—an exposé of alleged "malefactors of great wealth." After Sanders had been taken away, No. 2 remarked that he was disappointed to find that Sosthenes Behn, in Lundberg's opinion, was a less important villain than the Rockefellers, Morgans, and du Ponts. It was a pity, he said, that I had given him so little information concerning Behn's Wall Street "confederates."

"After all," he added, "it was in your own interest to tell me everything you could. We arrested you only because we couldn't arrest Behn. He's the real criminal; you're just one of his lackeys."

When I insisted that my dissertation on Abner Yokum and Senator Claghorn had exhausted my knowledge of Behn's "confederates," No. 2 ordered his subordinates to take me back to my cell. He must have made some joke about me, for Mrs. X's shrill laughter followed us down the corridor.

Gábor Péter emerged from his office as we approached the main stairway. He was wearing a green overcoat and a green Austrian hat with a *Gemsbart*, a tuft of goatsbeard, stuck in the band. My escorts clicked their heels and stood at attention until the chief of the AVH had passed. As we followed him down-stairs, I noticed for the first time that Péter walked with a limp. It was then about three in the morning, and he was just going home. Evidently he observed the same office hours as Stalin.

On Saturday, February 4, after receiving my weekly shave and shower, I was led out to the first floor of the main building to be fingerprinted and photographed. The photographer sat me on a swivel chair in a little cubicle equipped with a swinging gate, which he shut as soon as I had been seated. He said something to me in Hungarian which I failed to understand, and the moment he had taken my picture I stood up and swung back the gate. As I did so, I noticed that it bore the number 04381 R. Apparently, to judge from the photographer's angry remarks, I was not supposed to have left the cubicle until he had hooked back the gate in order to conceal my number. I might have forgotten it otherwise, but, since he called it so forcibly to my attention, I decided to commit the number to memory. It was easy enough to do, for the fourth power of three is eighty-one, and R, of course, is my first initial.

As I thought things over, I became more and more depressed. The fact that I had been given a number could mean only that I had already been convicted by "administrative decision" and that my forthcoming trial, if any, would be meaningless except as a demonstration of Hungary's ability—and indeed the ability of any Russian colony—to humiliate the United States.

My pessimism, as I have since discovered, was not unwarranted. The State Department, in a subsequent communiqué, announced that Mátyás Rákosi had finally received Nathaniel Davis on January 19, 1950. He had informed the American minister that

. . . under Hungarian law an espionage trial could be held in secret. He stated, however, [that] he had advised the Minister of

Justice that, in order to show the correctness of the Hungarian position, Robert A. Vogeler, who is accused of espionage and sabotage,
should have a public trial which all the world could see. He said that
it would be a fair trial and that Mr. Vogeler would have every opportunity to defend himself, even to speak in English, for which proper
arrangements would be made.

These assurances that Mr. Vogeler will be accorded a fair trial
have, however, been belied by the wholly inconsistent and prejudicial
speech made by Mr. Rákosi before the Central Executive of the Hungarian Workers' (Communist) Party on February 10. . . . On that
occasion, speaking with reference to the case of Mr. Vogeler and Mr.
Edgar Sanders . . . Mr. Rákosi asserted, among other things, that
"these spies are in point of fact the vilest and most dangerous enemies
of the Hungarian People's Democracy." He then added that while
"for some time in the past we have been rather lenient toward these
heinous and dangerous enemies of our people," and "often let them
[escape] . . . or were content to expel them," "we shall see to it
that these gentlemen who are spying in Hungary on the instructions
of their American, British, or other masters do not find this job to be
without risks. If their activities are discovered, they will receive the
severe sentence meted out by the laws of Hungary."

Mr. Rákosi has thus clearly impugned his own assurances about a
fair trial and not only asserted the guilt of Mr. Vogeler before he is
brought to trial but also assumed the role of the court by announcing
that he will be severely punished. . . .

On February 10, the very day that Rákosi thus anticipated the
court's decision, I was taken to No. 1's office (now occupied by
No. 2) for my first audience with Vilmos Olti, one of the two
magistrates who alternately presided at Hungary's political trials.
Olti was the man who had sentenced Cardinal Mindszenty to life
imprisonment. His colleague, Péter Jankó, had sentenced László
Rajk to death. It was now Olti's turn to sentence me to whatever
punishment that Rákosi, on Stalin's instructions, might recommend.

Olti had once been a member of the *Nyilas*, or Arrow Cross,

the Hungarian National Socialist Party, but he had betrayed the
Germans in time to make himself acceptable to the Russians.
He was a tall, slender man with Germanic features, a suave manner, and a resonant baritone voice. He was wearing a dark brown
suit with a fawn-colored waistcoat; a yellow silk handkerchief
protruded from his breast pocket. On his desk were two copies
of my final confession. He had marked them with a blue pencil
to indicate the portions that were to become my answers to the
twenty-three sets of key questions that he would ask me in court.

"Let's go over them," he said, "to hear how they sound. These
aren't the only questions I'll ask you, by any means, but they're
the most important, and your answers will have to be convincing."

He now addressed me in Hungarian, through an interpreter
who was present, and told me to respond to his questions in
English. Up to then we had spoken German.

"When and under what circumstances did you commence your
espionage activities?" he asked.

"In Chicago, in 1942," I heard my voice reply, "I became a
member of the FBI—the Federal Bureau of Investigation—and
was initiated into espionage work."

We continued in this vein for an hour and a half. At last Olti
called in No. 2, who had left the office, and told him to coach me
for several days until I had become "letter-perfect."

That night I was given a copy of my indictment. With Alex
looking over my shoulder, I read:

Robert Vogeler has been an agent of American intelligence since
1942. He was trained at a special spy school by the FBI. He admitted
in the course of the preliminary investigation: "I was trained in the
theory and practice of espionage, intelligence, and counter-intelligence, the building up and maintenance of spy networks."

In view of his training as a spy he was appointed, with the en-
dorsement of the Joint Chiefs of Staff of the USA, as head of all

Standard subsidiaries in Eastern Europe, with his headquarters in Vienna. Before his departure for Vienna, Col. Behn, one of the executives of the corporation, and at the same time one of the high-ranking American officers in key positions with ISEC, instructed him to put himself entirely at the disposal of the American military intelligence in Vienna. In order better to fulfill this assignment, Vogeler was promoted to the rank of a colonel. Accordingly Vogeler made the following statement on his activities in the course of the preliminary investigation: "I myself carried on extensive espionage activities, partly through the employees of the ITT and ISEC subsidiaries under my control, partly by availing myself of agents specially selected for the purpose."

The secret data thus obtained were assembled in regular reports and forwarded to the intelligence organizations of the United States. About the operation of these organizations, he admitted during the preliminary investigation that, while carrying on espionage activities for the CIC and ODI [Office of the Director of Intelligence], he availed himself of the services of the officials of the US legations and some of the American citizens residing in these countries.

About his activities in Hungary he admitted that, according to his instructions, his job was: "1. To carry on political, economic, and military espionage. 2. To carry out acts of sabotage and diversion in the Hungarian subsidiary of the Standard."

Robert Vogeler, a colonel in the US Army, making use of his experience acquired at the espionage school of the FBI, built up a network of spies composed of pro-fascist executives in the Standard plant and of adventurers greedy for money. . . . From all of them Vogeler continuously [sic] received intelligence material. He received copies of the reports forwarded by Sanders to the British Intelligence Service. All the material he obtained, Vogeler submitted to his chiefs. He organized the escape of such spies as were in danger of being exposed.

Taking advantage of *his official post* in this way, he spied out State secrets, seriously endangering important economic and international interests of the State, and surrendered them to *the authorities of a foreign state* [italics mine].

The second part of the crimes committed by Robert Vogeler, Colonel in the US Army, consists of his acts of sabotage consistently carried out in accordance with the instructions of Col. Behn. These instructions were supplemented by Col. Behn at the secret meeting that took place in October 1948 at the Hotel Gellért in Budapest, attended by Edgar Sanders and Imre Geiger among others.

It was on Vogeler's instructions that the Standard plant submitted a false balance sheet and made payment of unwarranted claims. Besides the details of his acts of sabotage exposed during the preliminary investigation, a further crime of Vogeler was that he instructed Zoltán Radó, one of his agents, in connection with the negotiations carried on by the Hungarian government with the Standard plant to commit a breach of his official duties and carry out diversionist activities.

By violating the provisions of the law relating to production, he committed sabotage.

Not a single one of the foregoing statements was true. I was not even a Navy officer, much less an Army officer, and my one and only contact with the FBI occurred in 1942, as I have explained, when I was denounced for criticizing the arrogant behavior of the Russian inspectors in the Kellogg factory. I was in no sense the "head of all Standard subsidiaries in Eastern Europe." Colonel Behn had retired from the Army immediately after the First World War. Neither of us had any connection, official or unofficial, with any agency of the United States government.

I had many friends in USFA, it is true, and I told them what I could about industrial operations behind the Iron Curtain. I considered it my duty and my privilege as a private citizen to do so. The type of information that I supplied was freely available to the public in all but Communist countries. It involved no military secrets. My dealings with Radó, who had never once given me cause to suspect that he was anything but a loyal Stalinist, were at all times open and official. The people whom I was supposed to have helped to escape from Hungary were innocent victims of political persecution. They had every right, in my opinion, to seek asylum in foreign countries.

I asked Alex what he thought would happen if, in the midst of the trial, I suddenly told the truth—namely, that it was all a barbaric hoax and that my codefendants and I were entirely innocent of the crimes to which the AVH had forced us to confess.

Alex was aghast. "I hate to think of what would happen," he said. "The careers of so many people depend on your conviction that they'll do anything—literally anything—to prevent you from queering the trial."

That night, when he was taken out for questioning, he must have reported what I had said, for the next day No. 2 issued a solemn warning.

"Your entire future," he said, "will be determined by your behavior at the trial. If you fail to answer the president's questions in the proper spirit, you will be removed from the courtroom and taken to a special hospital. There you will be given treatment that will make you happy to come back and answer the president's questions. But it will also make you a cripple for life."

As I pondered the meaning of what he had said, No. 2 took from his pocket a bottle of pills. He asked a guard to bring him a glass of water. He then took one of the pills, drank the glass of water, and put the bottle back in his pocket.

"Actedron," he said with a smile. "According to the press of your country, we've been drugging you with actedron. It just goes to show how much your people know about our methods. It's we ourselves, the examining magistrates, who take actedron, not our prisoners. We have better methods than drugs to obtain the truth."

And with that remark he sent me back to the Orpheum to digest the full meaning of his threat. Only one man, so far as I know, has ever dared to repudiate his confession before a Hungarian Communist court. He was Bálint Arany, an engineer employed by SKF, the Swedish Ball Bearing Company, who was a defendant in the first conspiracy trial in 1947. President Péter Jankó immediately called a recess. It was a week before Arany reappeared, and when he did he was a changed man. He groveled before the court and answered Jankó's questions with lunatic precision.

For three days I rehearsed my answers to Olti's questions in the presence of No. 2 and his interpreter. Then No. 2 announced that the time had come for me to select my defender. He produced a list of lawyers and told me to select any one of them. The only name I recognized was that of a lawyer who had done some work for Standard Budapest following the escape of our regular attorney, Tamás Mezei, who had turned up in Vienna unexpectedly.

"I don't think he's the man you want," said No. 2. "He's not reliable."

"Then why not let the American Legation select a lawyer for me?"

"You seem to have forgotten," said No. 2, "that your government has expressed no interest in your case."

Long afterward, following my release from prison, I learned that my wife and father and some friends, at the suggestion of I.T.&T., had retained Morris L. Ernst, of New York, as my defense attorney. Indeed, on February 13, the same day that No. 2 brought up the question, the legation had formally requested a postponement of my trial until such time as Ernst was permitted to confer with me in Budapest.

Two days later the State Department issued a communiqué:

Mr. Ernst, whose passport has been validated by the United States Government for travel to Hungary, has applied at the Hungarian Legation in Washington for a visa to enter Hungary and has also requested through the Legation that the Hungarian Government postpone the trial to enable him to arrive in Budapest in due time

to interview Mr. Vogeler prior to the start of the trial. Mr. Ernst
has notified these steps directly by cable to the Hungarian Minister
for Justice, Mr. István Ries. The Hungarian Minister for Foreign
Affairs has also been informed of them by the American Legation
in Budapest.

The United States Government has previously, in a note of February
1, made formal representations to the Hungarian Government request-
ing the entry of a private American lawyer into Hungary to represent
Mr. Vogeler. The Hungarian Government, in a reply of February 6,
refused this request. . . .

The United States Government does not regard the Hungarian
reply to its legitimate and reasonable request as satisfactory. In the
light of the theory and practice of justice which now prevail in Hungary, as well as of the duties toward the Communist regime now imposed on Hungarian lawyers and judges, there is grave doubt that,
in the absence of American legal counsel, Mr. Vogeler will be properly
defended and his rights adequately safeguarded by a Hungarian
lawyer. Moreover, in view of Mr. Vogeler's present situation and the
treatment experienced by other American citizens who have been
detained by the Hungarian police, there is serious doubt that he is in
a position to make a free choice of Hungarian legal counsel for his
defense.

Mr. Vogeler . . . has now been held incommunicado by the Hungarian police for three months. At no time to date has he been permitted access to American consular representatives or, so far as is
known to this Government, to legal counsel of any kind. This in-
excusable treatment of an American citizen by the Hungarian Government gives rise to apprehension that his rights will be flouted as
outrageously at his trial as during the period of his incarceration before trial and fully justifies the request that an American lawyer be
permitted to assist in his defense.

It is of interest to recall that the Bulgarian Communist leader Georgi
Dimitrov, when brought to trial in the Reichstag fire case, demanded
of the German Government the right to be represented by foreign
lawyers of his own choosing. He actually named two Bulgarians, an
American and others as his counsel. Although the Nazi Supreme Court
denied Dimitrov's request that he be represented by foreign lawyers,

it permitted such lawyers to be present at the trial, to send communications to the court, and to publish communications. On this issue the Hungarian Communist regime apparently wishes to outdo even Nazi "justice" in denying rights to the defendant.

Furthermore, in United States Courts the Constitution is interpreted to permit choice of counsel by the accused even outside the bar of jurisdiction. It is in accordance with international comity, especially where the defense of basic human rights may be involved, for courts to permit a foreign lawyer to appear *pro hac vice*. Such a practice exists in all United States courts which, otherwise, are, like Hungarian courts, governed by statutes limiting practice at court to those lawyers who are admitted to the local bar. A distinction thus exists between a lawyer's practice of his profession and his appearance in a single case. Attention is called to the fact that the Hungarian Government's reply completely ignores both this distinction and the circumstance that association of an American lawyer with the Hungarian defense counsel of record . . . would not contravene any Hungarian law of penal procedure limiting to members of the Hungarian bar appearance as counsel of record. Mr. Ernst's request, moreover, is not insistent on his appearance in court as counsel of record, but pertains to his entry into Hungary to protect his client's interests in every proper way. . . .

The Government and people of the United States are deeply concerned and indignant at the intolerable attitude and behavior of the Hungarian Government in the case of Mr. Vogeler. They take an increasingly serious view of the treatment of this American citizen, wherein the Hungarian Government has violated both its specific international obligations and generally accepted principles of humanity. . . .

Hungary's "specific international obligations," on its compliance with which its diplomatic relations with the United States legally depend, include, in addition to the Peace Treaty of 1947, the Hungarian-American Treaty of Friendship, Commerce, and Consular Rights of 1926, which was renewed in 1948, and to which Davis referred in the note he delivered to Kállai on January 3, 1950. The friendship treaty provides, among other things, that

Americans in Hungarian territory shall receive "the most constant protection and security for their persons and property and shall enjoy in this respect that degree of protection that is required by international law." Article 9 of the UN's Declaration of Human Rights, moreover, provides that "no one shall be subject to arbitrary arrest, detention or exile." Article 11 provides that "everyone charged with a penal offense has the right to be presumed innocent until proved guilty according to law in a public trial, *at which he has had all the guarantees necessary for his defense* [italics mine]."

Ernst, who embodied the most important of such guarantees—namely, my right to be defended by counsel of my own choice—flew to Vienna to await his Hungarian visa. It was withheld on the specious ground that I had already retained a Hungarian lawyer named Imre Bárd.

Actually I had nothing to do with the selection of Bárd. He was selected for me by No. 2, whose sense of humor was such that he thought it would be a good joke for me to be "defended" by a lawyer with the same last name as one of the persons whom I was accused of having helped to escape to Austria.

No. 2 left us alone in his office the next morning for exactly forty-five minutes. He left us "alone," that is, in the presence of two guards and two female secretaries who may or may not have been able to understand English.

Bárd turned out to be a fat, bespectacled shyster, who had the habit of patting his paunch, across which hung, or rather lay, a heavy gold watch chain.

"If you don't like me," he said, reading my thoughts, "you can always ask for someone else."

I knew it would be a waste of time to do so. Any Hungarian lawyer who attempted to defend me honestly would himself be persecuted as an "enemy of the state."

"Have you confessed to any serious crimes?" asked Bárd.

When I told him what he already knew—namely, that my "confession" had been extracted under duress and was therefore null and void—he looked at me in mock dismay.

"You don't mean to tell me that you intend to repudiate your confession?"

"You're my lawyer," I said. "What do you suggest?"

He suggested that, in view of the "serious nature of my crimes," the only thing to do was for me to throw myself on the "mercy" of the court. He obviously had no intention of defending me. His function was merely to assist the state prosecutor, Gyula Alapi, in obtaining a "legal" conviction.

As he was about to leave, I asked Bárd how many years he thought I would get. He looked at me with an owlish expression on his face.

"What do you think?" he said.

I told him that I had been threatened with everything from five years to death. Bárd hemmed and hawed and finally allowed that he would be very happy if he could get me off with life imprisonment. That was the last I saw of him until the day I went on trial. He left me with the feeling that, though my conviction was certain, my sentence had yet to be decided. Perhaps there was still some thought of exchanging me for Valentin Gubitchev; or perhaps it was merely that my sentence depended on some as yet unformulated demand.

Later that day I was taken to see Alapi again. He was seated, as before, behind a cluttered desk. As soon as I had been seated, he began to dictate to the curly-haired albino, who was seated at a typewriter to the left of Alapi's desk. The albino translated tonelessly as he went along. It was as if he were translating an application for a dog license rather than the official accusation against a prisoner charged "with the crime of espionage, once and continuously committed, in violation of Article 60, Section 1, of Statute III (1930) . . . qualified according to Article 61, Section 3; [and] furthermore charged with the crime, once committed, of jeopardizing the execution of the [Three-Year Plan] in violation of Article 7, Section 1, of Edict No. 8800 (1946) of the Ministry of Economics, as well as Article 1, Section 1, of Government Edict No. 14,200 (1947) and Article 3 of the same . . . qualified according to Article 9, Section 4."

The accusation, as I have since confirmed, was legally as well as factually bogus. Even if I had committed the crimes of which I was accused, I was guilty of neither espionage nor sabotage according to Hungary's penal code.

Article 61, Section 3, fixes death as the punishment for *treason* committed by "whoever misuses his official position . . . and whose act gravely jeopardizes the interests of the State." Article 60, Section 1, fixes five years as the punishment for *treason* committed by "whoever spies or unjustly acquires military or other secrets relating to other important interests of the Hungarian State, especially those affecting its international economic position."

According to Article 9, Section 4, of Edict No. 14,200 (1947), "it is a felony punishable by not more than five years' imprisonment to raise prices illegally or to jeopardize [in any way] the public welfare." The punishment may be raised to ten years' imprisonment if large sums of money and large quantities of materials are involved, and to death if the "economic system" as well as the "public welfare" is "gravely jeopardized."

In other words, anyone may be condemned to death for doing anything that "gravely jeopardizes" the Communists' economic policies, *provided* (and again I quote Edict No. 14,200) the culprit is either a "Hungarian citizen," an "indigenous legal entity," an "alien resident in Hungary and possessing an employment permit," or an "alien legal entity . . . with assets in the territory of the Hungarian State."

It was impossible, therefore, to convict me lawfully of the crimes of which I was accused. I was not a Hungarian citizen. I was not even a resident of Hungary. I was not a "legal entity," alien or indigenous, and I had never possessed an employment permit.

Sanders, unfortunately, had. In pointing out that I was to be convicted of violating laws that did not apply to foreign visitors, however, I wish to make it absolutely clear that I have no intention of suggesting that Sandy's conviction was in any way more lawful than mine. We were both innocent of the crimes to which we had been forced to confess. So were our Hungarian codefendants. It just so happens that, whereas the laws under which we were all to be convicted applied to Hungarians and foreign residents possessing employment permits, they did not apply to a foreign visitor who was under no obligation to assist the Communists in fulfilling their Three-Year Plan.

My trial, of course, was not to be affected by such considerations. Indeed, it was not to be a trial at all but a sort of *auto de fe*, in which the techniques of the Spanish inquisition were adapted to the needs of Russian imperialism. The purpose of the trial was not to establish guilt or innocence, but to teach a political lesson at the expense of the defendants. The lesson, in short, was that all Westerners, and especially Americans and Britons, were to be regarded as enemies of the Hungarian state in particular and of all Cominform states in general. All who regarded them as friends, therefore, were themselves to be regarded as internal enemies of the new Russian Empire.

It was perhaps a coincidence that I was to be tried, like Cardinal Mindszenty, together with six "accomplices." It was by no means a coincidence, however, that my six codefendants were who they were. Each of them symbolized, as I did, a specific bugaboo, each of which would be symbolically destroyed in the crude political allegory of the trial. That two of us would be condemned to death, and the rest of us to long terms of imprisonment, was only natural, since we were but gladiators in a court that was literally as well as figuratively an arena. A playbill of the drama, or masque, that was now unfolding (*"das Spiel der sich jetzt entwichelt,"* as Péter had put it) would, if published, have been approximately as follows:

JOSEPH STALIN

presents

ROBERT A. VOGELER and EDGAR SANDERS

in

"STANDARD ELECTRIC"

by

MÁTYÁS RÁKOSI

Directed by Gábor Péter

Lighting and Settings by AVH Associates

THE CAST

(In order of their appearance)

The bourgeoisie . . . . Imre Geiger

National Communism (alias "Trotskyism," alias "Titoism")

Zoltán Radó

The United Kingdom (alias "British Imperialism") . Edgar Sanders

The United States (alias "Wall Street Imperialism," alias "Dollar Diplomacy") . . . . Robert A. Vogeler

The German minority . . . . Kelemen Domokos

The clergy . . . . Dr. István Justh

The landed gentry . . . . Edina Dőry

To judge from the way our scripts were written, it was more important to establish our allegorical identities than it was to establish our "guilt." Each of us, in his testimony, was obliged to "unmask" himself for the benefit of the Cominform press and radio, whose task was to draw the necessary Stalinist conclusions. The pertinent dialogue, as it appeared in the official white book,* ran as follows:

* *R. Vogeler, E. Sanders and their Accomplices Before the Criminal Court,* Budapest, 1950, *passim.*

GEIGER

The President: Now please tell us something of your political convictions. How did you come to undertake this work? Did you hold beliefs opposed to the political direction of this country?

Geiger: Yes.

The President: From what sort of family do you come?

Geiger: I come from a middle-class family and my education, as well as my social surroundings, made me into a supporter and defender of the middle-class regime. That is why I watched with great hate the continuous upward development of the Soviet Union and the People's Democracies. I knew that the regime could not be overturned without foreign aid because of its political and economic achievements, and in consequence of my political convictions I readily agreed to carry out the espionage and sabotage orders given by the American intelligence. I knew that with this activity I was supporting the American government and its war policy against the Soviet Union and the People's Democracies.

RADÓ

The President: Please tell us when and under what circumstances you came to Hungary.

Radó: I came to Hungary, to Budapest, in August 1945, commissioned by the British Intelligence Service. I didn't live in Hungary, I was born in Czechoslovakia, and lived there. In 1939, before the Second World War broke out, I emigrated to England. In London I got in touch with Trotskyites, and through them I came in contact with two agents of the British espionage service, who brought me into their organization and on their instructions I worked as an informer among the Hungarians living in England. . . .

The President: What instructions did you get about the contacts you were to make on your arrival in Hungary?

Radó: First of all, the agents of the British espionage service instructed me to hide my anti-Soviet and anti-democratic attitude on my arrival in Hungary, and to try to infiltrate into the Hungarian Communist Party, because this was the way to carry out espionage and sabotage most successfully in the interests of the British Intelligence Service. . . .

The Prosecutor: Answer me the question, what financial reward did you get from the British Intelligence Service?

Radó: When in May 1949 I accepted Scudder's proposal to enter the American espionage service, and he on the same occasion took me into the organization, I found it very useful to get in touch with the American espionage service, because the British Intelligence Service paid me rather badly. For the last time they transferred to me £120 in 1948. On the contrary Scudder promised me . . .

The Prosecutor (interrupts him): Did he promise more than the British espionage service?

Radó: Yes, more.

The Prosecutor: I have no more questions. . . .

The President: When you were asked for data for the first time, you could have refused, since you knew that they are spies like you, and there was the danger of being discovered, both for them and you.

Radó: Apart from the financial gain, of which I have spoken already, I was led also by political consideration [*sic*], to get in touch with the American espionage service. It was my conviction, that the Americans represent the anti-Soviet and anti-democratic policy with much more consistency and energy and this suited my views. Besides, the Americans seemed to me much stronger and safer masters than the British.

SANDERS

The President: Did you have instructions to collect political information?

Sanders: Political no, but . . . I had instructions, as I travelled in the country, to organise [*sic*] or carry out a sort of quiet propaganda for the Anglo-Saxon side. The aims at that time, of the Anglo-Saxons, were to cause a split between the Government and the Communists . . . to oppose the formation of the democratic government as led by the Communists. For that purpose they were backing the right-wing reactionary parties . . . in hoping to keep the Communist Party out of the Government and furthermore, to make a break in between [sic] Hungary and the Soviet Union. For this purpose when Nagy Ferencz [sic] went about 1945, if I remember rightly, to America, soon afterwards you could see the supplies of UNRRA cars arriving in Hungary, then the Red Cross with medical supplies. Then there was the return of Hungarian National Bank gold, and also . . . a train arrived with hospital equipment belonging to the Hungarian Government which was taken away by the Nazis. In order to obtain their aims, the Anglo-Saxons . . . they went firstly . . . they started political espionage. In other words, they were obtaining information from various walks of life. Obtaining information as to the combat, so to speak, of various political parties and got agents in Government circles or . . . who had high posts in parties, and through these people they were hoping to obtain true financial and economic help, they were hoping to obtain their aims.

VOGELER

The President: At this time, what type of information and material did you collect in Central Europe?

Vogeler: The information I collected was mostly of a technical nature, inventions, processes and patents, and general economic, financial, military and political information.

The President: What political aims did you have at this time here in the people's democratic states?

Vogeler: Well, at this time our policy was to assist the reactionary elements and support . . . to support them.

The President: When did this political line change?

Vogeler: About 1947 when relations between the U.S. and the Soviet Union deteriorated . . . it became evident that the People's Democracies were rallying round the Soviet Union.

The President: Under these altered political conditions what changes did you execute in the espionage organisation [sic] of the U.S.?

Vogeler: As I mention up until that time the espionage work was of a general character. After that time when the American policy became more aggressive, the work in the intelligence organisations took on a more aggressive character. . . .

DOMOKOS

The President: Who enlisted you to work for the American intelligence service and when?

Domokos: I was enlisted into the American intelligence service by Imre Geiger in January 1947. But before giving a detailed account of my enlistment, I should like to explain my political convictions, my attitude, which induced me to lead a life of crime.

The President: Go ahead and explain, but briefly.

Domokos: On my father's side I am of the German minority by descent. My name used to be Krausz [Kraus] until 1936 when I changed it to the Hungarian-sounding Domokos. My political convictions make me a fascist. During the war I sided with the Germans, supported the fascists and did my best to promote the victory of Hitler's Germany. After the war, seeing that Hungary had set out on the road to Socialism, I tried to contact the delegates of the American trust in Budapest, who, as I already knew, made it their aim to undermine Hungary's economic situation. . . .

JUSTH

Lipót Konta (Counsel of Defense for István Justh): Please tell us, that although the financial compensation you received was disproportionately small, what was your chief reason for turning against your country?

Justh: My chief motive was my political conviction. By birth, education, and high clerical office I was strongly opposed to the policy pursued by the country after the Liberation. 2,000 *holds* [a *hold* is slightly larger than an acre] of my own estate, and about 2,000 *holds* of my sister, together with 800 *holds* of my eventual inheritance were distributed, and so were several thousand *holds* of near relatives; all this was a great financial shock to me. By birth, I belong to one of the oldest noble families of Hungary, my mother came from the aristocracy, my sister was married to an aristocrat, and all these developed in me a sharp antagonism to the present system of government.

DŐRY

Dőry: At first, Vogeler did not trust me. After I had told him that my sister, Ilona Dőry, was married to the U.S. agent well known also in Hungary, Lieutenant Colonel György Kovács, he took me into his confidence.

The President: Your father had a canned goods factory, didn't he?

Dőry: Yes. Besides, he had an estate of 3,400 *holds* in the county of Fejér.

None of the foregoing bits of dialogue bears any relationship to the truth. Even the facts and figures are imaginary. I have quoted them only to show how each of us was made to serve the purposes of the Ministry of People's Culture (Propaganda).

As my friend and colleague Goodwin Cooke remarked, in a memorandum to Morris Ernst,

All of the so-called "trials" conducted by Russia and her satellites have been in the nature of political demonstrations, sometimes for internal purposes and sometimes for the purpose of having a calculated effect upon opinion in the Western World. It has been well said that you may believe anything you like about a political trial behind the Iron Curtain except the facts. The facts simply do not matter: the "confessions" are undeniably false, but, false or not, they have served their purpose if they have some degree of plausibility. . . . Always the pattern is the same: an abject confession aimed at discrediting some phase of internal or external opposition, followed by a trial which is merely a way of publicizing the confession. . . .

It is certainly significant, in the Vogeler-Sanders case, that shortly before the defendants were brought to trial the Hungarian Government announced that all foreign-owned enterprises, including, of course, Standard Electric Budapest, were to be nationalized immediately because, it was said, foreign representatives were engaged in espionage and sabotage. It may well be that other purposes of the Cominform were served by the trial. It is significant, for example, that following the convictions all of the Iron Curtain countries have been engaged in a process of whittling away the British and American representation, both governmental and business. Hardly a day passes but one of the satellite countries announces a trial, either of a foreigner or some of their own nationals on the same general charges. . . .

Ernst, for his part, invented a new word—"legicide"—to describe the evil of which my codefendants and I were but seven of several hundred victims, if we count, as we should count, everyone who has been tried and convicted in similar demonstration trials since 1923.

In that year, it would seem, legicide was committed for the first time in Moscow when Monsignor Buchkevitch and several other Polish priests were unlawfully tried, convicted, and executed for invoking a higher authority than that of the state. The Buchkevitch trial was widely denounced as "judicial murder," which of course it was, but that it was even more than that has been proved by scores of subsequent demonstration trials.

Just as the new crime, genocide, implies a calculated effort to obliterate a segment of society, so legicide implies a calculated effort to obliterate the law itself, which is the very essence of society.

Fifteen | My Day in Court

For two more days I rehearsed my questions and answers with No. 2. Then, on February 16, the day before the trial, we held a formal rehearsal with Olti in the presence of Alapi's assistant.

That night I was taken to see Gábor Péter, who told me that if I played my part well he would personally see to it that I was made comfortable in prison. I asked him what my sentence would be. He disclaimed any knowledge of that phase of the trial, saying it was a question that could be decided only by the court. He then went on to paint an idyllic picture of what my life in prison would be like—no more interrogations, no more interruptions of my sleep, plenty of books to read, and plenty of food to eat.

"Remember," said Péter as he dismissed me, "the way you conduct yourself at the trial will determine the sort of life you lead in prison."

I was then taken in to see his deputy, the fat colonel, whose office opened off the opposite side of the antechamber through which I had to pass to enter Péter's office. Unlike his chief, the colonel was not equipped with an executive switchboard; his desk and the windowsill behind it were cluttered with a score of telephones. Whenever one of them rang, he had to lift up several receivers before he found the one he wanted.

In between telephone calls he told me that I would be given a

207

cellmate in prison if the "proper person" could be found. It would all depend, however, on how I behaved at the trial.

Later, after being escorted back to the cell I shared with Alex in the Orpheum, the lymph glands in my neck began to swell. Alex, who feared that I might be coming down with mumps, wanted to call a doctor, but I told him not to. Secretly I hoped it would be mumps, for then, I thought, it would be impossible for me to abase myself at the trial. Unfortunately my symptoms were psychosomatic; by morning the swelling in my neck had disappeared.

Before breakfast I was taken out to be showered and shaved. On my return to the cell I found the warrant officer awaiting me with my striped black suit and a clean shirt and tie. My shoes, I noticed, had been shined and provided with laces. Alex spoke enviously of all the good food and drink that I would receive in the course of the trial. As soon as I had dressed, the warrant officer led me out into the courtyard and locked me up in a large prison van with my six codefendants.

The van, which was apparently of Russian design, looked more like a meat truck than a paddy wagon. It was divided into two sections. The forward section contained six windowless steel compartments, three on either side, in which it was possible for a prisoner to stand but not to sit. The rear section was open, with a wooden bench on either side. My five male codefendants and I were locked up in the steel compartments. Edina Dőry was allowed to sit on one of the benches with the guards. Not a word was spoken from the time we left 60 Stalin Avenue to the time the doors were opened in the courtyard of the Criminal Courts Building on Markó Street.

There we were lined up with a guard between each one of us, warned not to speak, and then marched up a back stairway to an anteroom on the fourth floor, where we were seated in a row of plain chairs facing the wall. Guards in the green uniform of the Ministry of Justice walked up and down, silently serving us sandwiches, excellent *espresso* coffee, and fairly good Hungarian brandy.

Gábor Péter presently appeared with his fat deputy. They examined each of us to make sure that we were properly dressed and "in the right frame of mind." Then, after another round of brandy, we were marched into the courtroom, arraigned before Olti and his four assistant judges, one of whom was a woman, and marched back into the anteroom. There each of us with the exception of Geiger was rewarded with another sandwich. Geiger had been held in the courtroom to be cross-examined.

It all took place so quickly that I hardly realized what had happened until Péter said to me, "I think you made a mistake." It wasn't until later that I understood what he meant. Like each of the others, I had been asked a few questions, and with one exception I had given the expected answers. The exception occurred when Olti asked, "Did you serve in the Army?"

My answer, which was broadcast by Radio Budapest and recorded by the Blue Danube Network in Vienna, was a simple "No."

My mistake was not recorded, however, in the white book subsequently issued by the Hungarian State Publishing House. According to that officially doctored version of my trial, the following imaginary interchange took place:

The President: Did you serve in the army?
Vogeler: I served in the Navy.
The President: What rank did you hold?
Vogeler: I was Lieutenant-Commander in the Reserve.

To judge from the white book, I was at one and the same time a lieutenant commander in the Navy, a colonel in the Army, an agent of the FBI, and an assistant vice-president of I.T.&T.

My codefendants and I were tried before a "criminal" rather than a "people's" court, I suppose, in order to give an illusion of legality. The fact remains that the judge, who acted as prosecutor, and the prosecutor, who acted as his assistant, behaved exactly as they had behaved in the Mindszenty and other cases tried before a "people's court." It was a distinction without a difference.

Although Péter had told me that I would be the third defendant to be cross-examined, the order was changed at the last minute for a reason that is typical of the Communist mentality. The trial began on Friday, the 17th, and lasted until Tuesday, the 21st. It was decided that, if I was examined on Saturday instead of Friday, more industrial "activists" would be free to witness the ignominy of a real, live American "Fascist Beast." Hungarian factories, to save coal, were then working on the basis of a forty-eight-hour, five-day week—nine and a half hours, Monday through Thursday, and ten hours on Friday.

Thus it was that Geiger, Radó, and Sanders were tried on Friday while I was tried on Saturday along with Domokos, Justh, and Dőry, in that order. Mrs. Zádor, Ödön Gergely, and seven other persons subsequently testified as witnesses for the prosecution. There were no witnesses for the defense; indeed, as will presently be seen, there was no defense at all. Neither I nor any of my codefendants was allowed to hear the others' testimony prior to being cross-examined. It was impossible for us to know what had previously been said against us. We were not only presumed, individually and collectively, to be guilty in every detail, we were given no opportunity to suggest that we could possibly be innocent. All the advantages were thus given to the prosecution. It was the classical game of Communists everywhere: Heads I win, tails you lose.

Each defendant was prompted by his inquisitor, who sat behind him in the dock. Péter and his fat deputy acted as stage managers throughout the entire performance. Their standing in the party hierarchy apparently depended on the success of their production.

A physician and two medical orderlies joined Péter in the

anteroom before I went on stage. The doctor was under orders, I gathered, to declare me *non compos mentis* in the event that I attempted to repudiate my confession.

"Now don't be nervous," said Péter, clucking like a mother hen. "Just answer the questions as you did at the rehearsals, and everything will be all right. As soon as it's over, you'll be made very comfortable, I promise you, and you'll never be bothered again."

The night before I was released from prison, seventeen months after my arrest, Péter gave me a copy of the white book to read. It was only then that I learned that five representatives of the American Legation, four representatives of the British Legation, and six representatives of the Anglo-American press corps had been present. I was in such a daze at the time of my trial that I was unable to discover who was in the audience, and it would probably have done me little good if I had.

Of the six American and British correspondents who were present, only one—Leo Murray, of the Manchester *Guardian*—sympathized with the defendants. The others included Mark Gayn, of the *New Republic*, a man who had been involved in the *Amerasia* affair; Peter Furst, of Reuter's, Ltd., who contributes to the Communist publication, *Masses and Mainstream;* Paul Terry of the London *Daily Worker;* Peter ("Wilfrid") Burchett, then of the *Times* of London, and now an accredited correspondent with the Chinese Communist forces in North Korea; and Alexander Kendrick of the Columbia Broadcasting System.

My face, as I testified, reminded Kendrick of a "frightened rabbit." I wonder what Kendrick's face would have looked like if our roles had been reversed. No. 2 was sitting right behind me, and I knew as I spoke that, if I deviated noticeably from the lines that I had been taught to repeat, he would immediately signal Olti, who would call a recess. No. 2, in the meantime, would contrive to make it seem that I had collapsed. The doctor and the orderlies would then rush in, and I would be carried out for the "hospital treatment" that No. 2 had so convincingly described.

Perhaps I should have tried to repudiate my confession anyhow. At the time of my trial, however, I was in no condition to do anything but recite my lines. I had been imbued with such a feeling of desolation that my one desire was to say my piece and have done with it. My voice quavered as I spoke into the microphone that was placed before me. It sounded to me like the voice of another person, and in a sense, of course, it was. It was the voice of my Svengali, No. 2.

The text of my testimony as given in the official white book differs in several places from the portions of my testimony that were broadcast over Radio Budapest and recorded by the Army in Vienna. According to the white book the following interchange took place [italics mine]:

The President: When did you first enter *military* school?

Vogeler: I entered the *U. S. Naval Academy* in 1928 and . . .

The President: For how many years did you study at this *naval* academy?

Vogeler: I was there for *four years.*

What was really said, as can be proved by the Army's recording of the broadcast portions of my testimony, was [italics mine]:

The President: When did you first enter *military* school?

Vogeler: I entered the *United States Military Academy* in 1928 and . . .

The President: For how many years did you study at this *military* academy?

Vogeler: I was there for *four years.*

Thus, as far as the audience was concerned, I had attended the Military Academy at West Point for four years—a demonstrable falsehood that I gladly repeated in the knowledge that it would tend to invalidate the rest of my fabricated testimony. Even the edited passage printed in the white book was a lie. As the reader knows, and as it can easily be proved, I attended the Naval Academy not for four years but for two and a half years, and I enrolled as midshipman not in 1928 but in 1929.

Throughout my cross-examination I used plurals like "informations" and "equipments" that do not exist in the English language. I made no effort to correct the AVH's faulty English. Neither did I make any effort to correct my intentional errors, of which the following is a typical example:

The President: For instance, do you know of any instances where such specialist physicists were smuggled out of other countries to the U. S.?

Vogeler: Yes, I know of a case of a Dr. Etzler, who was an Austrian scientist, who was smuggled out through Germany to the U. S.

Etzler was a Czechoslovakian Communist who was still in Czechoslovakia.

At no point in my testimony did I admit a single act of espionage or sabotage committed in conjunction with any agency of the United States government. I falsely admitted working for the FBI, the ODI, and the CIC. But the reader will search the white book in vain for a single example of the services that I was supposed to have performed for these organizations.

Geiger: In May 1946, in his office in Nádor Street, Ogilvie gave me a nine-point questionnaire, which dealt with questions of air transport and aerodromes. He instructed me to procure for him intelligence material based on the questionnaire.

The President: And did you procure it?

Geiger: I obtained the intelligence data, listed it according to the questionnaire, had it translated into English . . . and handed it over to Ogilvie.

The President: This is the text from which the translation was made, and here is also a copy of the English translation. Please examine it. "Subject for June 5, 1946: civil air transport, communications and shipping." Is this the letter?

Geiger: Yes.

The President: This was also seized by the State Defense Authority in the course of the investigation. I note here that, among other things, you supplied the following facts as the fourth point of the letter: "There are only empty buildings on the aerodromes of Debreczen and Szombathely which are absolutely empty, with no equipment whatsoever. Point 1: to date we have had returned to us two aerodromes, that is the ones at Debreczen and Szombathely, etc." So this was the first concrete assignment which you carried out: to report on the state of Hungarian aviation at the time, about aerodromes and their equipment, which you handed over to him?

Geiger: Yes.

The President: What other data did you supply to Ogilvie?

Geiger: I supplied Ogilvie with other intelligence information in connection with the Philips works. But apart from that, without receiving a concrete request, I regularly collected and handed over to Ogilvie material on the position of the political, economic and military conditions in Hungary. . . .

The President: Now let us discuss the American so-called Telcom-plan [*sic*].

Geiger: It was the ambition of the ISEC concern to gain control over the Hungarian post office, telephone and telegraph network in order to be able to influence Hungarian political and economic life. It was also its intention to establish a base here for its espionage and destructive activities. In the interest of this triple purpose Ogilvie brought the so-called Telcom-plan with him when he arrived. The essence of the plan was the offer of the ITT concern to rebuild the Hungarian post office, telephone and telegraph network with the proviso that while the loan was being repaid—estimated at roughly a period of ten years—the work of the Hungarian post office would be supervised by an American committee. In the interest of the realisation [*sic*] of this Telcom-plan, and on the instructions of the concern, I took the necessary steps together with Ogilvie at the Ministry of Transport [Communications]; later, when the plan was rejected by the Ministry, I took indirect steps to realise the plan both on Ogilvie's orders and independently from him. . . .

I remember recruiting Kelemen Domokos, head of the Standard factory bookkeeping department [sic] at the beginning of 1947 so that I could satisfactorily carry out Pinkney's espionage and sabotage directives, and to pass them on to others. I knew that Domokos was of Swabian origin and of Anglo-Saxon orientation and also knew that he would carry out the espionage and sabotage work given him. He was, in fact, a considerable help in the espionage and sabotage work.

The President: What data did you collect with his assistance?

Geiger: He procured intelligence material on factories under the aegis of the Commercial Bank, in the first place on the Tungsram and Orion factories; it was he who collected [sic] about the banks that were to be nationalised. . . .

The President: What material did he obtain on the factories mentioned by you, which are of great importance to Hungarian production?

Geiger: The data which he obtained on these factories partly concerned their productive capacity, number of workers employed, partly the stock of orders, and future plans.

The President: Did Pinkney give you specific directives as to the collection of information about these factories?

Geiger: He gave specific instructions, because he was in the first place interested in telecommunication companies.

The President: Did you continue to prepare the monthly reports during Pinkney's stay here?

Geiger: As he was ailing at that time, I prepared them in May, June, and July and after signature gave them to Pinkney at his office in Nádor Street.

The President: When?

Geiger: In May, June and July of 1948.

The President: Here is a copy of the May report. Was this it? (*He holds it up.*)

Geiger: Yes.

The President: So that was it. These reports contain a whole series of absolute figures. For instance: figures showing that industrial investment had considerably risen in the previous two months of April and May, that altogether 16.5 million forints [florins] were spent on the reorganization and rebuilding of the mines, and about 18 million on the electrical power station of Mátravidék. How capital investment of 18.3 million was spent on other electrical power stations instead of the 13 million originally appropriated. How did you get hold of these absolute facts?

Geiger: Partly through my personal contacts in the economic field, and partly through the authorities . . .

The President: That is from officials?

Geiger: Yes, from officials.

The President: From persons whose official sphere of work covered these questions?

Geiger: Yes.

The President: Here is, for instance, the enclosure with the sign 1/10. Here, for instance, you supply data on the railway [telegraph] system's three year plan. The attached drawing . . . Did you also send drawings?

Geiger: Yes.

The President: This drawing shows the long-distance [telegraph] equipment. "Under the Three Year Plan the following railway lines will be built: Budapest-Hatvan, Budapest-Szolnok, Budapest-Székesfehervár. The following facts about the railway [telegraph] network are included: the railway signalling equipment, signal and communication equipment, the telegraph network, local and short distance network, and telephone and long-distance telephone network." Then follows the detailed description of the five networks.

Geiger: These are all details of the three year plan of the Hungarian State Railways, whose three year plan I procured and handed over to Pinkney in its entirety.

The President: In its entirety. They were facts which were not made public.

Geiger: Yes.

The President: As these are confidential facts and significant to national defense, it is of great importance from the point of view of the vulnerability of the respective networks where these critical points are [sic]. So you acquired this knowledge and sent it out through Pinkney. How long did Pinkney stay in Budapest and who succeeded him?

Geiger: Pinkney stayed in Budapest until November 1948, when he was relieved by Vogeler on the instructions of Colonel Behn, the head of the concern.

The President: Now please say something about Vogeler, about his person, how you met him, when you met him, and who this Vogeler is; what do you know about him and what directives did you receive from him?

Geiger: I met Robert Vogeler some time before the war when he was sent to Budapest by the concern. After the war Vogeler became the American representative at the Standard factory in Vienna, and came to Hungary during the years 1946-47 and 1948 and more frequently in 1949; from February 1949 onwards he became the American representative at the Budapest Standard factory. I heard about Vogeler from his predecessors Ogilvie and Pinkney that he served in American intelligence organs [sic] during the war and continued his espionage work also after the war. He himself told me that he was a member of the American Secret Service [sic] and in this capacity often travelled in Central and Eastern Europe. When Vogeler came to Budapest for the second time with Colonel Behn in November 1948, I gave him the monthly intelligence reports for September and October, afterwards prepared these intelligence reports regularly on my own as ordered by him, and handed them over to him usually at his office in Nádor Street.

The President: Since the order received from Colonel Behn in October 1948 at the Gellért, you prepared these monthly reports yourself then already as general director of the company?

Geiger: Yes.

The President: In the office?

Geiger: No, at my flat.

The President: So that no one should know about it?

Geiger: Yes. The instruction was that we should be increasingly careful, on one hand because of the very important facts contained in the reports and, on the other hand, because of investigations held in the factory and the arrest following.

The President: So you had instructions to prepare the monthly report yourself and hand it to him personally?

Geiger: Yes.

The President: Did you not keep a copy afterwards?

Geiger: No, I had to give the copy to Vogeler.

The President: How many copies of it?

Geiger: Five copies.

Geiger had helped me, as he had helped my predecessors, Pinkney and Ogilvie, to prepare monthly reports on the Hungarian economy with special reference to developments affecting the future of Standard, Dial, and Telefongyár. The reports were prepared in quintuplicate, and one copy of each was in the court's possession. How did the court obtain a copy of each and every one of these "secret" reports? As Morris Ernst, if he had been allowed to defend me, would surely have pointed out, the reports were obtained by the simple process of seizing ISEC's files in its office on Nádor Street. The reports were the usual monthly reports that every subsidiary of ISEC was required to send to the parent company in New York. There was nothing secret about them. The information they contained was indispensable to any company that hoped to continue profitable operations in Hungary. Would we, if we had been spies, have made *five copies* of our monthly reports, and kept one of each on file?

That we should have collected information about the airports at Debreczen and Szombathely may, at first glance, strike some readers as suspicious. May I remind such readers of the following demonstrable facts? In May, 1946, when the information was collected, Hungary, a defeated power, was jointly occupied by Russia, Britain, and the United States. It had no military secrets to conceal. Furthermore, Ernö Gerö (alias Singer), the Communist Minister of Communications, had officially requested ISEC to submit a bid for the installation of landing equipment.

How could we have submitted a bid without informing ourselves as to the conditions that prevailed at both of these civilian airports?

As for the "intelligence" that we collected about the Hungarian communications network, Ernst, if he had been permitted to defend me, would have submitted the following cablegrams as exhibits:

The first, dated February 28, 1947, was from Pinkney to Behn in New York. It read:

IN CONVERSATION TODAY WITH MINISTER OF COMMUNICATIONS WE DISCUSSED TELECOM PLAN. HE INDICATED HIS PREFERENCE FOR OUR PROPOSAL TO THAT OF OTHERS AND SAID IT WAS HIS OPINION THAT BEST . . . PROCEDURE WOULD BE FOR ITT TO INVITE HIM TO VISIT COMPANY IN NEW YORK IN ORDER TO DISCUSS REHABILITATION AND MODERNIZATION OF TELEPHONE NETWORK TOGETHER WITH RE-FINANCING AND POSSIBILITY OF TECHNICAL CONTRACT. MINISTER PLANS TO ATTEND INTERNATIONAL COMMUNICATIONS MEETING TO BE HELD IN ATLANTIC CITY. . . . HE BELIEVES TRIP SHOULD ALSO BE OCCASION TO REACH AGREEMENT WITH US. HE STATED THAT UPON RECEIPT OF YOUR INVITATION HE WOULD PLACE IT BEFORE COUNCIL OF MINISTERS AND WOULD EXPECT TO OBTAIN APPROVAL FROM COUNCIL TO NEGOTIATE WITH YOU. I WAS GIVEN COPIES OF PLANS DRAWN UP BY [POST TELEPHONE AND TELEGRAPH SYSTEM] COVERING PROGRAMS OVER A THREE-YEAR AND ALSO OVER A TEN-YEAR PERIOD. THESE WILL BE SENT TO YOU AS SOON AS TRANSLATED. PLEASE AIR-MAIL LIST OF STATISTICAL DATA YOU WILL REQUIRE TO ENABLE YOU TO MAKE THE STUDY FORESEEN UNDER TELECOM PLAN SO THESE CAN BE COLLECTED AND FORWARDED TO YOU PROMPTLY. . . .

The second cablegram was from Sosthenes Behn to Ernö Gerö. It read:

THE INTERNATIONAL TELEPHONE AND TELEGRAPH CORPORATION HAS THROUGH REPRESENTATIVES DISCUSSED WITH YOUR EXCELLENCY

THE MATTER OF REHABILITATION MODERNIZATION AND EXPANSION
OF THE HUNGARIAN TELECOMMUICATIONS SYSTEM. WE FEEL THAT
THE MATTER MIGHT BE EXPEDITED TO THE SATISFACTION OF THE
HUNGARIAN GOVERNMENT IF WE COULD DISCUSS THE MATTER WITH
YOU PERSONALLY. I UNDERSTAND THAT YOU ARE CONSIDERING AT-
TENDING THE WORLD TELECOMMUNICATIONS CONFERENCE TO BE
HELD AT ATLANTIC CITY STARTING MAY 15 AND I DESIRE TO SUGGEST
THAT YOU AVAIL YOURSELF OF THAT OPPORTUNITY TO DISCUSS THE
WHOLE MATTER WITH US INCLUDING ITS FINANCING. . . .

Among the other documents that Gerö gave to Pinkney, and
which Pinkney forwarded to New York, was a map of the Hungarian telecommunications system. The same map was later reprinted in a propaganda leaflet issued by the Ministry of Education. Other copies of the same map are on file in every major
telephone exchange throughout the world. Yet I was to be convicted of espionage because Pinkney sent the map to New York
along with other documents supplied him by Gerö, Rákosi's heir
apparent as Stalin's viceroy of Hungary.

The President: Now just in brief, so we can see just with a few
examples, what sort of material did you get from the various agents?
Take for instance Imre Geiger. What sort of material did you receive
from him?

Vogeler: From Imre Geiger I received the monthly reports from
the Standard which gave a survey . . . a monthly survey of political, economic, financial and military changes in Hungary. Further
through his connections with official organisations [sic] I received
information regarding the organisation of various industries. . . .

The President: Did you, for instance, receive data from Geiger on
the possibilities of manufacturing military pilot microphones?

Vogeler: Yes, I questioned Geiger on products that were of a military nature, I mentioned to him pilot throat microphones and also
military radio equipment. . . .

The President: Among the written material of the trial are proofs that at one stage you showed Geiger in your office at Nádor Street a plan of the Tungsram works?

Vogeler: That is to . . .

The President: From whom did you receive this photostat copy?

Vogeler: In October, one day I was sitting with Colonel Kraft who was present . . . who was then military attaché at the Legation, and Air Attaché Griffin showed me the photostat of the Tungsram factory. . . .

The photostat referred to was a photostat of an "artist's conception" printed on the back of an advertising brochure that was freely distributed to the public at the Budapest Trade Fair in September, 1949. Pál Aschner, the president of Tungsram, was an old friend of Colonel Behn's, and he was justly proud of his newly reconstructed plant. Since the brochure was exhausted by the time I arrived in Budapest, I borrowed a copy which I had had photostated to send to Behn in New York. Neither Kraft nor Major Griffin had anything to do with my decision to photostat a published non-technical drawing, which was far from being a "plan." I knew that Colonel Behn would be interested because I.T.&T., together with the General Electric Corporation, owned a block of stock in Tungsram, a company that Aschner had founded with American assistance in a successful effort to break the old German-Swedish light-bulb monopoly.

One day at lunch, in the spring of 1949, Aschner invited Scudder, Cooke, and me to visit the factory to see what he had done. We obtained the necessary permits from the government and were given a two-hour escorted tour through the factory grounds. Among the other "military secrets" that we were shown were the landscaped picnic grounds that Aschner had provided for his workers and a Rube Goldberg device for making the glass envelopes that enclose the filaments of light bulbs. The machine was interesting only as an example of clever improvisation; in

point of fact it was a crude adaptation of a better machine produced in the United States.

Our authorized visit to a factory that was partly owned by
I.T.&T. was in no way illegal. No. 2, however, to make it seem
that the crime of espionage had been committed, forced me to
admit that we had spied out "military secrets" in the course of
our visit. Hence my reference to pilot throat microphones. Tungsram, like Standard Budapest, was manufacturing throat microphones for the Russian Air Force. Standard, in fact, had supplied
Tungsram with the necessary drawings, for the instruments in
question were identical to those that Standard had been forced
to manufacture for the Germans during the war. So much for
the "secrecy" involved in Tungsram's manufacture of outmoded
German throat microphones.

The President: Erzsébet Blum left the country illegally. Did you
and Vogeler have any share in helping Erzsébet Blum leave the country illegally?

Geiger: Yes. In May 1949, Vogeler instructed me to secure permission from Zoltán Radó, that is, to get a passport for Dr. Erzsébet
Blum, official of the Standard works. He requested this, because I
had informed him of Miss Blum's abilities as well as her political
attitude and after this he thought they could make good use of her
in the London factory. Later I received instructions from Vogeler,
after the passport was ready, to secure permission, again from Radó,
to enable Blum to take with her certain blueprints and espionage
material, secret documents. . . .

The President: For example, what documents did she take with
her?

Geiger: Among these the most important one was the detailed map
of the telephone network of the Hungarian Postal Services, which is
very important from a military point of view, for its use during a
war might cause heavy damage to the Hungarian State.

The President: So she took this out with her. This map obviously
comprised material treated with the strictest confidence.

Geiger: Definitely.

The President: For instance you at the enterprise also handled this confidentially.

Geiger: Most confidentially.

It would have been comic if poor Geiger's life had not been at stake. The map he referred to as "the most important" of the "secret documents" that Erzsébet Blum had taken to London—with the express permission of the government—was the very map that Gerö had given to Pinkney to forward to Behn in New York and which, as I have explained, was on file in every major telephone exchange throughout the world.

Erzsébet Blum left Hungary legally, not illegally, as the dialogue itself reveals. She was a member in good standing, moreover, of the Hungarian Communist Party. Neither I nor Radó had anything to do with her trip. The plans and drawings that she took with her were either her own property or the property of Standard Budapest. None belonged to the Hungarian government, none was a military secret, and the map, as it happens, was *not* among them. The documents were itemized on an official list in Dr. Blum's possession, a list that was stamped and signed by responsible Communist officials, and which, if Ernst had been permitted to defend me, he would have submitted as proof of the absurdity of the prosecution's case. He would also have submitted the following deposition, freely sworn to by Dr. Blum in London:

The sole reason for my visit to England was because the Hungarian Government were pressing Standard Budapest to manufacture transmitter [tubes], because it had delivered to them transmitters with foreign-made [tubes] and they were anxious that they should be manufactured in our own factory. It was therefore decided that I should be sent to London to get manufacturing information. . . . The only papers of any sort which I brought were blueprints (all of them old issues dating back from periods between 1943-47) of items on which we needed up-to-date information. . . . These documents were stamped by the Directorate of Light Electrical Industry, and were read and signed either by Bíró or Nádas of that [directorate], who were the engineers who normally checked such papers. . . .

When I left Hungary there was no thought that I would not be returning. My exit was quite legal in every way and known to everybody. It had not occurred to me that I might want to stay in England, and I came only with two small handbags. I had a home of my own for the first time in years, a good job, and a good salary —more than I needed for my simple wants. It was only after I was here and realized what life meant here and that in England was the real democratic way of life, that I decided that I could do no good by returning, and announced to Mr. Cooke and Mr. Wibmer of Standard London that I wished to make application to stay here. . . . The Standard people in London were shocked and told me I must go back—that if I tried to stay they would not help me and they would not give me a job. . . . I did not receive any instructions from Mr. Vogeler or Mr. Scudder. . . . I feel they did not even want me to come, and I certainly had no discussions with them. . . .

I did not bring with me any map of any sort. I have never seen such a map. . . .

There was more, much more, of the same sort of testimony. The only "evidence" against us was the "evidence" that we were forced to give against ourselves. Dates and names were confused, and individuals and organizations were mistakenly identified. The prosecution's case was presented in such a slovenly manner that, even if we had been guilty, we would have been able, in a true court of justice, to win a dismissal by proving that we could not possibly have committed the crimes of which we were accused when, as, and how the prosecution said that we had committed them.

This is what it must have been like during the French Revolution, I thought, as I listened to the cross-examination of Domokos, Justh, and Dőry. The facts were unimportant. All that mattered was that each of us should be convicted on the basis of his own false testimony. Every now and then, as one of the defendants "unmasked" himself, the Communists in the audience would sigh and groan and cry, "For shame," whereupon Olti would rap his gavel and warn them against further "demonstrations," which continued to occur in response to the obvious cues embedded in the testimony.

On Monday, February 20, Péter belied his previous assertions by revealing that he had known all along the sentences that each of us, by the grace of Stalin, would receive. Geiger and Radó, he told me, would be sentenced to death. Sanders and I would be sentenced, respectively, to thirteen and fifteen years in prison. Domokos and Justh would be given ten years and Dőry five.

"Oh, don't take it so hard," said Péter as I buried my head in my hands. "You'll get time off for good behavior. Look at me! I once spent nine years in prison."

Even No. 2, who had spent seven years in prison, tried to comfort me when I was taken to his office to prepare my final plea. "Our leader, Mátyás Rákosi," he said, "spent fifteen years in prison, and look at him now! He's the boss of Hungary."

I was so despondent that No. 2 had to write my final plea himself.

"I am sincerely sorry," I intoned in court the next day, "for the subversive activities that I carried on against the People's Democracy of Hungary. Especially as I was sent here from a big country, America, to Hungary, a small country, to interfere and undermine its efforts in rebuilding and rehabilitating itself from the effects of war. I wish to avail myself of the privilege of the last word to state that I gave testimony freely and openly, without coercion or maltreatment. . . . I would like to state that I have been treated correctly and fairly throughout the investigation and my trial. I hope that my testimony will serve in some small measure to show the remorse I feel at my guilt. I know that I must be punished, but I hope that the Court will consider my plea for clemency, and also the defense that was put up for me by my attorney when it passes judgment on me."

Every word, as usual, was a lie. I was not sorry for the subversive activities that I had not carried on against a tyranny that was anything but a "people's democracy." I had testified neither freely nor openly, I had been treated neither correctly nor fairly, I had been subjected to every form of coercion, and I felt no hope of any sort.

As for "my" attorney, Imre Bárd, that paunchy hypocrite "defended" me as follows:

Honoured Court, Honoured President!

After the statement of the State Prosecutor and the Defense speeches of my colleagues, I consider nearly superfluous on my part to point out that it is Anglo-American capitalist imperialism that sits in the dock, that sends its spies and destructive agents to us. Indeed there hardly exist words adequate to express the indignation felt over the meanness of those who, in order to impede the magnificent constructive efforts of the people of a peaceful country, support institutions of espionage. . . .

The defense realises all this and is aware of the difficulties of its task in defending the spies, the destructive agents, sent here from the countries mentioned. But the defense is fully up to the demands of its profession. We must not hesitate for a moment in fulfilling our constitutional task and we stand fully by the principle that without any generalisation, everybody is responsible only for his own crimes, that without any generalisation no one may be punished with a penalty different from that for the violation of the Law that he himself commits. . . .

In the defense of Robert Vogeler I do not have to deal with anything else but his person: that is with the criminal acts committed by Robert Vogeler [who] has penitently and fully confessed to committing this criminal act. The accomplices of the accused testified against him in their confessions in which they accused themselves, too. The unprejudiced testimonies of the witnesses have confirmed this. The documents produced by the prosecution and presented at the trial have proved all this. Far be it from me that under such tremendous, and I should say absolute weight of evidence, I should even attempt to prove the accused innocent of the crime. . . .

Human feelings started to awake in Robert Vogeler when he sincerely and contritely repented the criminal act committed by him. It is possible, and surely it is so, that one of the aims of punishment is reprisal, but we must not forget that the human basis of the whole modern criminal law is to correct. Vogeler, a spy who failed, will no longer be employed by the U.S. as a spy and it is not likely that he would ever entertain the idea of continuing this trade, which cannot be enough condemned. I trust, Honoured Court, that holding in view the principles of both punishment and correction you will find the measure for the punishment of this defendant. I am also confident that the Honoured Court will give evidence of its high human conception in this case, too, by giving an opportunity to this young man to be at some time a useful member of society, doing honest work.

Sixteen | How I Served My Time

Tuesday evening, after being sentenced, we were herded into the van and driven to a former army barracks that was then being used as a training school for non-commissioned officers of the AVH. Sanders and I were locked up in cells on the second floor of the south wing of the old two-story barracks. Our male Hungarian codefendants were imprisoned on the floor below us. What happened to Edina Dőry and Mrs. Zádor I was never able to learn. A month later two other male prisoners—Gergely and Kozma, I believe—were incarcerated on the first floor, making eight of us in all.

A few minutes after Sanders and I had been locked up, Gábor Péter and his fat deputy paid us each a visit. I had assumed it was Sanders who occupied the other cell because Sandy was the only one of us who wore shoes with crepe rubber soles. I knew it was Sanders the moment I heard him say to Péter, "*Guten Abend, Herr General.*"

A little later my own door was unlocked and in stepped Péter, followed by his uniformed deputy. Péter had no trouble squeezing through the low and narrow doorway, but the colonel was so ungainly that he bumped his head painfully on the lintel as he entered. He took off his cap and stood there rubbing his bald head as he translated Péter's remarks into German. Bárd had appealed my sentence, Péter said, and in due course the Supreme

Court of the Hungarian People's Republic would review my conviction. In the meantime he would do his best to find a "suitable" cellmate for me.

"What about Sanders?" I asked.

"He wouldn't be suitable," said Péter, changing the subject by patting the mattress on my bunk. "You see?" he said. "I always keep my word. I told you that you'd be given a comfortable cell."

If there was anything I wanted, he explained, I had only to knock twice on the steel door, pointing to the left if I wanted to go to the toilet, and pointing to the right if I wanted to speak to the agent who supervised the guards. The agent, he said, would transmit to him any written requests that I wanted to make and, if my requests were reasonable, he would see that they were granted. And with that he nodded and left the cell, followed by the fat colonel, who was still rubbing the bump on his head.

My cell measured ten feet by seven. It contained a bunk, a table, and a chair, each cemented into the floor, and a small cabinet bolted into the wall. There was no plumbing—not even a slop can—and so I had to knock on the door whenever it was necessary to visit the toilet and washroom at the end of the corridor. Once a week I would be shaved and showered and once a month the barber would cut my hair.

A small barred window, covered on the inside with a heavy wire grille, was my only source of daylight. The usual electric light was kept burning at all times, and at night two searchlights were trained on the wing of the barracks in which my companions and I were imprisoned. Later, as an additional precaution, a spotlight was set up in the courtyard and trained on the barred window of my cell. The light was so bright that it projected the external bars onto the ceiling. It was months before I grew accustomed to the weird effect.

At the foot of my bunk was a tile stove, fed with briquettes from the corridor, which was fired on winter mornings and which kept me warm until the middle of the afternoon. By evening, however, I was often so cold that I had to go to bed.

Only once in fourteen months was I removed from my cell for more than an hour or two at a time. It was during the second winter of my imprisonment. Several tiles in the stove became loose and I was almost suffocated by smoke. I was transferred to the next cell on my left, in the opposite direction from Sandy, until some masons had rebuilt the stove, whereupon I was returned to my original cell.

The wooden slats of my bunk were covered, as Péter had remarked, with a thin hair mattress. The bedclothing consisted of two cotton-flannel blankets and a rough canvas sheet, which was changed in theory (but only in theory) once a month. My jailers never tired of commenting on their liberality in permitting me to sleep on a mattress covered with a "sheet." It was an unheard-of luxury, it seemed, in Hungary's political prisons.

Sanders and I were never once permitted to see or talk to one another. Our cells were separated by an intervening cell that was used as an office by the agents in charge. Even they and the guards were not supposed to speak to one another, except when necessary, and then they whispered in Hungarian. I was never able to determine whether this regime of silence was a part of our punishment or merely a precaution designed to prevent us from corrupting the prison staff. I suspect that the latter was the more important consideration, for, as I shall presently explain, several attempts would be made to enlist one or another of the guards in an effort to help me to escape.

During the three months that I was confined at 60 Stalin Avenue, Alex and I were given an hour of exercise ("to put color in my cheeks") on three successive days before my trial. At the

barracks my fellow prisoners and I were exercised for thirty to
forty minutes every other day except when it rained. We were
always exercised alone and were never permitted to speak. I
could usually tell which of my fellow prisoners was being exercised, however, by the way he walked. Sanders walked very
rapidly on his crepe rubber soles; Geiger walked very slowly on
leather heels that produced, until they were worn out, a distinct
clacking sound; Radó shuffled; and Father Justh, who had been
an army officer before he became a priest, walked with a military
gait. Domokos was the only other prisoner, but he was seldom
exercised and then only for a few minutes at a time; perhaps he
was too ill to take much exercise. On sunny days I could identify
the others not only by the way they walked but by the frequency
with which their shadows crossed the patch of light reflected on
the ceiling of my cell. Prisoners, I discovered, quickly learn to
make use of all their senses. My own powers of perception were
much more acute than they had ever been before.

The barracks occupied an entire block that was surrounded
by a high stone wall. Inside the enclosure were several court-
yards, each separated by similar stone walls. One courtyard was
used for drills and soccer games by the AVH men who were
being trained in other parts of the building. The main entrance
faced a landscaped courtyard, with plots of grass and a single
chestnut tree, in which we were exercised whenever it was inconvenient to use the courtyard surrounding the prison wing.
I noticed that we were never exercised in the prison courtyard
when any construction work was going on, apparently for fear
that we might be able to receive communications from the
workers on nearby roofs. Once, I remember, I was immediately
removed the moment a chimney sweep appeared. I was sorry not
to have been able to watch him, for in Europe it is supposed to
be lucky to see and be seen by a chimney sweep.

At either end of the prison courtyard was a tower occupied
by guards armed with tommy guns. Depending on the whim of

the agents who accompanied me, I was permitted to walk in an oval at one end or the other. One agent stood in the center of the oval and the other at the end beyond which I was not allowed to walk.

Of the two, I preferred the northern oval, which was longer. It consisted of sixty-four paces, and I was able to make a complete circuit every thirty-nine seconds. I timed myself by repeating the gunner's chorus that I had learned as a midshipman at the Naval Academy: "If I weren't a gunner, I wouldn't be here. Ready. Aim. Fire!" According to Navy tradition, it took exactly five seconds to complete the chorus, and I usually managed to complete each circuit just before I whispered the eighth "Fire!" I had to repeat the chorus in a whisper, for every time I was heard talking to myself the agents would threaten me with punishment.

To keep from going crazy, I whispered an average of a hundred prayers a day. I calculated the number of days that I had been alive and decided that I owed at least that many prayers to God, Whom I had too often ignored in the thirty-eight years preceding my arrest.

I also worked out Euclid's plane geometry in my head, as I imagined that Euclid had done himself. I had to do it in my head because I was allowed no writing materials except as a special favor. Once a month I was allowed to write a one-page letter to my wife. I was also allowed to address occasional requests to Gábor Péter, and every now and then, as I shall explain, I had to answer certain lists of questions.

Once I secreted a bit of paper on which I drew up an annual calendar, but I was later forced to surrender it. Thereafter I calculated the days and seasons by observing the angle of the sun's rays as they struck the wall of my cell. It was not difficult to check my calculations by comparing them with the Catholic church bells that still rang three times every Sunday.

Beyond the north end of the courtyard was a large building

with a red tile roof that I took to be an old tobacco factory. Beyond the west wall I could see the chimney pots of a row of
tenement houses on the opposite side of the street. At night,
when the wind was right, I would hear switch engines shunting
cars along the Danube waterfront. Every morning and evening,
and three times on Sundays, I heard the bells of what I assume
was the Ferenczváros Church. On all but one Sunday, in addition
to the church bells, I heard a xylophonist practicing in one of
the tenements across the street. He was not a very good musi-
cian, but I enjoyed listening to him, and I felt especially sad on
the one Sunday that he failed to practice.

The name of our prison was a carefully guarded secret. On
my return to the United States, however, I was able to establish
its location on a prewar map of Budapest. It had once been
known as the Maria Theresa Barracks.

The food at the barracks was not too bad. I was served meat—
usually pork—three times a week. Every morning for breakfast
I was served ersatz coffee with boiled milk and a white roll. My
only utensils were a mess kit and a soft pewter spoon. The spoon
was so flexible that I had to hold it by the bowl in order to prevent the handle from bending double.

My weight leveled off at approximately 130 pounds—forty
pounds under normal. I soon began to suffer from pyorrhea, as
well as constipation, and before long a number of gumboils
formed in my mouth. One day a physician was called in to
lance the largest of my gumboils. He performed the operation
so badly that I never complained again. From then on I treated
myself by massaging my gums with my fingers. My American
toothbrush had worn out and the Hungarian toothbrush that I
had been given to replace it was worse than no toothbrush at
all. Its bristles came out in tufts. I was also given some tooth
powder, but it was so full of sand that I used it only once.

I was issued a package of stale American cigarettes, but no
matches, every other day. The cigarettes were Philip Morrises,

the only American brand distributed by the Hungarian tobacco monopoly. Before I could receive another package, I had to surrender the twenty butts that I had already smoked. This precaution, I suppose, was intended to prevent me from committing suicide by eating my cigarettes.

In the entire seventeen months of my imprisonment, I was not once permitted to see a single newspaper or magazine in any language or to learn of a single event that had occurred since the day of my arrest. I learned of the war in Korea, for example, only after I had been released. I also learned that Debe, my first wife, had died while I was in prison.

I had repeatedly asked for a Bible, but it was not until September, 1950, that I received one—a small volume published by Oxford University for the British and Foreign Bible Society. During the first three months of my imprisonment, despite my repeated requests, I was given nothing whatever to read. In May, however, following No. 2's second visit to the barracks, I was given several books by Dickens—the first volume of *Dombey and Son,* the first and third volumes of *David Copperfield,* and *Oliver Twist* and *The Pickwick Papers* complete. I was also allowed to read a French translation of Tolstoy's collected short stories and an English translation of Gogol's *Dead Souls,* complete with a happy ending supplied by somebody else. Other books that I was allowed to read included Shaw's *Man and Superman,* Galsworthy's *Forsyte Saga,* Louis Bromfield's *The Rains Came,* the second volume of Molière's collected plays and, for comic relief, the collected wartime speeches of J. V. Stalin.

Although I read *Pickwick* two or three times, the other novels of Dickens, especially *Oliver Twist,* were so depressing that I could read them only once. The Bible, in spite of certain depressing chapters, gave me the greatest solace of all. I now know that, if I were marooned on a desert island, the Bible is the one book above all others that I would most like to possess.

I also received, after months of waiting, a deck of playing cards and a cheap Czechoslovakian fountain pen. I was allowed to keep the cards in my cell (they were counted at regular intervals) but the agents kept the pen and allowed me to use it only for the purpose of answering questionnaires. I was never given more than two or three sheets of paper at a time, and I was required to surrender as many sheets as I had been given. It was in vain that I pleaded for scratch paper with which to work out mathematical formulas as a means of recreation. My jailers obviously feared that if I were allowed to keep any paper I would contrive to smuggle notes either to my fellow prisoners or to my friends outside. Nor was I allowed to engage in leatherwork, as I desired, or any other form of handicraft. It was apparently forbidden to let me have any tools.

I received exactly six visits during the fourteen months that I was confined in the Maria Theresa Barracks. In March, May, and September, 1950, it was my second inquisitor, No. 2, who came to see me. No. 2, on his first visit, asked me to identify some of the defendants in the Plocek trial in Prague. When I had convinced him that I was unable to do so, he then asked me to write him a history of ISEC's negotiations with the Czechoslovakian government.

I asked him if the Supreme Court had acted on my appeal, but he told me that only four weeks had elapsed and that the court seldom acted before the end of the sixth week. I also asked him if I had received any letters. He shook his head, saying that my mail was obviously being "censored" by the American authorities in Austria.

On his second visit, No. 2 asked me to write everything I knew about the methods and organization of the American police. I obliged him with as nonsensical a dissertation on the subject as my layman's mind could devise. I again asked him if I had received any letters and if any action had been taken on my appeal. He told me to forget about letters, that I would never receive any; and as for my appeal, he said, I would be officially notified the moment any action was taken.

My appeal was rejected, as I later learned, in May. But I was never informed of its rejection by the Hungarian authorities. In September, when No. 2 again came to visit me, he gave me to understand that the Supreme Court was still considering my case. I am at a loss to explain the reluctance of the AVH to let me know the truth.

I had long since given up any hope of receiving letters, but I was still hopeful of being allowed to have a cellmate. No. 2, however, informed me that it had been decided not to let me have one after all.

On his third visit, he asked me to provide him with a list of all the people I had ever known in Hungary. I took my revenge by drawing up a list of all the Hungarian Communists I could think of, most of whom I had never even met.

In October, 1950, a polite young man, who later turned out to be Gábor Péter's new interpreter, questioned me on the subject of wire tapping. It was something that neither of us knew very much about. He also asked me to tell him everything I knew about "stereophonics." I had never heard the word before, and neither, I gathered, had he. But I told him what I had done, as an engineer, to improve the quality of sound transmission, and he was apparently satisfied. It was only after I returned to the United States that I learned what his question about stereophonics meant. The AVH was apparently interested in learning how to listen in on telephone conversations without actually tapping wires. The Russians, I gathered, hadn't yet learned how.

The warrant officer from the Orpheum, who had been promoted to the rank of second lieutenant, was the deputy commandant of the Maria Theresa Barracks. One day in December, 1950, he escorted me downstairs to the conference room to meet a man whom he identified only as "the major." The major turned out to be the swarthy man with the two missing fingers who had always been present at my audiences with Péter. He spoke to me in German with a heavy Russian accent, from which I concluded that he was a major of the MGB rather than the AVH.

"Have you adjusted yourself to your new life?" he asked. I merely shrugged. "Good," he said, squeezing my shoulder as if we were old buddies.

"There comes a time," he continued, "when you can no longer live in the hope that you will eventually be released. You should realize now that your country can do nothing for you. You must therefore adopt a new philosophy of life."

I must have grimaced, for he said, "Oh, I know it's hard to be a prisoner, but you are not alone. There are millions of prisoners all over the world. You should make use of your time to study."

"How can I study," I asked, "when I haven't been given any textbooks?"

I had repeatedly asked for books on mathematics and physics, but none had been forthcoming.

"When you go back to your cell," the major said, "write another list of the books you want and send it to the general. I'll see that you get them. Ask for books on foreign languages, too. It's always useful to know another language. Rákosi studied languages when he was in prison. You ought to do the same."

After a few more pleasantries, the major came to the point of his visit. Russian DP's, he said, were being smuggled back into Russia as American agents. He wanted me to tell him who they were and how they were getting into Russia. I was pleased to know that the MGB was worried about the problem, but it was something about which I was entirely ignorant, and so my answers were of little value. I hinted, however, that many of our agents had disguised themselves as members of the MVD-MGB.

In February, 1951, the sixth and final visitor appeared. He was one of the captains from 60 Stalin Avenue. He brought me a list of naturalized Hungarians who were believed to have returned to Hungary as American agents and asked me to identify as many as I could. I recognized none of the names on the captain's list, but one of them, I recall, was Schultz. I told him that Schultz was a well-known gangster whose cover name was "Dutch."

I do not know to what use, if any, my answers to such questions were put, but I hope that at least some of them led the Cominform astray.

Seventeen | Lucile Appeals for Help

On February 23, 1950, two days after I had been convicted and sentenced, Fish Karpe was murdered while traveling from Vienna to Paris on the Arlberg Express.

Captain Karpe had been recalled from Bucharest shortly before my trial, and had stopped off in Budapest and Vienna on his way to Washington to see if he could arrange for my escape. Always a Scarlet Pimpernel, he had the romantic notion that it might be possible for a group of anti-Communists to rescue me and my codefendants by breaking into our prison at night. My third cigarette lighter, which Fish had borrowed from Lucile, and which was found on his mangled body in the Pass Lüg Tunnel, was to have been used as a recognition piece in carrying out my rescue.

During the nine days that he spent in Vienna, Karpe consulted numerous agents and double agents, and whoever murdered him must have done so at the orders of persons whose duty it was to frustrate his plan. Otherwise it is difficult to account for the telephone call that Lucile received the day after Karpe was murdered.

At intervals all morning the same woman called, only to hang up after asking Anton Brugger, our new house man, whether she had been given the right number. Finally, when Lucile answered the telephone, the woman asked, "Have you heard about your friend?"

"Yes."

"Well, you'd better keep his fate in mind if you want to see your husband again."

Lucile received a number of such anonymous telephone calls, all of them to the effect that, if she wanted to see me again, she should do nothing that would embarrass the Cominform.

The rumor that Karpe was drunk and had fallen out of his compartment as the Arlberg Express went through the tunnel was a libel. He was not drinking at the time, because of gout, and he was completely sober in the dining car before his death. The CIC experimented with sandbags of the same weight as Karpe (200 pounds) and thus confirmed, beyond any possibility of doubt, that he had been thrown from his compartment. His body caromed off the side of the tunnel and fell beneath the wheels of the train. In order to achieve the same result with a sandbag, it was necessary for two CIC agents to hurl it out of a similar compartment with all the force at their command.

Fish Karpe was a fun-loving bachelor who had enjoyed considerable success as a ladies' man. He had often traveled between Bucharest, Budapest, and Vienna on the Orient section of the Arlberg Express and he told Lucile that on several trips he had met the same Hungarian blonde. He had met her again on his last trip to Vienna, and as usual she was on her way to Paris. Fish had made a date to meet her there on his way through to Washington. It was impossible, given the AVH's passport regulations, for anyone, even an attractive blonde, to travel repeatedly between Paris and Budapest except on official business. Fish had evidently been hoping to learn what her official business was.

Later, when Lucile herself became involved with the Vienna underworld, she learned of Mátyás Rákosi's mistress. Old "Potato Head" was officially married to a Soviet "citizenness" of Mongolian origin. His unofficial wife, however, conformed exactly to the description of the blonde whom Fish had intended to meet in Paris. Even their Budapest addresses were the same. Lucile concluded, therefore, that Rákosi's mistress had something to do with Karpe's assassination. A young Rumanian, Rian Tarescu, has since confessed to the Swiss police that he and two other Communist students, on orders received from a "foreign organization," overpowered Karpe and pushed him to his death.

Inasmuch as Rákosi had once spent fifteen years in prison for his illegal Communist activities in prewar Hungary, Lucile addressed no fewer than three appeals to him in the hope that he would be moved to clemency. She submitted her first two appeals, just before and just after my trial, through the American Legation in Vienna. Neither was ever acknowledged. She submitted her third appeal through the Hungarian Legation a week before Christmas, 1950. It read:

Your Excellency!

In this letter I enclose a small note to my husband . . . an American citizen charged with espionage and condemned to fifteen years' imprisonment in Hungary.

Since November 18, 1949, I have received no word from him, nor he from me. I have already written twice to plead with you to send my husband back to me and our two little boys. Your Excellency, I am sure it is not your intention to make me suffer so, when even a short note from my husband would make my lot easier to bear. Won't you please do that for me? I only want him to know that I love him and that I shall wait for him, even if it takes fifteen years.

I have spoken with people who have met you and talked with you. They are unanimous in saying that you are a kind person, pleasant, with a good sense of humor. I therefore feel confident that you will eventually grant my plea. I do not care about political things. All I want is my husband because I love him and because my children need him. Please, Your Excellency, make 1951 a wonderful year for me. For you it is a small thing; for me it is my whole life. Just think of it that way and send my husband back to me.

Ten days later the appeal was returned to Lucile with the explanation that the Hungarian Legation was "not in a position to forward [her] letter to Budapest."

Earlier, in London, Lucile had met an Englishman who had once saved Rákosi's life by pushing him from in front of a speeding automobile. Rákosi invited the Englishman to dinner and, over drinks, had told him that if he ever had occasion to ask a favor, he would grant it, no matter what it was. The Englishman, following our conviction, wrote to Rákosi to remind him of his promise and to ask that Sanders and I be pardoned. He sent three copies of his letter, one through the open mail, one through the British Legation, and one through a Hungarian friend. None was ever acknowledged.

It may be interesting at this point to compare our treatment at Rákosi's hands with his own treatment at the hands of Admiral Miklós Horthy, the dictator of Hungary between the two world wars. Rákosi's death sentence in 1925 caused a "worldwide uproar," according to John Gunther; "liberals everywhere, particularly in Great Britain and the United States, protested at the extreme severity of the sentence." *

The uproar saved Rákosi's life. His sentence was commuted to ten years in prison. In 1935, when his first sentence had been completed, he was retried on another charge and again sentenced to death. Again his sentence was commuted, and in 1940, thanks to the Nazi-Soviet Pact, he was deported to Russia in return for some battle flags that the Russians had captured from the Hungarians in the First World War.

On the day of my cross-examination, the official newspaper of the Hungarian Communist Party, *Szabad Nép* ("Free People"), recalled that, when Rákosi was being tried, his sister was re-

* *Behind the Curtain,* New York, 1948, pp. 200-201.

moved from the courtroom for shouting, "I'm proud of you!" Not even my lawyer, much less my wife or any other member of my family, was allowed to be present when I was being tried.

Szabad Nép, quoting the Moscow *Pravda* ("Truth"), went on to recall that, in the words of a "counter-revolutionary" correspondent, "Rákosi could see before him those observers who had arrived from abroad, which is the reason why he spoke so bravely. He felt and could make them feel that he was not alone."

It was undoubtedly for that very reason that I was held incommunicado from the day of my arrest until the day of my release. I could neither feel nor make others feel that I was not alone.

But the most important difference between the two trials was a difference that *Szabad Nép* neglected to mention. Whereas my codefendants and I were forced to plead guilty to every false charge against us, Rákosi was permitted to plead not guilty and to protest his innocence to the very end, even though his guilt was evident.

It was not until after my release from prison that I learned of my wife's untiring efforts to keep my case alive. I am satisfied that, within the limits of our weak policy toward Russia, Nathaniel Davis did everything he could to procure my release. But if it had not been for Lucile and my father and the publicity they received in the American press—and particularly in the Scripps-Howard newspapers—I would probably still be in prison.

Lucile's idea was to impose an economic boycott on Hungary, and if she had received any real support from Washington in this endeavor it might have been effective. It was not entirely ineffective, even so, for she managed, with the help of certain British friends, to prevent Hungary from selling 5,000 tons of dressed turkeys to the United Kingdom during the Christmas season of 1949. With the help of the late John G. Erhardt, the American minister to Austria, and Culbert L. Olson, the former governor of California, she also prevented Hungary from perchasing 30,000 bales of cotton from the United States in the spring of 1950.

In general, though, our diplomats took a very dim view of Lucile's "interference," as they called it, and tried in vain to persuade her to give up her battle and return to the United States. Thomas Blake, I.T.&T.'s former Washington representative, made the mistake of telephoning in an effort to bring her round to the State Department's point of view. Lucile was so annoyed that she wrote him the following letter:

Dear Mr. Blake:

You seem to be laboring under the impression that I am . . . a senseless and hysterical woman who is doing everything possible to handicap our government in its business of getting my husband released.

A transatlantic telephone call is not ideal for an argument of this sort, and so I am going to take up a few points that I want to make clear to you.

You said, "Please try to get it through your head that our government is very interested in obtaining your husband's release." It may amaze you, Mr. Blake, but I was convinced of that fact even before you told me.

Quote No. 2: "You should have blind faith in our government." I presume this to be a very blissful state to be in, but I am unable to achieve it. I do have faith in our government, but there is nothing blind about it, as I have personally known too many incompetent people working for it.

Quote No. 3: "You should keep quiet." Let me assure you, Mr. Blake, that I am not the type who gets told to "keep quiet." Neither Mr. Truman nor Mr. Acheson could make me do so. I shall keep quiet only when I am convinced that the right action is being taken. . . .

Quote No. 4: "Our government doesn't need the suggestions of a . . . yearling." As I told you . . . I have never meant to be disrespectful, but I have been given to understand that we are a democracy, a government for the people and by the people, etc. I happen to be one of the people . . . and so I feel I have the right to speak up when I feel so inclined.

Quote No. 5: "Our diplomatic representatives know how the Russians work." This statement may be true but, as we can all see, they don't know how to handle the Russians, or the world would not be what it is today. Many Americans have been sent to Europe in the past few years to get a picture of the situation to take back home. Even the wives of fifty farmers came this year to have a look at the agricultural side of Europe, so they went to Rome, Paris, Brussels, etc., which are hardly the places to learn about farming. Many congressmen and senators have been here. Most of them have looked at the famous Iron Curtain through a haze of receptions and cocktail parties given in their honor in Vienna. These people go back to the States as experts on the Russians. . . . Perhaps you can see why it is such a strain on me to have any faith at all. . . .

Lucile, as my wife, was undoubtedly prejudiced. She took the view, which was not without precedent in American history, that it was shameful for a great power like the United States to permit any country to victimize one of its citizens and particularly one who happened to be her husband. It was doubly shameful, she thought, for the United States to permit a defeated power like Hungary to do so in open violation of its peace treaty. The State Department took the view that it was not worth the risk of war with Russia to attempt to enforce the peace treaty on behalf of a lone American prisoner. The upshot of the argument was that Lucile, in defiance of the State Department, opened direct negotiations with the Communist underworld, offering to raise $500,000—by subscription, if necessary—to pay for my liberation.

A kidnaping attempt, after all the threatening letters and telephone calls that Lucile received, seemed an imminent possibility. The *Österreichische Volkstimme*, in fact, announced that my family and I would thenceforth be considered as "*Vogelfrei.*" The *Volkstimme's* pun was a veiled threat meaning that the Fowlers (Vogelers) would be considered to be as "free as fowls" —that is, outlaws, or, in another sense, "fair game."

Lucile armed herself with one of my pistols and announced that she would shoot anyone who attempted to molest her or any other member of the family. No one did—less for fear of Lucile's marksmanship, I suspect, than for that of Sergeants Roy Greer and Hollis Graves of the Secret Investigation Service. Greer accompanied Lucile and her sister Pia wherever they went. Graves and assistants maintained a twenty-four-hour watch around our house for the next five months.

Bob and Bill, before they were taken out of school, had several fights with other little boys who referred to their father as a "jailbird." Their reply was to distribute copies of the white book among their classmates in the hope that it would convince them (or their parents) that I was not the criminal that the Communist press had been trying to make me seem.

Lucile eventually made contact with certain Russian agents who agreed to negotiate my release. Before long they offered definite terms. The State Department, however, refused to take their offer seriously, and so Lucile announced, in May, 1950, that she would fly to London to beard Dean Acheson himself. Lucile, I think, was justified in thus dramatizing my predicament. But the State Department, I think, was also justified in expressing its annoyance.

Mr. Acheson had gone to London to attend the fourth meeting of the North Atlantic Council, and I am sure that he had more important things to worry about than my imprisonment. But Lucile had her way, in spite of our diplomats, and certain friends of ours arranged for her to be flown to London in an Army air-plane.

Mr. Acheson had no alternative but to receive her. As soon as the pleasantries were over, and the inevitable photographs had been taken, Lucile asked him, point-blank, if he had a feasible plan for procuring my release. The Secretary of State admitted that he did not.

"Then you'll have to negotiate."

"How can we negotiate," said Mr. Acheson, "until we know what we're going to negotiate about?"

As Lucile remembers their conversation, she then submitted the ransom terms that she had obtained from the Russian agents: $2,000,000 worth of ball bearings, radio tubes, and special steels from Western Germany; the reopening of the Hungarian consulates in Cleveland and New York; and the rescinding of the ban on private American travel to Hungary.

Mr. Acheson, she recalls, said that such a proposal was "out of the question." The United States government could not allow itself to be placed in the position of paying ransom.

Lucile explained that she had been given to understand that the $2,000,000 figure could be shaved to $500,000, which she hoped to raise privately. The important thing, from the Communist point of view, was to humiliate the United States by forcing our government to submit to extortion.

"I'm sorry," said Mr. Acheson, "but it can't be done."

"If we had a decent foreign policy," Lucile remembers saying, "this would never have happened. But I'm not going to let my husband be the victim of your mistakes. We should have issued an ultimatum, but we didn't, and so now we've got to crawl. If you won't agree, I'll go to President Truman; and if he won't agree, I'll tell the whole story to the press. I'll say that you had five months in which to make up your mind about the ISEC agreement, but that you waited until Bob had gone back to Budapest alone before you decided to disapprove it. I'll say that it was criminal negligence on your part not to have warned him in time to get out of Hungary before the agreement was disapproved."

"What you're suggesting, Mrs. Vogeler, is sheer blackmail."

"I don't care what you call it. It's my position, and I'm going to stick to it. I can be very stubborn, you know."

"I can be stubborn, too," said Mr. Acheson.

"But not as stubborn as I am," said Lucile. "I was born in Flanders, and the Flemings are the most stubborn people in the world. Look it up in the Encyclopaedia Britannica, and you'll see."

I had often kidded Lucile about the Britannica's repeated use of the word "stubborn" in reference to her people. In this instance, as in so many others, her Flemish stubbornness won out. Mr. Acheson, after consulting Washington, agreed to authorize immediate negotiations. Lucile in return agreed to make no public statements for at least three months.

And she kept her word in spite of several disquieting events. In London she received a telephone call from Kate Field, Hermann's wife, a naturalized American of British origin, who begged her to remind Mr. Acheson that she, too, expected him to procure her husband's release. Lucile delivered the message, but without apparent effect. Mr. Acheson indicated that he saw no solution to the problem of the Fields, whose record, he said, was "not entirely spotless."

Earlier, in Vienna, Erle Cocke, the commander of the American Legion, had called on Lucile to assure her of his organization's wholehearted support. The legion had been holding rallies on my behalf, as it had earlier held rallies on behalf of Angus Ward, the American consul general in Mukden, who had been imprisoned by the Chinese Communists. Cocke was worried, he said, by Washington's pessimism. He had been told in confidence by a high government official that my own record was "not entirely spotless," for which reason it might not be possible to procure my release.

It was that remark, more than anything else, that prompted Lucile to fly to London to demand an audience with Mr. Acheson. And now, having heard it a second time, in connection with the

Fields, it renewed her determination to force the State Department's hand. It may well be true, though not necessarily relevant, that the Fields' record was "not entirely spotless." In my own case, though, the remark was neither true nor relevant. Lucile knew that I had done nothing in Vienna, Prague, or Budapest of which there was any reason to be ashamed.

Kate Field told Lucile that she had been advised to keep quiet and let the State Department handle things in its own way, with the result that her husband was still among the missing. She urged Lucile not to make the mistake of accepting such advice, but to go on fighting in the interests of all Americans who were prisoners of the Cominform. Lucile vowed to do so.

Soon after her return to Vienna, she was astonished to discover that the United States, without reference to my imprisonment, was preparing to restore the Hungarian property that the Nazis had removed to the American zone of Germany. She immediately protested to Erhardt, the American minister, suggesting that the least the government could do would be to make the restoration of Hungarian property conditional on my release. Erhardt, who agreed with her, transmitted her complaint to Washington. Thus it was that on June 16, 1950, the Hungarian government agreed to release me in return for the reopening of its consulates, the rescinding of the travel ban, and the restoration of Hungarian property in the American zone of Germany.

According to the State Department, "premature publicity" was solely responsible for the Hungarian government's failure to live up to its agreement. Until Drew Pearson and others mentioned the Crown of St. Stephen, the department said, this relic of Hungary's Catholic kings had not been a part of the price demanded for my release. Later, following the invasion of South Korea, Hungary raised its price to include the crown as well as the termination of the Voice of America's broadcasts to Hungary from Germany.

Whatever the cause of the Hungarians' failure to keep their

word—the Crown of St. Stephen, the Voice of America, or the Korean War—Lucile kept quiet for four and a half months. Then, when nothing happened, she publicly accused the State Department of "writing off" my case and treating her as if she were a "widow." The department denied her charge, of course, but gave her no reason to hope that it was prepared to take any further action on my behalf.

At Roy Howard's suggestion, therefore, Lucile told her side of the story to Allan Keller, who wrote a series of articles for the Scripps-Howard newspapers. A similar series of articles had helped to free Angus Ward and other Americans who had been imprisoned in China. It was hoped that the result in my case would be the same. It was, but not until after Howard had published a second series of articles signed by Lucile and written by Wellington Long, the Vienna correspondent of the United Press.

Meanwhile, to the State Department's dismay, Lucile reopened her negotiations with the Communist underworld. All sorts of schemes were devised, including a plot to kidnap me as I was being transported from one prison to another. The only trouble was that I was never moved from the Maria Theresa Barracks.

The man who organized the plot was a Russian intelligence officer who had been secretly working for one of our allies. All of Lucile's eighteen contacts were interested in "going west," as they called it, but Major Nikita Kobiakov was the only one who was not also interested in money. The others included smugglers, kidnapers, and black marketeers. One of them worked for USIA, the Russian importing and exporting trust. He assured Lucile, in the name of Colonel General V. P. Sviridov, the then chief of the Russian forces in Austria, that I would be released the moment she supplied him with a kilogram of uranium.

"For that much uranium," he said, "you could buy Stalin himself."

It wasn't true, and the MGB proved it by arresting the man a few weeks later. He has never been heard of since.

Another Russian intelligence officer who, unlike Nikita, was playing a double game with her, told Lucile, "If we can take people east, we can certainly bring them west. It's only a question of making it worth our while."

Uranium, of course, was out of the question, even though minute quantities of the metal were probably available in Vienna. My freedom was not worth a micromilligram of stolen American uranium, and Lucile knew it; but she was not so sure about the ball bearings, radio tubes, and alloy steels that had been mentioned as acceptable tender in payment of my ransom. It was Nikita who finally brought her to her senses.

"You're a fool," he said. "These people you're dealing with are crooks. They're only after your money. Nobody can do a thing for your husband except the Soviet government."

"But what about you? Can't you do something?"

"I'm not so foolish as to get myself mixed up in such a business. Besides, I have a wife and children."

Nikita was a tall man with dark hair and a long, sad face. He worked in the Belaria Building, the headquarters of the Russian intelligence corps, and almost always wore civilian clothes.

Lucile had been introduced to him by two Austrian contacts who were eager to prove that they were actually working for the Russians. One of them, as a matter of fact, was also working for the Americans. He turned out to be even more of a scoundrel than Nikita thought he was. I am not at liberty to reveal his true identity, and so I shall refer to him merely as Erich. He is an excellent example of what is known in Eastern Europe as a *Hochstapler*, or highbinder, the sort of person who takes pride in never having done an honest day's work in his life. Erich is a distant cousin of a distinguished Austrian aristocrat, a relationship on which he has traded shamelessly all his life. Lucile was indeed foolish to have trusted such a man, and so, for that matter, was the CIC.

Erich and his friend wanted $5,000 as a retainer fee, and they brought Nikita to see Lucile in the hope that he would help them to persuade her that such a fee was justified. Nikita spoke to her in English, which neither of them understood, but they were sharp enough to realize that what he told her was far different from what they had expected him to say. They admitted defeat but made it clear that they intended to take revenge.

A few days later Nikita came to call with his wife and two little boys. Milush, his wife, was a Czechoslovakian girl whom he had met in Prague. They have since married, but they were not married at the time because Russians were forbidden to marry foreigners. Milush's parents had fled to Vienna, following the Communist *Putsch* in Prague, and had opened a dry-cleaning establishment in the American sector of the city. Nikita and Milush lived in the Russian sector.

They often visited Lucile and Pia after that, and Nikita brought numerous little presents for Bob and Bill. Once he gave them some Russian coins; later some medals bearing Stalin's profile; and finally some belt buckles embossed with the hammer and sickle. The boys, who had returned to school, made the mistake of wearing their new belt buckles in public, with the result that they were now accused of being "Reds." It was only then that they understood what Lucile had meant when she told them that Nikita was a Russian.

One day Nikita announced that he was going to Budapest on business. While he was about it, he said, he would see if there was anything he could do to help me. Lucile, overcome, offered to pay him any amount of money, but Nikita said that all he wanted was permission, when the time came, to emigrate with his wife and family to the United States.

On his return to Vienna, he told Lucile that it would be very difficult to do anything for me, but that a fellow Russian officer, who also hoped to "go west" one day, was looking into the possibilities. After his second trip to Budapest, Nikita reported that two of the guards at 60 Stalin Avenue had indicated their willingness to help me to escape in return for the equivalent of $800 each and safe passages to Vienna. On his third trip to Budapest, Nikita paid the men, obtained their receipts, and gave them my photograph and a cryptic message from Lucile. The message, which was to serve as a recognition piece, was *"Sneulen pompeleuten en palingsputen,"* a bit of nonsense in bad Flemish that had to do with "eels' feet." Lucile knew that only I could understand it, for it was a family joke designed to put a stop to children's foolish questions.

It was Nikita's plan, after rescuing me from the Maria Theresa Barracks, to disguise me as a Russian officer and send me to Vienna with false travel orders. And the plan might have succeeded if his apartment had not been raided by the MGB. Fortunately Nikita and Milush had spent the night in the apartment of some friends, leaving their children with Milush's parents in the American sector. The next morning, on her way home, Milush noticed several jeeps parked in the vicinity of their apartment building. Instead of entering, she prudently went to a café to telephone some neighbors, who confirmed her fear that the building had been surrounded. Milush returned to the Ferdinand Bridge to wait for Nikita, whom she expected home for lunch, and when he appeared she told him what had happened. They fled to a different sector of the city, reported their plight to Nikita's Allied superiors, and were soon provided with false Austrian passports.

A week later Erich telephoned to say that he had an entirely new plan for procuring my release. "And, by the way," he added, "our Russian friend is no more."

Lucile, feigning ignorance, asked him what had happened.

"Oh, there was some trouble, but don't worry. They didn't take him alive."

"Did he get away?"

"No, he committed suicide by swallowing some poison that he carried in his cigarette case."

Lucile has never doubted that it was Erich who denounced Nikita to the MGB.

Nikita's position became so precarious that he asked Lucile to help him and his family to enter the United States. It was finally arranged for him to be given an interrogation by the CIC. In spite of the favorable recommendation of the Allied intelligence corps for which Nikita had been working, the CIC decided to intern him as a "doubtful" case. For eight months Nikita, Milush, and their two children were confined in an overcrowded barracks for displaced persons.

Finally, in December, 1951, I managed to persuade the authorities to let them come to the United States. I agreed to pay for their transportation and to be responsible for them here until Nikita could find a job. They were accordingly sent to Bremerhaven, and were preparing to board ship when they were arrested and taken back to Austria. Three weeks later they were released for lack of evidence. Again they were sent to Bremerhaven, and again they were arrested and taken back to Austria. I am still trying to convince the American authorities that Nikita deserves to be allowed to come to the United States. But someone (and I suspect that he is Erich) continues to denounce Nikita on the basis of new "evidence," all of which has so far proved to be false.

I have told Nikita's story not only because I want to help him, in return for his effort to help me, but also because I think his problem is typical of thousands of worthy Russians interned in the American zones of Austria and Germany. Spies have undoubtedly been planted among them, and every effort should be made to weed them out. But the vast majority, I am convinced, are people like Nikita who, if we would only trust them, could be of great help to us in the psychological war against Stalinist imperialism. I sincerely believe that Nikita's case deserves the support of the American Committee for the Liberation of the Peoples of Russia, Inc. As Admiral Kirk, our former ambassador to Russia, who recently became chairman of the group, has said, the anti-Stalinist exiles are "the first and most persecuted victims of Communism and potentially the first allies of the free world in its struggle against the Communist menace."

Eighteen | The Nightmare Ends

Shortly before noon on April 26, 1951, the former warrant officer, now a second lieutenant, came to my cell with a clean shirt, a pair of shoelaces, a can of shoe polish, and a clothes brush. When he told me to spruce up, in preparation for an important visit, I was naturally excited. Could it be that the Supreme Court had finally answered my appeal? Was Rákosi going to receive me? Or was I now to be taken from Budapest to Prague or Moscow, as Péter had threatened, for another trial?

Early that afternoon my question was answered. The lieutenant led me down to the main courtyard of the Maria Theresa Barracks. My second inquisitor, No. 2, was waiting for me in a new black Chevrolet sedan. An agent whom I had never seen before was sitting in front with the chauffeur. I was placed in the rear between the lieutenant and No. 2, who pulled down the familiar black curtains before we passed through the barracks gate and out into the street.

The sun was so bright that I could detect occasional landmarks through the translucent curtains. We drove around the rings of Pest and crossed the Danube into Buda. We ended up in the basement garage of what proved to be the brand-new Ministry of Internal Affairs—significantly one of the most splendiferous architectural projects of the Communist regime.

I was led up a stairway and through a steel door into a ro-
256

tunda edged with marble columns. Near the entrance from the street were a bank of elevators, but my escorts avoided them and led me up a back stairway to the second-floor gallery. I was then led down a corridor and through a busy anteroom into an inner office at least forty feet long.

At the far end of the office, behind a desk from which a conference table projected in the latest Hollywood manner, sat General Gábor Péter. The ensuing interview was more like a conference with a movie mogul than an audience with the chief of the Hungarian section of the Russian political police.

On the paneled walls of Péter's office were the usual portraits of Lenin, Stalin, and Rákosi in new mahogany frames. Through the windows to the right of Péter's desk I could see the trees on Margaret Island, which were just turning green, and several people walking in the park. On Péter's desk were the silver knickknacks that I remembered from 60 Stalin Avenue—including the horse and the flamingo—and behind his desk was the same executive switchboard, with which, I noticed, he was still having trouble.

I sat in a red leather armchair at the far end of the projecting conference table. No. 2 sat on my left, next to Péter, and in between us sat No. 2's new deputy, a major, who had joined us in the anteroom. Next to Péter on my right sat the young interpreter who had questioned me in October, 1950, about stereophonic eavesdropping. The chair between us was empty.

"Now that you've been in prison for seventeen months," said Péter, "how do you feel?"

"As you can easily imagine," I said, "the last seventeen months have seemed much longer to me than they have to you."

Péter was his usual dapper self. His gray mustache had been carefully trimmed and his hands were freshly manicured. He was attired, as always, in a dark gray suit.

A flight of Russian jet bombers thundered overhead, and for a moment I wondered if the Third World War had begun. But

Péter paid no attention to the bombers. He merely asked me if I had been comfortable in my cell and if there was anything I wanted.

I asked once again to be allowed to communicate with the American Legation. All I wanted to know, I said, was how my wife and family and my father were getting along. Although I had been allowed to write monthly letters to Lucile, I had received no replies. The reason, as I later discovered, was a simple one. My letters had never been mailed.

"I'll see what I can do," said Péter, "but I must remind you once again that your government has not once expressed the slightest interest in your case."

He never tired of repeating the same cruel lie.

"How much longer will I have to serve?" I asked.

"You'll get time off for good behavior, of course, and the people's authorities may even give you an amnesty—but we'll speak of that in a few days. In the meantime, if there's anything you want, you have only to write a request and I'll do what I can to see that it is granted."

His offer was a little late. There was no time, as things developed, to supply me with the dictionary and the books on physics and mathematics that I once again requested. The Russian major with the missing fingers had failed to keep his promise. I had received none of the textbooks with which he had promised to supply me.

On the night of April 27, half an hour after I had gone to sleep, the lieutenant came to my cell to tell me to dress at once. No. 2 and his deputy drove me back to the new Ministry of Internal Affairs, this time without bothering to draw the curtains. It was only eleven o'clock, but the streets of Budapest were already deserted. Night life, along with so many other aspects of the old regime, was now a thing of the past. Instead of driving into the basement garage, the chauffeur parked in front of the ministry and we walked in through the main entrance. We avoided the elevators, as before, but this time we walked up the spiraled main stairway to the gallery above.

Péter received me in the presence of no one except the young interpreter. He shook hands with me, to my surprise, offered me one of his Player cigarettes, and told me to be seated in the armchair that No. 2 had occupied the day before.

"The people's authorities," he said, "have expressed their willingness to consider the question of your release. But you'll have to co-operate if you want their decision to be favorable. It will help you if you sign the letter that I am about to dictate."

He took a Parker 51 out of his vest pocket and handed it to me along with a sheaf of writing paper.

"Date the letter, 'Budapest, February 15, 1951,'" he said, "and address it to me."

As I have explained, I was still unaware of Péter's identity, and so I gave the interpreter an inquiring glance.

"Just address it to the general," he said in English.

"But what's the general's name?"

The interpreter looked surprised. He said something to Péter in Hungarian. The latter smiled and nodded.

"Péter Gábor," he said.

Now it was my turn to be surprised. I was of course familiar with the dreaded name, but I had somehow failed to connect it with the mild little man whom I had known as "the general." I had expected the chief of Hungary's political police to be a more impressive person.

"Péter Gábor or Gábor Péter?" I asked. It is always a problem to get the names of Hungarians straight, especially when they are such transparent pseudonyms as "Peter Gabriel" or "Gabriel Peter." Hungarians, in speaking foreign languages, often forget that they and the Chinese are among the few peoples in the world who normally use their last names first.

"It doesn't make any difference," said the interpreter. "In Hungarian it's Péter Gábor; in English it's Gábor Péter."

The general's real name, I knew, was Benö Ausspitz, but at his own dictation I wrote (to the best of my recollection):

General Gábor Péter, Chief
State Defense Authority (AVH)
Ministry of Internal Affairs
Budapest

My dear General:

I wish to state that my arrest, my investigation, and my trial were conducted in a fair and just manner. At no time, during or preceding my imprisonment was I mistreated in any way. During my imprisonment I was shown every possible consideration. I was supplied, for example, with English books, writing materials, American cigarettes, and every sanitary convenience.

In recognition of the kind treatment that I have received, I wish to express my gratitude by presenting you with a token of my consideration—the gold ring that you have kept for me during my imprisonment.

From our conversations I have learned that you, as a representative of the Hungarian People's Republic, are interested in world peace. I therefore promise to meet at any time with your designated representative, who will make himself known to me by means of the ring that I have given you. I promise further to inform him whether the United States government plans to go to war with the people's democracies of the world. I understand that this promise in no way obliges me to reveal any other secrets.

"That's the letter," said Péter. "I suggest that you study it while I am gone. I won't be very long."

He limped out of the office and left me alone with the interpreter, who looked at me with a puzzled expression on his face. I was equally puzzled. I could understand the bit about the "kind treatment" that I had received. It was obviously designed to clear Péter and his underlings in the event that they should be tried, as I hope they will be, in the not too distant future, for their systematic violations of the human rights provisions of the peace treaty of 1947.

But I have yet to understand the part about my ring. It was my class ring, of course, from the Massachusetts Institute of Technology. It had always puzzled No. 2, who apparently believed that it possessed some cryptic significance. Perhaps Péter wanted to retain it as "proof" that I was an American agent. I know that No. 1 questioned Sanders at length about my ring, for it was mentioned in Sanders' original confession, which was read aloud in my presence at the time of our second confrontation. Sandy testified that I had once explained to him that you could always tell a professional Army or Navy officer by his class ring from one or the other of the two academies. No. 2, however, had refrained from questioning me about my ring and probably would not have believed me if I had explained to him that MIT was not a training school for spies.

As a matter of fact, in my own confession, I purposely failed to mention MIT by name. I merely stated that I had attended "the university" in Boston. The result, as I hoped, was the white book's erroneous implication that I was a graduate not of MIT but of Boston University.

As for the meeting I was supposed to have some day with his "designated representative," did Péter really believe that I would tip him off in advance of a Third World War? If so, he was mad, which was always a possibility, and one that would help to explain a number of the more bizarre passages in my confession. But perhaps Péter was merely ignorant. Communists, I have observed, are often surprisingly ignorant of the motives of their chosen enemies.

When he returned to his office, Péter asked me, rather doubtfully, if I would sign the letter that he had dictated. I signed it without another thought. I would have signed anything, I suppose, in order to be freed.

"Before you go," said Péter, "there's another request I have to make. My representative will telephone to say, 'A friend from Budapest is here to see you very urgently.' This will mean that you are to meet him in the bar of the leading hotel of the city in which you happen to be. For the purpose of recognition, you will both wear white flowers in your buttonholes. And, if you should meet in New York, I would suggest the bar in the basement of the Waldorf-Astoria."

I was about to ask him which one, but decided to keep my mouth shut.

Péter added that he would trust me not to mention the ring or the contents of the letter to anyone. I was expected to betray my country, I gathered, out of gratitude for being released from prison after seventeen months of unlawful confinement.

Before leaving the Ministry of Internal Affairs, No. 2 invited me into his new office for a chat. He spoke of the "kind treatment" I had received and told me that, all things considered, I was a pretty "lucky" man. I was unable to share his complacency. Going downstairs, on our way out of the ministry, we passed a fat Russian general with medals all over his chest. It was apparently no longer a secret that the AVH was a mere subsection of the MGB.

No. 2 escorted me back to the Maria Theresa Barracks. A few minutes after the lieutenant had locked me in my cell, Péter's interpreter appeared with a copy of the English version of the white book. He told me to read it that very night and to give it back to the lieutenant in the morning. Apparently the white book was supposed to fill me with a proper sense of remorse.

It was then about one o'clock. I read and reread the incredible document until the lieutenant came in to collect it just as dawn was breaking. No one seems to have slept that night. A few minutes before six, on the morning of April 28, the major in command of the prison himself escorted me downstairs. Péter, No. 2, and the interpreter were waiting for me in the major's office.

"I have seen my superiors," said Péter, who looked rather wan, "and they have agreed to release you within an hour."

He then gave me three documents to sign. The first was a formal statement reiterating that I had not been mistreated, that I had confessed voluntarily, and that I had been justly sentenced to fifteen years in prison.

None of it was true, but I signed it anyway.

The second document was an itemized receipt for the personal property that would be returned to me. It consisted of my wallet, minus my dollars, pounds, and florins; the cheap Czechoslovakian fountain pen that had replaced my gold Sheaffer pen-and-pencil set; my chromium wrist watch; and one of my two cigarette lighters. No mention was made of I.T.&T.'s Buick sedan, my platinum pocket watch, or the $2,000 that I had been carrying at the time of my arrest. Only two of my three suitcases were returned. The best one, along with my better articles of clothing, had disappeared. The company and I were thus robbed of currency and possessions worth at least $6,000, but I decided not to complain.

The third document was an itemized account of the expenses that the AVH had allegedly incurred on my behalf—soap, tooth-brush, tooth powder, laundry, playing cards, and Bible. Total: 1,400 florins. The remainder of my 7,500 florins, Péter said, had been turned over to the American Legation. I later discovered to my surprise that Péter, for once, had told the truth. The florins were converted into shillings and deposited to my credit in Vienna. Ambassador Walter Donnelly, at my request, donated the credit to the Austrian Children's Friendship Fund, an American relief organization.

"In Vienna," said Péter, "and later in New York and Washing-ton, you will be asked many questions about the treatment you have received in Hungary. We shall be very interested in what you have to say. I would advise you to be cautious, for we are young men and our arm is long."

He then stood up, bowed, and said good-by, but this time he made no effort to shake my hand.

The lieutenant took me down to the basement for my last shower and shave. Then he brought me the black striped suit in which I had appeared at the trial. He also brought me a clean shirt and some socks and shorts, none of which were mine. As soon as I had dressed, we joined the major in his office, where a pot of coffee, a porcelain cup and saucer, and a plate of cookies had been placed on a table and covered with a towel.

"*Tessék! Kérem szépen!*" said the major, bowing and scraping like an overly solicitous waiter. "Help yourself! Pretty please!"

The lieutenant poured my coffee for me and handed me the plate of cookies. It was amusing to observe their sudden change of manner. Until that moment they had both been petty tyrants.

No. 2, an interpreter, and a tall captain dressed in riding breeches and boots accompanied me to the border in the black Chevrolet sedan. Ten miles out of Budapest we joined a tall major and a tall civilian in another black Chevrolet sedan. At the Hegyeshalom border station we were met by ten or fifteen men and women, apparently writers for various Communist newspapers, who stared at me curiously but asked no questions. As soon as my passport had been stamped, No. 2 handed it back to me, saying, "You're free. You may go."

I started back toward the Chevrolet in which I had traveled from Budapest, but the tall civilian, who turned out to be an undersecretary of the Ministry of Foreign Affairs, said, "No. We walk."

The chauffeur placed my two suitcases in the middle of the asphalt highway. The civilian indicated that I was to carry them across the border. I picked them up and staggered off in the direction of Austria, like Charlie Chaplin in the fadeout of almost any of his films. It was my final humiliation as a prisoner of Stalin's political police.

The tall civilian walked beside me, followed by the tall captain and the tall major. They had evidently been selected for their height and elegance of dress in order to emphasize my own bedraggled appearance. I was so weak, after my long confinement, that I was tempted at intervals to put the suitcases down and rest. But I resisted the temptation in order not to give my captors pleasure. I struggled on as best I could until we had rounded a bend in the road and were lost to view from the Hungarian side of the border.

A green Chrysler sedan approached us from the direction of Nickelsdorf, the Austrian border station. Two men alighted. One of them was Arthur F. Tower, the American consul general; the other was Halvor Ekern, whom I had known as a major, and who was now the director of the Four-Power Secretariat in Vienna.

Ekern handed the tall Hungarian civilian a document stamped with the great seal of the United States and entwined with a yard of red tape. It was the official receipt for my safe delivery.

The Hungarian attempted to introduce himself, but Ekern turned his back on him and said to me, "Climb in. I'll put your suitcases in the trunk."

Tower and Ekern drove me to Vienna, where they delivered me to the door of our house on Max Emmanuel Strasse. Bob and Bill rushed out to greet me, followed by Lucile and her sister Pia. Egbert Kus, my physician, and his wife Thilde, my secretary, were waiting for me inside. The first thing I did was to drink a glass of milk. Then I went upstairs with Kus for a physical examination. Except for my loss of weight, and my weakened eyes and gums, Bert said, I was in surprisingly good condition.

The next day I called on Donnelly, from whose office I dispatched formal messages of thanks to President Truman and

Secretary Acheson for the government's efforts on my behalf. The following morning, with Colonel Grant Williams, who had succeeded me as I.T.&T.'s Vienna representative, we flew to New York and thence to Washington, where I entered the Naval Hospital in Bethesda. I was not given free hospitalization, as some readers may suppose, because of any past connection with the Navy; I received this courtesy thanks to an old act of Congress, passed in the days of the Barbary pirates, extending military privileges to all citizens held as hostages by foreign powers. I might just as well have recuperated in the Army's Walter Reed Hospital, except that the Naval Hospital was the one to which civilians were customarily sent.

The aged Cordell Hull, with whom I had several talks in the solarium overlooking the capital, was one of my fellow patients. The former Secretary of State spoke at length of his "losing battle," as he described it, to prevent the creation of the conditions that had been responsible for my imprisonment.

Mr. Hull and I occupied rooms on the floor above the room in which the late Secretary of Defense, James Forrestal, had once been confined. The conditions of which Mr. Hull complained would never have developed, in my opinion, if Mr. Forrestal had been victorious in his battle with the men whose unjust criticism prompted him, in an unbalanced moment, to take his life.

Six weeks later I retired with Lucile, Pia, and the boys to Grand Lake, Colorado, where the series of articles that resulted in this book were written. Thanks jointly to the excellent care I received in Washington, plus the curative effects of a summer in the Rocky Mountains, I soon regained my normal weight. By November, 1951, I was well enough to begin a lecture tour.

Nineteen | The Oatis Case

The worst shock I received on being released from prison was to learn how great a price had been paid for my redemption: Fish Karpe was dead, William Oatis was in prison, and the United States had been ignominiously forced to rescind its ban on private travel to Hungary, reopen Hungary's consulates in Cleveland and New York, restore Hungary's property in the American zone of Germany, and terminate the Voice of America's broadcasts from Germany to Hungary.

I was deeply aware of the great debt of gratitude that I owed to everyone who had been instrumental in procuring my release. Yet I felt that I owed it to the memory of Karpe, and even more to the future of Oatis, to say exactly what I thought, even though I might be accused in some quarters of ingratitude. I therefore published a series of six articles in the *Saturday Evening Post*, and in the last of these articles, which appeared on December 1, 1951, I wrote:

The Administration fumbled my release, and I am afraid it will fumble Oatis' release unless it adopts new and more courageous tactics in dealing with Russia and its colonies. It is absurd to pretend that Hungary and Czechoslovakia are independent countries. If they were, neither Oatis nor I would ever have been imprisoned. We were both imprisoned, on orders from Stalin, by local representatives of the MGB. The men who arrested Oatis were members of

267

the same organization as the men who arrested me. I was released, on certain conditions, by Stalin's Hungarian stooges. Oatis was arrested five days earlier, in flagrant violation of those conditions, by Stalin's Czechoslovakian stooges. My release, therefore, was meaningless to everyone except poor Oatis and myself and our respective families. The United States was tricked into making a series of humiliating concessions, and, though I was released, Oatis was imprisoned. . . . It was just another example of the Soviet principle of heads I win, tails you lose.

The SNB, as the Czechoslovakian section of the MGB is known, had been waiting impatiently to emulate the sordid triumph of the AVH in Hungary. The SNB had been privileged to kidnap Noel and Herta Field, of course, and it had also imprisoned two naturalized Americans, Jan Hvasta and Imrich Solar.

Hvasta, a young Navy veteran, was unlawfully convicted of "espionage" and sentenced, in October, 1948, to three years in prison. His sentence was later increased to ten years as punishment for his temerity in daring to appeal it. Hvasta, like Solar, had returned to Czechoslovakia to visit his relatives and, while there, had made the mistake of falling in love with and marrying a Slovakian girl. His "espionage" consisted of taking photographs of public buildings in Bratislava.

Solar, who had worked as a dishwasher in New York, was sentenced in December, 1949, to a year in prison for saying to a waiter, "In the United States we throw away better food than you eat here."

But these were minor triumphs for the SNB. The Fields, for reasons best known to Stalin, were removed to Russia, where they have yet to be brought to trial, and neither Hvasta nor Solar was qualified to act as the leading scapegoat in a demonstration trial against the United States.

Dana Adams Schmidt, the Prague correspondent of the New York *Times*, would have made an ideal scapegoat, especially since his wife was a daughter of Russian fugitives who had settled in Turkey following the Bolshevik *coup d'état* in 1917. Schmidt, however, managed to escape from Czechoslovakia just as he was about to be arrested in June, 1950. Otherwise he would almost certainly have suffered the fate that was to befall Oatis, the correspondent of the Associated Press, in April, 1951.

Two of Oatis' predecessors in Prague, Nathan Polowetzky and Richard Kasischke, had been expelled for "unobjective reporting." At his trial, in July, 1951, Polowetzky and Kasischke, along with A. I. Goldberg, an earlier AP correspondent in Prague, would be accused *in absentia* of the same charges of which Oatis would be convicted in person. What had been defined as "unobjective reporting" one year earlier had been re-defined as "espionage" by the time of Oatis' arrest. "Espionage" was defined as "attempts to obtain state secrets with the intention of betraying them to a foreign power. . . ." And a "state secret" was defined as "everything that should be kept secret from unauthorized persons in an important interest of the Republic, particularly [a] political, military, or economic interest." In other words, anyone could be convicted of espionage if he acquired or transmitted information of any sort that had not been officially released by the Czechoslovakian government.

Such had been the attitude of the Russian government for many years. Scores of Moscow correspondents, including Leigh White, who collaborated with me in the preparation of this book, were forced to leave Russia because they refused to confine themselves to innocuous quotations from and interpretations of official Russian "news." But Oatis was the first correspondent to be indicted, in Russia or any of its colonies, for the "crime" of reporting news according to the best traditions of journalism. Indeed, as his indictment revealed, it was not he, William Oatis, who was being tried, but American journalism in the name of the Associated Press. The indictment read in part:

The United States is waging war against the Soviet camp of peace. Officials of its missions and agencies in the People's Democ-

racies are espionage agents. One of the espionage agencies in Czechoslovakia was the so-called news agency of the Associated Press. This
agency abused the right of free collection of information. Masquerad-
ing as a press agency, the Associated Press for years carried on extensive espionage activities and obtained reports of a military, economic,
and political character.

As most Americans know, or should know, the Associated Press
is a cooperative newsgathering organization owned and operated
by and for the independent American newspapers that constitute
its membership. Most of its member papers are owned by Re-
publicans who are so opposed to the statist tendencies of the
Truman Administration that they have refused to permit the
AP to sell its news to the Voice of America or any other agency
of the United States government, even though it has long sold
news to TASS, the Telegraphic Agency of the Soviet Union, and
to news and propaganda agencies owned or subsidized by other
foreign governments.

If the AP has faults, submission to government domination is
certainly not among them. Whoever wrote Oatis' indictment confused the function of the AP with that of TASS, and he did so
with a purpose. It has long been a fundamental tenet of Russian
foreign policy to accuse the Kremlin's enemies of the very crimes
that the Kremlin commits, or intends to commit, in order to put
them on the defensive.

By imprisoning William Oatis just as I was about to be released, Stalin won a triple victory over the United States. First,
by nullifying the effect of my release in Hungary, he saved the
face of Rákosi's dictatorship. Second, by convicting another
American, this time in Czechoslovakia, he further humiliated the
United States in a country where American prestige had perhaps
been higher than anywhere else behind the Iron Curtain. And,
third, by smearing the Associated Press and, through it, the British and American traditions of independent journalism, he so

dismayed our government that no effective reprisals were taken against his agents in the United States.

William Oatis, unlike Sanders, was not even permitted to wear his glasses in court. He was forced to submit to two days of cross-examination without being able to see his questioners or the "secret documents" that, from time to time, were submitted as exhibits by the prosecution. As at my own trial, the "documents," far from being secret, had been found in the defendant's office files. (Queer "spies," both of us, to have kept such voluminous records of our "espionage"!) Oatis, when he was arrested, even had a card in his wallet that "proved" he was a spy. The card showed that he had attended a military language school in 1944 in the expectation of being sent to Japan as a military government officer. The fact that he admitted having learned to speak the Japanese language was considered to be especially damning, since his knowledge of Japanese had obviously been of great help to him in Czechoslovakia, a country whose language Oatis was admittedly unable to speak.

The Czechoslovakians went the Hungarians one better in that they attempted to make it seem that Oatis' very occupation was a crime. Whereas I was convicted of engaging in imaginary activities foreign to my occupation, Oatis was convicted of engaging in real activities essential to his occupation.

No white book has been published in connection with the Oatis trial, and so I shall quote hereinafter from the verbatim record taken by Mary F. Horak, a bilingual stenographer, who was one of two representatives of the American Embassy who were allowed to attend the trial. As the first quoted passage will show, the prosecution, to strengthen its non-existent case, was forced to implicate Oatis in a "murder" said to have been committed by an associate of a man whom Oatis had never even met. It seems that the alleged "murderer," a man named Pavelka, was ac-

quainted with a man named Komarek, who was a friend of a
man named Libensky, who was a friend of Pavel Wojdinek, who
was one of Oatis' three codefendants. The others were Peter
Munz and Tomas Svoboda. All three had been employed in the
AP office in Prague—Wojdinek and Munz as clerks, and Svoboda
as a translator.

Q. Please tell us of your espionage activities with Tomas Svoboda.
A. Svoboda told me about the search of a writing desk of a cer-
tain high official.
Q. Of course, he gave you the name of this official.
A. Yes, he did.
Q. What did you do with this news?
A. Nothing.
Q. Other activities of Svoboda for you.
A. [He] often told me that people's militia [SNB troops] were
training near his summer home. He told me something of the state
of their training, which he considered poor.
Q. Were you yourself present at this training?
A. I don't remember.
Q. Svoboda claims you were. How did Wojdinek work for you?
A. Wojdinek gave me information on changes in [the] Ministry
of Foreign Trade.
Q. What sort of changes were they?
A. Changes in positions in the Ministry of Foreign Trade.
Q. What else was in the report?
A. Information on trade between Czechoslovakia and the Soviet
Union.
Q. You mentioned also a report which you received about [trucks].
A. I first received this from Wojdinek.
Q. So you first heard this from Wojdinek. Who verified this?
A. Peter Munz and Vlasta Pankova.
Q. The accused should be questioned again about Votavova.
What kind of news did you receive from her?
A. She helped Wojdinek and sometimes gave me [a] report on
frontier measures.

Q. Secret measures against attacks on Czechoslovakia?

A. No, illegal border crossings.

Q. What [*sic*] is also defense of the Republic. What did you do with it?

A. Nothing, except that I gave it to Colonel Atwood [an American army attaché]. (*Laughter in court.*)

Q. That is all?

A. That is all.

Q. That is news (*laughter*). Did you discuss this with Wojdinek?

A. Yes.

Q. Under what circumstances did this appear?

A. After Svoboda was arrested.

Q. He discussed this with Wojdinek?

A. He [Wojdinek] told me that he had expected this for a long time. He told me the family of Libensky were arrested. They used to visit Wojdinek. According to Wojdinek's reports, these two were in contact with a man whom Polowetzky mentioned to me in London, and I later found out that it was J. Komarek.

Q. Polowetzky did not mention his name?

A. He called him "Joe."

Q. Then you found out that "Joe" was Komarek?

A. Only after I was arrested [italics mine].

Q. Did Wojdinek tell you what the situation was and why the family of Libensky was arrested?

A. Yes, he said that a partner of Komarek had killed a security officer. Komarek himself was on his way back to Paris. . . .

Q. Was it important for our security organs to know all the contacts Komarek had here?

A. Yes, it was.

Q. On which side did you place yourself?

A. In this case I was against the National Security [SNB].

Q. And for whom?

A. For Wojdinek.

Q. And for whom else?

A. Komarek.

Q. You knew at the time that Komarek was in touch with murderers?

A. Yes, I did.

Q. To whom else did you give information on this matter?

A. I discussed this situation with [Tyler] Thompson, the counselor of the American embassy, and with [Alexander] Schnee, the first secretary of the American Embassy.

Q. What did Schnee tell you about the case?

A. He told me that the Voice of America had broadcast the arrest of Svoboda. He was sorry that this had happened and [said] that, if he had known about it, the Voice would not have broadcast it, because it could be unpleasant.

Q. For whom would it be unpleasant?

A. For Svoboda.

Q. And for all the murderers and gangsters who were in contact with him. What did Wojdinek say about the situation with Svoboda?

A. He wanted to leave the country.

Q. Was he afraid he would be arrested?

A. Yes, he was. He was arrested later.

Q. Did you inform anyone else in the American Embassy?

A. I told Thompson about it.

Q. Then Thompson knew that Svoboda was arrested in connection with murder.

A. I don't believe I told him that.

Q. If you informed him, it was necessary to tell him even this; otherwise you could not have spoken about the case.

A. I didn't go into detail.

Q. Murder is not just a detail. We don't regard it in our country as a detail. What did Mr. Thompson say?

A. After Munz was arrested, I asked him to look after my own person, as I believed I was to be arrested. I was afraid that security organs [SNB agents] were already in my office.

The "murder" charge was so patently groundless that it was not even mentioned by the president of the court in passing sentence against Oatis and his codefendants. It was injected into the trial only to make the equally groundless charge of "espionage" seem more plausible.

One of Oatis' first assignments, after arriving in Czechoslovakia in June, 1950, was to investigate a report that Andrei Vyshinsky, Stalin's Minister of Foreign Affairs, had gone to Carlsbad for "medical treatment." Actually, as Oatis soon discovered, Vyshinsky had visited Carlsbad to lay down the line to a secret meeting of Cominform delegates from fifty-five different countries. Since non-Communist foreigners were forbidden to visit Carlsbad, Oatis sent Wojdinek in his stead to see Lydia Votavova, a former AP employee, who was then working as a telephone operator at the Hotel Pupp.

Q. Can you remember the circumstances when you verified information obtained from Lydia Votavova?

A. Yes.

Q. Do not mention names concerned in this report. Please continue.

A. In June or August of last year I got orders to ascertain if secret meetings were taking place between [officials of] the Soviet Union . . . and the People's Democracies. I sent Peter Munz [to Carlsbad] to ascertain whether this high official was [there] and he found out that he was. I wasn't satisfied with Munz's report, so I [then] sent Wojdinek.

Q. What about Wojdinek?

A. I found out that he [Vyshinsky] left the day before Wojdinek arrived.

Q. Did Wojdinek and Munz check these reports themselves, or did they get it [*sic*] from someone else?

A. Wojdinek said he obtained [the] information from Lydia Votavova.

Q. Mention other incidents. . . .

A. [Once] I was told to find out if negotiations were carried on among military leaders.

Q. Is this the report that has to do with it? (*Exhibits a copy of one of Oatis' dispatches to the AP.*)

A. Yes, this has to do with the matter I am speaking of.

Q. Did you yourself write this report and send it out?

A. Yes, I did. I wrote this particular message in connection with a story we were after.

Q. How did you mark the news which you sent abroad . . . ?

A. With my own initials, WNO.

Q. How often were instructions received from London or New York? Regularly or seldom?

A. Regularly.

Q. You mentioned Engineer Pollak [the manager of the local Pan-American World Airways office].

A. That's right.

Q. What information did you receive from Engineer Pollak?

A. Information on arrivals and departures of visitors to Czechoslovakia by air. . . .

Q. You have a place name in your notebook (*exhibit*).

A. No, that is not the name.

Q. Do not give the name but its nature.

A. It pertains to uranium ore. I ascertained that uranium ore was found on this spot.

Q. So that you could further verify this?

A. That was the idea.

Q. What other espionage information did you gain?

A. I gained espionage information pertaining to Sling, Svermova, and Clementis. I got orders from New York and London. It was important to our espionage [news] service to learn which of our positions of espionage were uncovered, so that they could orient themselves [*sic*] to those who still remained.

Q. (*Exhibits copies of various cablegrams.*) Are these the orders which you received from London and New York?

A. This has to do with something else. This has to do with . . . other people.

Q. (*Exhibits other cablegrams.*) Here are original documents marked . . . L-23 [London, Message No. 23]. . . . They [concern] the anti-state activities of the Clementis group, at that time considered secret by our government. Your instruction . . . concerns not only Clementis but also others who were concerned with Clementis. What steps did you take?

A. First, I was to find out if Clementis [had] disappeared. I went to the American Embassy and got in touch with [Otto] Colclough, who gave me the address and number of Clementis' apartment. Then I went back to the office and got Svoboda and Wojdinek to go with me.

Q. Why did you take these two with you?

A. Because they could speak Czech.

Q. What did you three do?

A. We were investigating [sic] that Clementis was not in his apartment. We learned that he was not there and that security measures had been taken [Communist jargon meaning that a guard had been assigned to Clementis' apartment].

Q. What did you do with the information?

A. I sent the news to London.

Q. Did you file this item (exhibit)?

A. Yes, this is part of that item.

Q. Did you send more reports regarding Clementis? Is it . . . possible to say that there were quite a number of them?

A. I sent several such stories. Yes, that's true.

Q. Did you try to find out where Clementis was interned?

A. Yes.

Q. Your employers . . . were interested in Clementis?

A. They were highly interested.

And why shouldn't they have been? It was legitimate news that Vladimir Clementis, the erstwhile Minister of Foreign Affairs, had been arrested and charged, like Rajk in Hungary, with having led a "Titoist" conspiracy to overthrow the Stalinist rulers of his country. It was also legitimate news that Vyshinsky had met in Carlsbad with foreign representatives of the Cominform. And it was legitimate, too, for a correspondent to check on the arrivals and departures of individuals likely to be concerned in the news. Officially, at least, Czechoslovakia was not at war with the United States, and until war was declared, or unless a special decree prohibiting newsgathering was issued, Oatis had every right to obtain all the information he could, so long as he observed existing laws. At no point in his trial was he accused of having broken any law but one—the general provision defining espionage as "any attempt" to learn about anything that the government preferred to consider secret.

The conviction of Oatis not only made it possible for the SNB to share the vicious laurels of the AVH, it also established an artificial precedent for the official Soviet position that newsgathering is a governmental rather than a private function, and that every government has the right to determine, at its own convenience, what is, and what is not, legitimate news. A United Nations subcommittee, ironically charged with drafting an international treaty designed to protect the "freedom of the press," has come dangerously close to accepting this benighted principle. If it ever does so—and it can do so only against the opposition of the United States—then truly the Communist millennium of universal slavery will be at hand.

So that there could be no mistaking the significance of his trial, Oatis was called upon to "unmask" himself in the following terms:

The witnesses have given a picture of one class of people with whom I had connection [*sic*] in Prague: I mean the Czech citizens from the reactionary point of view. Now I would like to say something . . . about a second class of people: I mean in this case Western correspondents and Western diplomats here in Prague. I said yesterday that other Western correspondents were dealing in espionage news [*sic*]. I will give you some examples. Colonel Atwood . . . told me on two occasions that he obtained reports from Russell Jones [the correspondent of the United Press]. The first . . . was a story

that came out in January of this year to the effect that secret negotiations were going on in certain parts of Bohemia . . . dealing with
the Ministry of National Defense. The second case I heard in March
or April of this year. Colonel Atwood told me the names of some
army [officers] who had been arrested in . . . connection with the
. . . case [of Otto Sling, the ousted secretary of the Communist Party
in Brno]. He said that he got these cases [sic] from Jones. Robert
Bigio, the Reuter's correspondent, used to give information to the
American ambassador, Ellis Briggs. I was with him one day last
August when Briggs told Bigio that several people in a certain ministry
had been detained. Fournier of the [Agence France Presse] put out
a bulletin for diplomatic missions in Prague which contained espionage reports. It had the story of the arrest of the Minister of Agriculture. . . . All of these had reports of the disappearance of Clementis. *My own espionage activity resulted from trying to check on
stories that these other correspondents had [obtained] in Prague*
[italics mine]. . . . Usually it happened that when a correspondent
[obtained] a story that I didn't have, I got an order from London or
New York to get it too. Besides the correspondents, the Western
embassies in Prague used to get information from the British, French,
and Italian embassies and also had a contact with the Yugoslav Embassy in Prague. I used to get espionage reports of my own from
various embassies. For example, Tyler Thompson . . . of the American Embassy gave me a report in March on labor camps in Czechoslovakia. In this report there were names and locations of various
camps. . . . Thompson, as I have said, also gave me the first word
that Clementis was missing. Geoffrey Kirk, [the] counselor of the
British Embassy, gave me a story in January, 1951, to the effect that
[Marie] Svermova was dismissed from [her] post as deputy secretary . . . [to] Sling. He said that the wife of a high political leader
had been arrested in the same case, interrogated, and later released.
. . . Martin Bowe, [the] military permit officer . . . with the American Embassy . . . gave me a story last October of the secret trial of
. . . hockey players in Prague. In January of this year he told me
that several people had been dismissed from several ministries and
he gave me the details. These embassies collected information in index
files. . . . Atwood kept the military index . . . and . . . Schnee

kept the index on political figures. At the British Embassy these index cards were handled respectively by Captain Wheeler and Anthony Snellgrove. That's about all with [sic] my connections with Western diplomats. . . .

And all it was, as Oatis made clear, was a normal exchange of legitimate information between correspondents and diplomats, who often depend on each other to confirm the reports that they separately obtain. The prosecutor, however, chose to define such exchanges of information as "criminal activities . . . planned preparations . . . in the service of the bloody dollar trying to subvert the life of our happy people."

At another point in his cross-examination, the following interchange occurred between Oatis and the president of the court:

Q. Mr. Oatis, do you yourself hold any hatred to [sic] Czechoslovakia or do you hate the Czechoslovak people?
A. No, I don't.
Q. What compelled you to [engage in] these activities?
A. I did this on instructions from New York and London and under the influence of Western diplomats.
Q. Please make it clear before the court, your origin and background.
A. I am from a working-class family. My father and both my grandfathers were from the working class. One of my grandfathers worked in another man's glass factory, the other worked in another man's butcher shop. My father worked in another man's pharmacy. I am a worker myself. I earn my living by the work of my hands and brain. I am not a capitalist and don't own any factories. I am a worker.
Q. You are not a worker. You are a spy. . . .

In his final statement, again repeating the jargon he had been forced by his captors to recite, Oatis reverted to the same theme:

I am sorry that I went into espionage in this country. I didn't do it because I am an enemy of the working class. I am from the working class myself. I did it only because I listened to the wrong kind of orders from abroad and came under the influence of the wrong kind of people here in Czechoslovakia. I hurt myself, I hurt my friends, I harmed the Republic and helped its enemies. I repeat that I am sorry for all this. Your security organs . . . have treated me with great consideration, even though I don't deserve it. Your courts treated me courteously. I thank you for all that. I know that I did the wrong thing. . . . I am ready for your judgment. Thank you!

The court, true to the "humanitarian" principles of the Cominform, chose to be "lenient" in view of Oatis' "sincere" repentance. He was sentenced to only ten years in prison for the "crime" of accurately reporting as much of the truth as he could discover about Czechoslovakia's enslavement. The verdict, as a final slap at the United States, was handed down on the Fourth of July. Svoboda, whose name in Czech means "freedom," was sentenced to twenty years in prison for assisting Oatis to perform his duties as a foreign correspondent. Wojdinek and Munz, for the same "crime," were sentenced, respectively, to eighteen and sixteen years in prison. The State Department, in what was probably the angriest communiqué it has ever issued, aptly replied that "the present regime in Czechoslovakia fears truth, hates liberty, and knows no justice."

Czechoslovakia has made no secret of the ransom it hopes to obtain in return for Oatis' release—the termination of Radio Free Europe's broadcasts to Czechoslovakia from Germany. Radio Free Europe, the operating division of the National Committee for a Free Europe, Inc., is a private organization supported by contributions to the Crusade for Freedom. Its purpose is to bring about the eventual liberation of the seven countries that were the principal European victims of the disastrous treaty signed at Yalta in 1945. Every American who has contributed to the Crusade for Freedom has helped to finance Radio Free Europe's propaganda. The State Department is in no position to put a stop to its activities, and the department has so informed the Czechoslovakian government. But Czechoslovakia's Communist rulers are evidently convinced that, if they hold Oatis long enough, they will eventually be able to destroy a troublesome mouthpiece of the anti-Communist underground.

It is not for me, having been ransomed myself, to say that Oatis should not be ransomed. If Laurabelle Oatis were to demand, as Lucile demanded, compliance with her husband's ransom terms, I would not blame her in the least; indeed, I would feel obliged to support her demand. But until and unless Mrs. Oatis decides to do so, I think we should insist that the State Department make every effort to procure his release by less humiliating means. I shall make some suggestions as to what these efforts should be, but, before I do, I had better discuss the latest humiliation suffered by the United States at the hands of Mátyás Rákosi.

Twenty | The Four American Fliers

On November 19, 1951, an unarmed C-47 took off from Erding, near Munich, in the American zone of Germany, with a cargo of freight consigned to the American air attaché in Belgrade. The airplane, which was conservatively valued by the Air Force at $100,000, was equipped with radar. In addition to its cargo, it carried six parachutes, an equal number of life jackets, a life raft, nineteen blankets, four portable radio transmitters, and several boxes of emergency equipment, including waterproof rations, fishing tackle, and carbon dioxide for keeping the raft and jackets inflated in the event that the airplane was forced down over a large body of water. Its pilot was Captain Dave Henderson, of Shawnee, Oklahoma; its copilot, Captain John Swift, of Glen Falls, New York. Its other crew members were Sergeants James Elam, of Kingsland, Arkansas, and Jess Duff, of Spokane, Washington.

Weather conditions were far from ideal. None of the crew had ever flown to Yugoslavia before, and Captain Henderson lost his bearings. Instead of following the Sava River down to Belgrade, as he should have done, he followed the Drava River down to its confluence with the Danube. He became confused, flew over Rumania for a while and then, realizing that he was lost, turned back and flew across Hungary in the direction of Austria. He was within half an hour of Vienna when he was waylaid by a squadron of fighters and forced to land at a Russian air base near Pápa, in western Hungary.

In Moscow, exactly two weeks later, TASS announced that the four fliers were being held incommunicado in Hungary on charges of having "deliberately violated" the sovereign skies of Hungary and Rumania with the "criminal intention" of dropping "spies and saboteurs." In the meantime a P2V Navy patrol bomber had been shot down by Russian fighters off the coast of Siberia with the loss of all ten members of its crew.

In 1946 Yugoslav fighters, at the orders of Tito, had forced down one and shot down another unarmed C-47 with the loss of five American lives. In this instance the Truman Administration comported itself in a manner befitting the dignity of the world's greatest power. The then Secretary of State, James Byrnes, issued an ultimatum requiring Tito to free the survivors and deliver the bodies of the dead, with full military honors, within forty-eight hours. This was done. The ultimatum also fixed an indemnity of $400,000, which Tito grudgingly paid. In 1950, when Russian fighters shot down another Navy patrol bomber —a Privateer that was flying off the coast of Latvia—Dean Acheson issued an ultimatum that the Russians were allowed to reject. In 1951, therefore, when the second Navy bomber was shot down, all that Mr. Acheson could do was to issue a hollow protest to the United Nations, which the Russians ignored.

In the case of the four captured fliers, Mr. Acheson issued a note but not an ultimatum, addressed to Hungary but not to Russia, demanding their immediate release. Another two weeks were allowed to pass before Vyshinsky let the cat out of the bag at a meeting of the Political Committee of the United Nations in Paris. He said: "I venture to assure you that the fliers were arrested and that they received due attention from *our* border authorities, and I hope that due attention will be given to them by *our* military and judicial authorities, because [they] were flying over [Hungary] for a particular intelligence purpose in the interests of the Atlantic Bloc [italics mine]. . . ." When Representative Mansfield of Montana asked Vyshinsky to explain what he meant by *"our"* authorities, the latter replied that he had been speaking only for himself and not for the Hungarian government.

His statement was in fact a directive with which the Hungarian government immediately complied. It announced on December 21 that Henderson, Swift, Elam, and Duff would be tried for the "crime" of "violating" its skies. Although the radar, parachutes, life raft and jackets, portable transmitters, blankets, and other emergency items were standard equipment on all C-47's operated by the Air Force in military zones, the Hungarians, taking their cue from the Russians, chose to regard such equipment as "proof" that the airplane had been dropping spies and saboteurs.

Captain Swift, in writing about his experiences in *Life* on January 14, 1952, recalled how puzzled his Russian inquisitors had been about the nineteen blankets. He made no effort to explain, and would not have been believed if he had, that the blankets, like the other equipment, were intended to preserve the lives of the crew if they were forced to ditch their airplane. Nineteen blankets were perhaps more than four survivors would have required, but if the airplane had carried six crew members instead of four, and had crashed in a mountainous area, for example, nineteen would have been none too many. It was too much, however, to expect the Russians to understand. Russian airplanes are not normally equipped for emergencies; *ergo,* an American airplane so equipped had clearly been carrying spies.

The four fliers were tried and convicted by a military court and sentenced, on December 23, to three months in prison or the payment of "fines" totaling $120,000. The airplane was confiscated.

It was on Christmas Eve that I learned of their conviction. I thought it would be an error for our government to pay their "fines," but I also felt that I should offer to raise their ransom privately. I accordingly telegraphed Mrs. Swift, informing her of my intention, and asking her for the addresses of the next of kin of the others, to whom I sent similar telegrams. With the approval of all concerned, I then announced that I would personally contribute $1,000 and would accept contributions in any amount until I had raised the entire $120,000.

Within seventy-two hours I had received some $200,000 in cash, checks, and pledges from people in every walk of life. Their generous donations, and the messages accompanying them, revealed how strongly the American people felt about the humiliation of their fellow countrymen.

Senator Smathers of Florida had meanwhile proposed that 120,000 Americans of Hungarian origin be allowed to contribute a dollar apiece toward the payment of the ransom. It was Smathers' idea, and I think he was right, that by so doing we could convert our national humiliation into a propaganda coup that would demonstrate the solidarity of Hungarian Americans with the victims of Communist oppression in their unfortunate country of origin. Everyone knew that it was not the enslaved Hungarian people who were responsible for the savagery of their rulers, and it was important for the Voice of America, Radio Free Europe, and other propaganda media to say so at every opportunity. Otherwise the Cominform would sooner or later achieve its objective of alienating the American people from the subject nations of Eastern Europe, whose assimilation by Russia it was imperative to prevent.

But the Administration rejected every proposal that was made to raise the fliers' ransom privately. They were employees of the government, it was said, who had been captured while in government service; it was illegal for the government to accept contributions from private citizens; and it was also illegal for private citizens to deal with the representatives of a foreign government. A special act of Congress would have disposed of such objections, but before Congress could pass such an act, the State Department announced that the fliers' ransom had already been paid. After forty days of confinement, Henderson, Swift, Elam, and Duff were delivered on December 28 to the American authorities in Austria.

Mr. Acheson then issued one of the weakest statements in his career. "Because we value the welfare of the individual above all else," he said, "we have paid the so-called 'fines.' But we have not paid willingly, and we state clearly, in order that there may be no misunderstanding of our attitude in the future, that our patience is not inexhaustible." The State Department then announced that it would re-impose the ban on private travel to Hungary and close, once again, the Hungarian consulates in Cleveland and New York.

There was nothing to do but acknowledge the pledges and return the money that I had collected. I returned all the money except a ten-dollar bill, which I sent to the American Legion. The anonymous donor of the bill had instructed me, in the event that his money could not be used to buy the fliers' freedom, to turn it over to "a veterans' organization."

In short notes addressed to all who had contributed, or promised to contribute, I suggested that they would do well to support the efforts to free William Oatis and the other innocent Americans imprisoned in Czechoslovakia and elsewhere behind the Iron Curtain, including the thirty or more persons incarcerated in China. Twelve thousand citizens of Marion, Indiana—Oatis' home town—signed a petition urging the government to take any and all action necessary to free Oatis "except concessions and bargains." Common Cause, Inc., formed a "Free Bill Oatis" committee, of which Lucile became a member.

I joined a separate organization, known as "Operation Oatis," whose single purpose is to keep his case alive until such time as Oatis is released.

Before Russia admitted that the four fliers were being held as hostages, and while the search for their missing airplane was

still going on, the Hungarian government published a note addressed to the United States in which it denounced our government for its "failure" to live up to the terms of my release. Only
an "insignificant part" of the Hungarian property in the American zone of Germany had been restored, it charged, and the
United States was still in "illegal" possession of the Crown of
St. Stephen, which was being held at the request of the Vatican
and which, in any case, had never been a part of my ransom.

The note turned out to be the introduction to yet another
white book, 323 pages long, entitled *Documents of the Hostile
Activity of the United States Government against the Hungarian
People's Republic*. The chapter dealing with my own imprisonment read, in part, as follows:

After the failure of the Mindszenty conspiracy and simultaneously
with the espionage activity of the Rajk-gang [*sic*], the United States
secret service [*sic*] organized sabotage activities in Hungary under
the leadership of Colonel Robert Vogeler, aimed at paralyzing the
economy of the country. . . .

Vogeler's arrest by the Hungarian authorities led to a campaign of
slander and threats of the rudest sort conducted against Hungary by
the Government of the United States and its propaganda organs. The
United States Government, together with the British Government,
did not balk at any type of threat in its attempts to terrorize the
Hungarian Government and prevent the trial from taking place in the
case of Vogeler and associates. In the time beginning [*sic*] from
November 22, 1949, and the start of the trial on February 23, 1950,
the U.S. Legation in Budapest intervened on behalf of Vogeler by
means of 14 personal calls, 9 inquiries by telephone and 10 notes and
memoranda addressed to the Hungarian Ministry of Foreign Affairs.
The U.S. press and radio, and Secretary of State Acheson himself,
tried by means of crude threats and blackmail to force the Hungarian
Government not to call Vogeler to account for his crimes. The Hungarian Government in its notes and statements of views rejected the
unauthorised [*sic*] American intervention and exposed the aggressive
[*sic*] activity of the U.S. towards Hungary, an outstanding example

of which was Vogeler's espionage and sabotage activity. . . .

The American press and radio used the sentence on the spy and saboteur Vogeler . . . in order to indulge in further anti-Hungarian steps. The Hungarian Government, however, exposed the true purpose of this campaign of slander and pointed out that it was the U.S. Legation in Budapest that had been the directing centre of these subversive activities. Acting on the conclusions drawn from the trial, the Hungarian Government called upon the U.S. Government to reduce the unjustifiably large personnel of the U.S. Legation in Budapest, *which served exclusively the purposes of espionage and sabotage activity against Hungary* [italics mine]. The Hungarian Government moreover demanded that those U.S. diplomats who had been gravely compromised in Vogeler's sabotage activity be recalled.

The U.S. Government was compelled to comply with the demand of the Hungarian Government.

Twenty-one | "What Can You Do?"

At a press conference in Washington on Christmas Eve, 1951, President Truman was asked if he intended to do anything more than he had already done to procure the release of the four fliers who were still imprisoned in Hungary.

"No," he said. "What can you do?"

He paused and then added, "You're still trying to get Oatis out, aren't you?"

"What can you do?" In these words the President of the United States has expressed his inability to cope with the violations of the rights of American citizens abroad. But the American people, in my opinion, will never accept such an answer—or lack of one. They will insist that there must be something that we *can* do, and that ways and means must be found for doing it. In this concluding chapter, therefore, I should like to discuss three courses of action, short of open warfare, that are open to our government:

1. We can stop trading with the Cominform.
2. We can block the activities of Cominform agents.
3. We can put Russia on the defensive.

1. STOP TRADING WITH THE COMINFORM. In August, 1951, the Senate voted, 81 to 0, and the House voted, 362 to 1, to halt trade with Czechoslovakia in retaliation for the imprison-

ment of Oatis. Our trade with Czechoslovakia has since been considerably reduced, but it is still far from being halted altogether. Only three basic steps have been taken to date to fulfill the expressed desire of Congress: (1) the Allied High Commission has forbidden Czechoslovakian airliners to fly over Western Germany; (2) the State Department has abrogated our reciprocal tariff agreements with Czechoslovakia as well as with Bulgaria, Rumania, and China; and (3) the Commerce Department has prohibited the shipment to Czechoslovakia of a steel mill manufactured for that country in Youngstown, Ohio.

The State Department has also abrogated our reciprocal tariff agreements with Poland and Russia and prohibited the importation from those countries of some but not all types of furs, pelts, and skins. For reasons best known to the fur lobby and its friends in Congress, however, so-called Persian lamb pelts are still being imported from Russia at an annual rate of $5,000,000.

Our reciprocal tariff agreement with Hungary will not be abrogated until July, 1952, for the interesting reason that a clause in the agreement requires *a year's notice* to be given before the agreement may be abrogated by either party. Hungary, it seems, is free to violate its peace treaty, expropriate American property, and hold our citizens for ransom, but the United States is not free to abrogate its tariff agreement with Hungary except in accordance with this restricting clause.

Representative Battle's amendment to the Mutual Security Act requires its administrator, Averell Harriman, to take sanctions against any country shipping strategic materials to Russia and its colonies. Yet, as these lines were written, American automobile and truck parts were being shipped to Denmark for transshipment to Poland; aluminum oxide from Canada was being shipped to Belgium for transshipment to Hungary; and Chinese hog bristles and East German shotguns were entering the United States by way of Holland, Denmark, West Germany, and Sweden. Ball bearings were still entering Czechoslovakia and Russia by way of Sweden and France. Britain was still importing Russian lumber, grain, and crabmeat in return for manufactured products that were theoretically "non-strategic," and, until the International Longshoremen's Association (AFL) put a stop to it, Britain was dumping its Russian crabmeat in the United States.

As a spokesman for the War Department put it, trying to enforce an embargo against the Russian Empire under the present loose restrictions is "like trying to plug the holes of a sieve." The obvious answer to the problem is to tighten the restrictions and employ an adequate number of inspectors to see that they are enforced. The natural sentiments of the American people, and particularly of the working men through whose hands the goods will pass, will make the embargo effective.

The loud complaints of the Communist industrial bosses behind the Iron Curtain indicate that the half-measures already taken have begun to hurt. If full measures were taken, they might hurt so much that Oatis would have to be released.

Once upon a time, before the West began to suffer from what Pope Pius has described as "spiritual anemia," British and American trade unions refused to permit the importation of the products of slave labor. Prior to the Roosevelt-Litvinov Agreement, in 1933, it would have been unthinkable for either Britain or the United States to import crabmeat or lumber from Russia, for it would have been called to our attention that Russia's fishing and lumbering industries were both dependent for their labor on Gulag, the Central Administration of Concentration Camps. Isn't it about time for us to recognize that our past willingness to wink at Russia's concentration camps has prepared the way for the torture and imprisonment of American citizens?

2. BLOCK THE ACTIVITIES OF COMINFORM AGENTS. We should impose on all Cominform representatives in the

United States the same restrictions that are imposed on our own citizens behind the Iron Curtain.

During the Second World War, American military and diplomatic personnel, correspondents, and other visitors were graciously permitted to travel as much as 100 kilometers (62 miles) out of Moscow without special permission from the MVD. Only in Odessa, however, were the crews of American ships permitted to walk freely through the city streets. In Murmansk, if they were allowed to go ashore at all, they were confined to a small restricted area and forbidden to have anything to do with the city's inhabitants, most of whom, as it happened, were political prisoners. After the war even such limited "privileges" were withdrawn.

By 1948, Americans were forbidden to travel more than 50 kilometers (31 miles) out of Moscow, and by 1952 the free travel radius had been reduced to 40 kilometers, or 25 miles. The list of forbidden cities had meanwhile been increased by twenty-two, which meant that only four cities in addition to Moscow were accessible to Americans in Russia—Leningrad, Stalingrad, Odessa, and Tiflis. Kiev, the capital of disaffected Ukrainia, has been on the forbidden list since 1948.

Even the State Department agrees that the time has come to consider imposing similar restrictions on Soviet Russians and perhaps on all Cominform representatives in the United States. As these lines were written, however, the only Cominform representatives against whom such retaliatory action had been taken were the Hungarians and Rumanians, whose freedom to travel has been restricted—in theory, at least—to a 35-mile area surrounding Washington.*

In addition to travel restrictions, we should also apply legal restrictions based on a policy of "counter-capitulations." Such a

---

* In March, 1952, the United States, Great Britain, Canada, France, Italy, and Holland imposed the same restrictions on Russian diplomatic representatives, who must now request permission to travel more than 35 miles outside of Washington, London, Ottawa, Paris, Rome, and The Hague.

policy would be the reverse of the old policy of "capitulations" (or "extra-territorial rights") that was once applied in countries whose governments were unable or unwilling to enforce civilized standards of conduct. Under the capitulations that prevailed in the old Turkish Empire and in the so-called "treaty ports" of China—and which still prevail in Morocco and several other countries—the human rights of Americans and other foreigners were protected by treaties that provided for the enforcement, for and against them, in consular courts, of their own laws rather than the laws, if any, of the capitulating power.

The proposed counter-capitulations would make it juridically feasible for the United States to protect its citizens indirectly by reserving the right, *quid pro quo,* to prosecute representatives of the Cominform countries according to the same legal pretexts invoked in the persecution of American citizens behind the Iron Curtain.

We could do so, I think, without damaging in any way our own standards of justice. If our laws were strictly enforced, I dare say that we could lawfully convict ten foreign Communists for every American unlawfully convicted behind the Iron Curtain. Instead, we have hesitated to punish Russian agents who break our laws for fear of jeopardizing the non-existent safety of Americans in Russian-dominated countries.

In 1946, for example, Lieutenant Nikolai Redin was acquitted after being indicted on five charges of espionage by a Federal grand jury in Seattle. Was it because the Department of Justice was instructed not to press its charges against him? His acquittal, in any event, failed to prevent the subsequent imprisonment of scores of Americans in Russian-dominated lands.

Valentin Gubitchev was sent home to Russia, after being lawfully convicted of espionage, in the apparent hope that Stalin, in return, would order my release. He failed to do so. Stalin not only waited a year and then exacted concessions, but before I was released he saw to it that Oatis was arrested. It is difficult for me to believe that there are no more Gubitchevs among the Russian and satellite "diplomats" now in the United States.

In the winter of 1951-52, a fleet of thirty-two Russian trawlers, equipped with the latest electronic devices, sailed from Murmansk to Vladivostok by way of London, Gibraltar, Suez, Aden, Singapore, and Hong Kong. It was a "fishing expedition" on a scale and of a sort that had not been seen since the last fleet of Japanese trawlers, prior to Pearl Harbor, sailed around South America into the Caribbean and returned home by way of the Panama Canal. At every port of call the Russian trawlers were received with the courtesies normally extended to friendly ships on legitimate voyages. They were still in the port of London, in fact, when the *Star of Aden* docked in Newcastle with a cargo of Siberian lumber from Igarka, a prison settlement on the Yenisei River. Benjamin Wake, the captain of the *Star of Aden*, indignantly told the press:

In my twenty-seven years as a sailor . . . I have never been on a worse trip. The Russians turned my ship into a prison, and I was the principal prisoner. . . .

I had twelve nationalities in my crew of forty-three, [and] everything went all right until I reached Murmansk. Then the Reds took over. Two Russian pilots came on board to take us through the Kara Sea. They refused to let us see our own charts or to take sights of any description.

Later, two other Russians came on board to take us up the Yenisei. When all four were aboard, my officers and I were not allowed even to speak to one another. We were followed everywhere, and if the Russians didn't want us to do something, they merely smacked a revolver holster and said, "Please."

As everybody knows, or should know, by now, the principal function of the Russian merchant marine is not to carry freight but to carry couriers and provide floating message-centers for Stalinist agents in every country in the world. Is there any reason why, in accordance with a policy of counter-capitulations, we and our allies should not begin to treat the crews of Russian ships exactly as the crew of the *Star of Aden* was treated on its voyage to Igarka?

The FBI undoubtedly has enough evidence to obtain a lawful conviction of Mikhail Fedorov, the chief TASS correspondent in Washington. Fedorov, far from being a bona fide newspaperman, is in reality an aircraft engineer. His principal function, as the Kremlin knows we know, is the collection and transmission of secret information. As the representative of an official agency of the Russian government, he carries a diplomatic passport and is therefore immune to arrest. He is not immune to deportation, however, and there is nothing to prevent his being tried *in absentia*. The evidence that could be presented against Fedorov and his organization in a public trial would be so embarrassing to the Kremlin that it would probably agree to release Oatis, even now, in return for calling off Fedorov's trial. It would certainly have been worth more to the Kremlin, prior to Oatis' trial, to protect Fedorov than to convict Oatis and hold him for ransom.

Victor Kravchenko, the author of *I Chose Freedom,* won a memorable victory over the Cominform in 1949 by suing the French Communist magazine, *Les Lettres Françaises,* for libel. David Rousset, with the help of Valentin González, Alexander Weissberg, Elinor Lipper, and other former inmates of Russian concentration camps, repeated Kravchenko's victory over the same magazine two years later. Why not emulate what has been done in Paris by filing libel suits against Communist publications in New York, London, and other cities? Instead of idly bemoaning the "blackmail" of our own citizens, why not resort to some legal counter-actions of our own? The Kremlin's representatives are far more vulnerable than the Administration seems to think.

Finally, I should like to call President Truman's attention to Howard T. Oliver's letter in the New York *Times* of December 28, 1951. Oliver reminds us that Article III, Section 2, of the

Constitution of the United States provides that "the judicial power shall extend to all . . . controversies . . . between a state or the citizens thereof, and foreign states, citizens, or subjects." Why shouldn't Mrs. Oatis be encouraged to file suit for damages against Czechoslovakia for the unlawful arrest, conviction, and imprisonment of her husband?

The only reason, according to Oliver, is that "during the past twenty-five years it has been the custom of the Department of State to intervene in the courts of the United States in civil actions brought by American citizens against offending foreign governments, and induce the courts to deny jurisdiction, even though it was notorious that our government was convinced that injustice had been done to these American citizens." In other words, such suits embarrass our diplomats. But if the framers of the Constitution saw fit to grant our citizens the right to take civil action against foreign governments, why should the Constitution not be allowed to prevail?

3. PUT RUSSIA ON THE DEFENSIVE. Several senators and representatives of both parties have advocated the severance of diplomatic relations with Hungary. David Lawrence, the editor and columnist, has gone so far as to advocate the severance of diplomatic relations with all the Communist countries, including Russia. Such a step, Lawrence believes, would be "the forerunner of a campaign which ultimately must mean helping the freedom-loving peoples inside the Iron Curtain countries to get rid of their gangster governments."

The day may soon come when such a course of action will be effective. For the time being, though, in the absence of a well-conceived program of psychological warfare on our part, I doubt that a general rupture of relations would produce the positive results that Lawrence envisions. It would advance our national interests to sever relations with all the Iron Curtain countries only if we were prepared to engage in the psychological warfare necessary to liberate the peoples of those countries from the Kremlin's tyranny. We have refused to recognize Communist Albania and Communist China, and we severed relations with Communist Bulgaria in February, 1951, following the expulsion of Donald Heath, the American minister, and the torture and murder of Michael Shipkov and other Bulgarian employees of the American Legation. It cannot be said, however, in the absence of a strong program of psychological warfare, that we have thereby given pause to the Communist rulers of any of those countries, for they have yet to be convinced that we are either able or willing to exert the pressures necessary to undermine the Kremlin's dominance.

Propaganda, especially of the innocuous "white" variety to which the Voice of America has been so largely limited, is not enough. To achieve the results foreseen by David Lawrence, we must engage in the "black" propaganda of psychological warfare. We must make far better use of native anti-Communists than we have made to date. We must infiltrate the Cominform with American agents. And we must support our agents with vigorous propaganda, keyed not to "peace" as so much of our propaganda is today, but to "liberation."

The Kremlin's vehement attacks on the Mutual Security Act are indicative of its fears. It is especially fearful of the provision that authorizes the expenditure of $100,000,000 "either to form [Iron Curtain refugees] into elements of military forces supporting the North Atlantic Treaty Organization or for other purposes." The Polish delegate to the United Nations demanded the repeal of the act on the ground that it was intended to foster "spying, sabotage, and diversions against the Polish State"—that is, liberation. He was supported by delegates of the Civil Rights Congress, an American fifth column, who attempted to embarrass the United States by accusing our government of fostering "genocide" through isolated acts of violence against Negroes in the South. In Moscow, Andrei

Gromyko accused the United States of violating the Roosevelt-Litvinov Agreement of 1933, whereby Russia and the United States undertook to curb in their respective territories all activities whose purpose was "the bringing about by force of a change in the political and social order" of either country. And, in Paris, Vyshinsky himself delivered the following note to the United Nations:

This act provides for the financing by the Government of the United States of America of persons and armed groups in the territory of the Soviet Union and a number of other states for the purpose of carrying out subversive and diversionary activities within those states.

The act provides for the financing of traitors to their native lands and of war criminals who have fled from their countries and are hiding in the territory of the United States and a number of other states, for the financing of armed groups for the purpose of fighting against the Soviet Union.

The financing by the United States . . . of subversive organizations and diversionist groups, both in the territory of the Soviet Union and other peace-loving democratic countries and beyond the frontiers of their territory . . . constitutes an act of aggression towards the Soviet Union and the states of the People's Democracies.

In the meantime the four American fliers had been arrested, tried, and convicted in Hungary, and in each of five different countries—Hungary, Bulgaria, Rumania, Poland, and Russia—four alleged agents of the United States were condemned to death as a warning to the populace. Vyshinsky's understudy, Jakob Malik, insisted that our government's payment of the fliers' "fines" was a tacit admission of their "guilt." The Kremlin had apparently feared that the imprisonment of the fliers would result in far more serious reprisals than those that were actually taken. As usual, it organized a large-scale "diversion" of its own, and as usual it was successful. Philip Jessup, the American delegate to the United Nations, weakly denied Vyshinsky's charges and, in so doing,

confirmed their validity. What Jessup should have been instructed to do, if the Administration were equal to its responsibilities, would have been to call Vyshinsky's bluff.

If we had a conscious policy of putting Russia on the defensive, Jessup could have turned the whole argument against the
Kremlin by demonstrating, point by point, that the psychological
warfare in which we cannot deny that we are now engaged was
forced upon us by Stalin's systematic effort to subvert and
eventually absorb the whole of Europe. Instead of *denying* that
we have at last decided to combat the further enslavement of
the Eastern European peoples, we should have declared, boldly
and proudly, that our objective is nothing less than their eventual
liberation. Had Jessup done so, I think, he would have inspired
our friends and demoralized our enemies among the subject
peoples—including the Russians themselves—and he would have
increased the Kremlin's growing fear that the whole rotten structure of Soviet totalitarianism may soon collapse.

Vyshinsky's attack on the Mutual Security Act, like Molotov's
earlier attacks on its progenitor, the European Recovery Program, was a confession of weakness, not an expression of strength.
There is no need for us to remain on the defensive indefinitely.
As our own strength and determination increase, we shall be
able to stem the tide. But to stem it decisively we need to be
represented, at home and abroad, by men of resolution who
sincerely believe that our cause is just and that, being just, it
must prevail. It will never prevail so long as we tolerate the
barbaric treatment to which our representatives, official and
unofficial, are being subjected not only in Hungary and Czechoslovakia but in all the Communist slave states including Russia
itself.

In 1816, under James Madison's administration, Richard
Meade, the father of the Civil War general, was unlawfully im-

prisoned in Spain. When the American minister failed to procure
his release, Meade's wife appealed to Congress. A Senate committee resolved, in answer to her plea, that "any United States
citizen who [behaves] as becomes his character is entitled to
the protection of his government, and that whatever intentional
injury may be done against him be retaliated, if necessary, by
the whole force of this nation." Meade, whose predicament
closely paralleled my own, was released soon afterward. Spain's
power, in those days, was fully as great in relation to our own
as Russia's is today.

In 1853, under Franklin Pierce's administration, Márton Koszta,
a Hungarian fugitive from Austria who had applied for but had
not yet received American citizenship, was arrested in Turkey
and imprisoned aboard an Austrian brig. Captain Duncan Ingra-
ham, the commander of an American sloop, procured Koszta's
release merely by threatening to open fire on the brig in which
he was confined.

In those days our country was a relatively minor power. It had
relatively few diplomatic missions, yet our citizens were respected almost everywhere. Today we have diplomatic missions
everywhere, yet our citizens are respected nowhere in the one-
fourth of the world that has fallen under Russian domination.

On January 31, 1952, at a meeting of the Social, Humanitarian,
and Cultural Committee of the United Nations, our delegate
Channing Tobias announced that the United States would never
"cease to protest the use of William Oatis as a pawn in the sup-
pression of freedom." Russia's delegate Alexei Pavlov immediately rose to accuse Tobias of injecting "the manners of the
Chicago stockyards" into an international gathering. Espionage,
he said, is "inherent" in the traditions of American journalism.
All American correspondents are "spies." And if we insist on
sending them behind the Iron Curtain, they "will get what they
deserve, and many of them will envy those whose fate is only a

prison sentence. . . . The Soviet Union and the People's Democracies are not . . . your colonies, and if you stretch out your paws, we'll hack them off."

In 1904, when the Moroccan bandit Ahmed ibn Mohammed Raisuli kidnaped Ion Perdicaris, an American protégé of Greek nationality, President Theodore Roosevelt authorized Secretary of State John Hay to issue the now-famous ultimatum: "We want Perdicaris alive or Raisuli dead." Perdicaris, who was not even an American citizen, was promptly released. The Sultan of Morocco, in addition to refunding his ransom, paid the United States an indemnity of $4,000 to cover its expenses in procuring Perdicaris' release.

Our ultimatum, in the Perdicaris case, was reinforced by a demonstration of American sea power in the Mediterranean. If we had issued an ultimatum in my case, and reinforced it with a demonstration of American air power over the Western zones of Austria and Germany, I am inclined to believe not only that I would have been released but that Oatis would never have been imprisoned.

I was not the first American to be imprisoned by Stalin, and, unless we change our tactics, Oatis, I fear, will not be the last.

What are we going to do about Hvasta and the Fields and all the other Americans, naturalized and native-born, who are still imprisoned in Russia, China, and Eastern Europe? I am fully aware that the Fields are accused of being Russian agents, but after what I have been through I am no longer impressed by unsubstantiated accusations. If my treatment at the hands of the AVH taught me nothing else, it taught me the crying need for enforcing civilized standards of justice.

I believe more strongly than ever before that every man is innocent until he has been found guilty by a jury of his peers.

I was innocent, yet I was forced to confess to crimes that I had not committed. The same is true of Oatis. Who knows but what the Fields may also be innocent, or at least less guilty than we have been led to suppose? As American citizens they are as fully entitled to their day in court as Judith Coplon, and until and unless they have been lawfully convicted of treason or espionage they are entitled to the protection of the American flag.

If we continue to tolerate the unlawful imprisonment of American citizens, and if we continue to pay ransom for their release, it will increase, not lessen, the risk of a Third World War. Lucile put it well, I think, when she said that we must either demand or crawl. We are the greatest power on earth. Yet we have been crawling when we should have been demanding, and enforcing our demands, that Russia and its colonies abide by the standards of international law. Having crawled twice, however, once in my own case and again in the case of the four fliers, we seem to have convinced Stalin that we can be made to crawl again and again—and therein, I think, lies the greatest danger of a Third World War.

In my opinion, the risk of open war involved in defending the human rights of American citizens behind the Iron Curtain has been very much exaggerated. A secretary of our Budapest legation, it will be recalled, accurately predicted that if I were arrested the State Department's unsupported protests would be ignored. "The AVH," he said, "knows that we aren't going to war with Russia over a lone American prisoner." The secretary failed to draw an obvious corollary to his proposition. Just as we won't go to war with Russia to prevent the unlawful imprisonment of a lone American, neither will Russia go to war to keep him in prison. If the secretary's superiors in Washington had recognized that the proposition works both ways, I am confident that I would have been released much sooner and that Oatis would never have been imprisoned.

The importance of national honor has often been overestimated in the past. Today it is being so grossly underestimated that the future of our country is at stake. We must convince Stalin before it is too late that, though we won't go to war to save one American, we will certainly go to war to prevent the persecution of Americans from becoming a habit. Unless we do, we may find that we have lost the war that we have tried so hard to avoid before it even begins—which, of course, is Stalin's fondest hope.

As things stand now, what happened to me, and what has since happened to Oatis and the four fliers, could happen to any American in any Russian-dominated country, and no effective reprisals would be taken. I consider that a shocking admission for an American to be forced to make. Unfortunately it is true.

I am thinking, as I end this book, not only of Oatis and myself and the many other Americans who have been victimized by the oppressors with whom we are nominally at peace. I am thinking also of Edgar Sanders, Imre Geiger, and my other codefendants, and of Alfred Plocek, Jaroslav Peske, and the others who were condemned to death in Czechoslovakia within a month of my release from prison. These men were no more guilty than I was, yet they were equally the victims of our failure as a great power to enforce the human rights in the name of which so many of our young men gave their lives in the Second World War.

If we are to survive as a great power, I can think of no better rule to guide our conduct than the admonition contained in the Book of Common Prayer: "Grant us grace fearlessly to contend against evil, *and to make no peace with oppression;* and, that we may reverently use our freedom, help us to employ it in the maintenance of justice among men and nations."

Index

Index

307

11489